TEST *of* WILL

GLENN McGRATH

TEST *of* WILL

WHAT I'VE LEARNED FROM CRICKET AND LIFE

ALLEN&UNWIN
SYDNEY • MELBOURNE • AUCKLAND • LONDON

First published in 2015

Allen & Unwin
83 Alexander Street
Crows Nest NSW 2065
Australia
Phone: (61 2) 8425 0100
Email: info@allenandunwin.com
Web: www.allenandunwin.com

Cataloguing-in-Publication details are available
from the National Library of Australia
www.trove.nla.gov.au

ISBN 978 1 76011 280 6

Internal design by Simon Rattray
Set in 12.5/17.5 pt Bembo by Midland Typesetters, Australia
Printed and bound in Australia by Griffin Press

10 9 8 7 6 5 4 3 2 1

MIX
Paper from
responsible sources
FSC® C009448

The paper in this book is FSC® certified.
FSC® promotes environmentally responsible,
socially beneficial and economically viable
management of the world's forests.

To Sara, James, Holly and Madison

CONTENTS

1

THE CONTROLLABLES

In three words I can sum up everything
I've learned about life: it goes on.

—Robert Frost, poet

Whenever I was asked during my cricket career for the secret to my success, I had a standard answer that rolled off my tongue. I would always say that I 'controlled the controllables'. For the main I found it was an easy mantra to live by, especially on those occasions when I had a six-stitcher in my right hand and a batsman 22 yards down the pitch, giving some cheek and taking guard.

I'd learnt from years of practice in the nets that if I cocked my wrist and bowled the ball a certain way it'd hit a spot on the pitch that would cramp the batsman and strangle his flow of runs. I found if you bowled a persistent line and length, eventually it would be cricket's equivalent of water torture for some batsmen and no matter how good they were they'd eventually crack and succumb to the pressure by playing a rash shot. I could also grip the ball's seam in a particular way to fish for a nick off the edge of his bat; or if my attempts to up-end his stumps with a yorker didn't succeed, I always had a plan where I could tempt him to hook to a fieldsman who was strategically placed out in the deep.

Everything I did on the cricket field was aimed at controlling all I could; that allowed me not to stress about those things that were out of my hands. And that's a lot of things in cricket. For instance, if a catch was skied to a fieldsman, no matter how much I wanted him to take it, I knew there was nothing I could do to control whether or not he dropped the ball. Or if someone misfielded, there was absolutely nothing I could do about that. I never worried about the selectors not picking me, I didn't play my career looking over my shoulder and worrying about the 'next big thing', because I realised if I did my job and took wickets then I was doing everything that was required of me. If Australia's batting line-up was in the midst of a collapse, there was little point in me, the No. 11, sitting in the dressing room and stressing out or cursing the batsmen for getting out. That's cricket, and in cricket blokes get dismissed. All I ever worried about was how *I* would stand up to the test when the time came. I'd get kitted up in my pads and other protective equipment, and I'd practise in the dressing room getting behind the ball. Rather than dwelling on the negatives that could take root in my mind if I allowed them, I'd repeatedly tell myself that, come hell or high water, I wouldn't throw my wicket away. *That* was what I realised I could control in that particular situation. I couldn't control what the bowler was going to do when I faced him; I couldn't control what my batting partner might do or even what he might think about me as a batsman, but I could control *my* thoughts and *my* actions. I have no doubt that realising early in my career that all that mattered was what I did or how I handled a situation enabled me to escape a lot of the angst that can choke cricketers if they allow it.

An important element of controlling the controllable as a professional sportsperson—and it's not just applicable to cricket, the controllable concept can be applied to anything— was to leave nothing to chance during my preparation for a game. I ensured I ate well; I trained hard; I rested. I worked hard to fine-tune whatever was required to improve my bowling action—I'd stretch; I would treat my niggles; I would swim laps of the pool before leaving the team's hotel for the ground; and I would study the opposing batsmen's strengths and weaknesses in video sessions and come up with bowling plans. I also made a point of thoroughly under-standing what my role in the team's match plan was. On those days when things didn't go well out in the middle— and yes, there were those stinking hot days when it felt as though I was up to my knees in quicksand—controlling the controllables simply meant keeping my emotions in check so

I could focus on the job that's required of a fast bowler, and that's taking wickets!

All in all it was a pretty good philosophy to follow, and for the main it's served me well throughout my life. When I was a young boy growing up on my family's farm, Lagoona, just outside of Narromine, it wouldn't have occurred to me to describe my approach to life as 'controlling the controllables', but even then the process was a good friend to me when my father Kevin was forced to seek extra income by driving road trains between Dubbo and the Top End. My younger brother Dale and I were left to look after the farm, and now, as a 45-year-old, when I look back on that period of my life I realise it could easily have been a situation that overwhelmed me. After all, I was still a kid of 16 and Dale was 14. We were responsible for tending the crops and looking after the livestock, and without me even noticing it I got through each day by focusing on those controllables. Of course I missed my dad's guidance, but I accepted it was pointless to moan about his absences, when he was behind the wheel of a massive truck carting cattle to and from Darwin. So I woke early each morning, and I prepared for the day by having a decent breakfast. We'd plough the land, we'd harvest the crops or do whatever it was that particular day demanded. After that, my focus was set on the next job . . . and the one after that . . . and that . . .

Even as a cricketer I controlled when it was time for me to step down. I'm proud I went out on my own terms. Not too many players do. My farewell Test at the Sydney Cricket

Ground, my home ground as a New South Welshman, finished remarkably.

I can only recall bits and pieces of what was an emotion-charged five days. But I do remember a journalist asking me during a television interview, if I could take anything from the Test, what would it be? I answered that I'd walk away feeling very pleased if I took a wicket with my last ball. Well, perhaps the universe was listening—as it does from time to time—because that's what happened. I captured Jimmy Anderson's wicket when Michael Hussey caught him off my last ball, a slower one. I remember feeling happy when I saw the ball lobbing towards Michael Hussey because if I'd learnt one thing about him in all the years we'd played alongside one another, it was that he had a safe pair of hands. I remember the excitement that charged through my body as I stood on the middle of the pitch with my arms raised high in the air and feeling as if life, well, *life as a cricketer*, could not get better than that moment. Life was good. When I reflect on that happy day in 2007 and I remember how my late wife Jane gave me the thumbs up from her place in the crowd after I took Anderson's wicket, and then, how I walked around the SCG with our children, James by my side and Holly in my arms, it still makes me smile . . .

What I learnt when I retired from cricket was that controlling my destiny, and that of the people I love, wasn't as easy as it had been as a member of the Australian cricket team, being called upon by Mark Taylor, Steve Waugh or Ricky Ponting to get that breakthrough wicket. Jane . . .

well, she lost her battle with cancer not long after I left cricket. I had decided to give it away because we felt it was time for me to be at home. While neither of us ever wasted the time we had—or the energy we needed—by worrying about the 'what-ifs' and 'whys' of our situation, we definitely did everything possible to try and beat Jane's disease. While Jane had tremendous courage to fight, and God knows she fought hard, it wasn't enough at the end, and her passing was the beginning of a terribly sad time.

What I had to try to do, and at times it was impossible, was to control that sadness, because while I was grieving I was also the father of our two young children, and it was my job to ensure they lived as happy and healthy a life as possible.

Before Jane's death I'd struggled with the transition from international sportsman to fitting in with what I've heard described as 'everyday life'. Sometimes I wondered what the future held, and it worried me. While I had work—corporate speaking jobs, commitments with sponsors, and I was lucky enough to still have a profile I could use as leverage—I didn't have a 'regular' job, so it felt as though I was forever juggling time at home and work engagements. I found that tough, because as a member of the Australian cricket team, I had known exactly what I had to do to achieve my goals. I was used to a structure that allowed me to be productive and successful. That structure meant that I woke up at a certain time; I ate breakfast at a scheduled time; I trained when I was told to; I had time set aside by team management for media or commercial commitments; I ate lunch with my teammates; I had appointments scheduled in advance for physiotherapy or other treatments; and afterwards I ate dinner and then either studied my opponents by watching them on DVD, or I switched off. Looking at it in a different light, I view the life of an Australian cricketer as one long and demanding schedule, but it was well mapped out and such is my nature I liked that it ran like clockwork and that there were never any shades of grey.

Now I was away from that well-planned life, and while I wasn't unemployed—I still had my major sponsors; the McGrath Foundation was going well; and my manager Warren Craig still had things for me to do—I didn't have that regular job, so it felt as though I was going from here to there. Work, for instance, would be noted in my diary as: '[Wednesday week], attend a conference as a guest speaker from 3 pm to 6 pm'. I enjoyed that, but I found the change was tough going from having a very clear direction to basically none at all. And so much for controlling the controllables, because there were times throughout Jane's illness when the uncertainty of what I would be doing for work meant that everything seemed so out of control and I'd ask myself, 'What am I going to do?'

There were times during that period when I felt a bit lost and as though I wasn't achieving much: work-wise there wasn't a single thing for me to pour all of my energies into, as I had in my cricket career. But I don't live in the past and, in terms of cricket, I had moved on. I don't miss playing at all, but eight years after that farewell game at the SCG there are still times when I can't help but wonder if I've completely made the transition to 'everyday life'.

Those first few years were challenging after I bade farewell to a sport that I gave *everything* I had to offer. But I was very lucky because I had people I could rely on: my family and my friends. While my kids and I suffered the worst possible tragedy, I'm grateful that I didn't have to worry about how we would survive. I had seen how my parents battled during the lean times on the farm, and I'm certain not having to worry about financial issues at least spared me from a nightmare. At that stage of my life, I guess what I learnt about controlling the controllables in a dark time was that I had two children and I needed to stay strong for them.

Something else I realised during that period was that as much as there are times when you don't want the sun to rise the next day, the reality is it does. Regardless of anything that might be happening around you and how terrible things seem, a fact of life is that life continues and you have to make the most of it. Everyone has battles and challenges to face, but what matters is how you pick yourself up and carry on.

2

SARA

La vita è bella.

—Italian translation of 'life is beautiful'

Sadly, the cancer that Jane had fought so hard against returned and, despite her strength and immense courage, she was unable to beat it. Her death is something I don't wish to revisit but it was the beginning of a devastating time, a time when I never imagined I would meet anyone again.

What I was to learn during that period was how wrong I was in the past to have been so quick to form an opinion about people I knew who became romantically involved with someone else after they'd lost their partner. Knowing what I know now I can't help but cringe when I hear my old self ask: 'How could they?' 'What are they thinking?' 'What about so-and-so?' because, as I discovered, the reality is you can't possibly know what will happen to you after the death of a loved one unless you're thrust into that situation. You see, I met Sara and thankfully she challenged my thinking and ultimately changed everything for the better . . .

I met Sara in Cape Town, South Africa, on 15 April 2009 while I was playing in the second edition of the Indian Premier League (IPL). As a result of the 26/11 terrorist attacks carried out by extremists in Mumbai, the organisers decided to relocate the tournament to South Africa; the Indian general elections were about to be held and they couldn't guarantee the cricketers' safety because their nation's paramilitary forces were committed to the politicians and the polling stations. We were based in Cape Town for the start of the tournament, and one of my teammates, Paul Collingwood, had toured there the previous year as a member of the England team. During the tour, Kevin Pietersen had introduced the team to Mike Jefferies, an English movie producer who lived in an exclusive suburb called Clifton. Mike co-wrote and produced the movie *Goal!*, which told the story of a young, illegal immigrant who rose from poverty to become one of the world's greatest footballers. Paul invited us to Mike's home, a beautiful place which has the backdrop of Table Mountain and looks out over the Atlantic Ocean, for a birthday get-together for Mike's girlfriend, Frieda. There is a lot of time spent in the hotel during a tournament like the IPL, and I was one of many of the boys who jumped at the offer to get out of the hotel.

When we arrived at Mike's home we bypassed a room with a Celine Dion concert playing on a big screen and headed straight for the bar area, which boasted a pool table. I was sitting at the bar when I saw a good-looking brunette wander across the room; she exchanged a few pleasantries with David Warner before she sat next to me at the bar. She introduced herself as Sara Leonardi and we began chatting. The subject turned to the inevitable question of 'What do you do for a living?', and when I replied that I played cricket, Sara's response was memorable because with a confused look on her face she said, 'Sorry . . . no . . . what do you do to pay the mortgage?' I answered again with, 'I play cricket'. She had no idea about cricket—she had lived in Italy, America and in Europe where it's not dominating the airwaves yet—and I explained why we were in South Africa. When I told her about the IPL and Twenty20 cricket, I noticed that something about Twenty20 registered with her. It turned out she had been driving around Cape Town trying to work out why 'they' were talking up 2020 when it was only 2009.

I found Sara to be pleasant company and during the course of our conversation she told me that she almost didn't make it out that night because she felt exhausted and had wanted to stay home after a girlfriend visiting from the United States had flown home that day. She said the reason she'd ventured out was due to Frieda's insistence that it wouldn't be a party if Sara wasn't there, and I couldn't help but feel happy about Frieda's power of persuasion. Sara had been living in Cape Town for a few years, studying interior design at a local university. I learnt she was born in Miami in December 1981, her father was Sicilian and her mother Italian, but she had been born in Venezuela. Her father owned and ran businesses in Miami, including nightclubs and restaurants. They went back to Sicily for their holidays. Sara grew up speaking Italian to her father, Spanish to her mother and had learned English when she went to school. She completed a degree at a university in Rome before moving back to Miami, then Prague, before dropping anchor in Cape Town. We had an amazing night, finishing it off with shots of whatever was left behind the bar and exchanging phone numbers.

One night she invited me to her house and cooked dinner for me; she showed off her incredible culinary skills, a gift she inherited from spending time in the kitchen with her mother. Sara and I stayed in contact and we caught up a few more times before the tournament finished. It was a . . . *confusing* . . . time for me because after Jane passed away I never wanted to meet or fall in love with anyone, and I was adamant that I wouldn't. However, I knew I had met someone very special, because Sara had energy and an attitude I had never seen before. She was confident, fun loving and had so many ideas, it seemed to me that she was someone who couldn't wait to experience everything life had to offer. While she had an incredible effect on me, and I liked it, I did my best to suppress it. A month after the IPL finished I flew to the United Kingdom with James, Holly and my mother so the kids could spend some time with their grandparents. While there I received an email from Sara asking me if I would like to come and visit her in Sicily. Her mother was selling their family home and Sara had invited her friends from all around the world for a final get-together in the family *casa*. I was only a three-hour flight away and thought, Why not? I had a great time there with all of her friends. Sicily was so beautiful and the food was amazing, however there was a subplot to my time there—I found out afterwards that it was also a test to see if her friends liked me . . . apparently I got the thumbs up from all of them.

I met up with Sara once more on a trip to Johannesburg and upon returning to Sydney I was still doing my best to fight my feelings. Then came the day when I was walking through the mall in Cronulla and I was wondering why I felt so low. It was then that it struck me: I was lonely and I was missing Sara. I could no longer lie to myself about how I felt. I realised I didn't want to spend the rest of my life by myself. I realised I had fallen totally in love with Sara and wanted her to be with me.

I left for India the next day for the Champions League and during the stopover in Singapore I contacted Sara and asked her to move to Australia. I was ecstatic that she said 'yes' without any hesitation. Sara moved over, but she didn't move in straight away. I wanted to introduce her to James and Holly before she lived with us. We thought a great way to do that was a holiday to Disney World in Orlando. Sara had grown up in Miami and been to Disney World on numerous occasions. It was a great idea and Sara and the kids got on extremely well while we were there.

It was February before the first photograph of Sara and me appeared in the gossip columns. The photographer who took it sold it for $95,000—if I knew it would fetch that amount I would've sold one myself! Regardless, the cat was out of the bag. We hadn't tried to keep our relationship a secret, but we hadn't gone out of our way to let the media know about it either. What happened after that shocked me. We had six to seven cars of paparazzi following us daily; they were like shadows and we couldn't turn without a camera clicking or a flash casting more light on our relationship. I had never experienced anything like it before and I guess it provided me with an insight into what Shane Warne's life must be like. Sara took it very well, although there were times when she was overwhelmed by it all. I knew Sara was the one I wanted to spend the rest of my life with; I made that decision when I asked her to Australia. We were soon engaged and then married at our home in Cronulla on 18 November 2010. It was a very private ceremony, immediate family only. But unfortunately nothing is a secret in Sydney and the media found out about it. We had numerous journalists camp out at the top of our driveway, there were boats on the water and three helicopters hovered above the house for the entire time. The scenes outside belied the calm and happiness inside our house where, upon saying our nuptials, Sara became Sara Leonardi-McGrath.

We repeated our vows on 4 July 2011 in a beautiful church in Acireale, the small town in Sicily where Sara's family home had been.

Sara is an amazing wife and she is also an attentive stepmother to James and Holly. She looks after the children as though they are her own and I can see her love for them in the tears of pride she cries while watching such things as Holly performing in a play or reciting poems from memory on stage at school. It is very special—she loves them and they love her back. To know this reinforces that I made the right decision in asking Sara to become a part of our family, though I never had any doubts. The love that's within our family is the reason why we decided to add to it.

As someone with a business degree from the University of Rome, Sara values education and in doing so she shares my belief that Holly and James's schooling is a priority. Although I myself have long been a big believer in the need to keep learning and to improve ourselves. We train our bodies to keep healthy but we should be just as vigilant to keep the mind alert by feeding it.

Sara is the most loyal, passionate and caring person I know. She is very protective and has a no-nonsense, direct approach to handling things (I think that's the Italian combined with a touch of Latino in her). She says she likes it when I assert myself and take control of situations. She has an adventurous spirit; she loves to travel and prefers the chaos of India to the serenity of outback Australia. Sara is always searching for new experiences and is definitely an ideas person. She is the perfect wife and an incredible mother. I hope it's obvious that I love her with all my heart.

3

PARENTHOOD

*You can never say never, you don't know what
can happen in life. Glenn never thought
he was going to get remarried and I didn't
even think about kids until I met him. I never
thought to have them or not to have them but
when you meet that person you want to share
that gift with them.*

*But, we're not starting a family—we're
building on the family we already have.
I would not have adopted, I would not have
used eggs from anyone else because I already
have two [step]children who love me and adore
me and satisfy any parental need. People can
talk about biology but everyone loves what
they love, how they love . . .*

—Sara

One of the happiest moments after Sara fell pregnant was witnessing the reaction from James and Holly when they heard the news. James gave us both a loving hug and kiss, Holly was ecstatic and I'll remember it as a time that defined our sense of 'family'. As Sara said, we weren't creating a new family, we were simply building upon the one we had.

The thought of announcing our news to James and Holly (after Sara had endured the worst imaginable morning sickness every day for three months) made Sara nervous—although I know she'll say otherwise—and I found that funny, because by nature she's a very confident, very self-assured person. This was one occasion where she didn't know how the kids would react. Although she'd later rationalise there was never going to be a problem because during our time together we've provided the kids with an environment of safety, reliability, stability and reassurance so, as she said, there was no reason why they wouldn't be pleased with what awaits us.

Regardless, she broke the news in her own unique way—by writing each of them a beautiful card to express the happiness she felt at being pregnant and how she hoped having another sibling would add even more to their lives. It really was a special time and, as it turned out, she needn't have had any concerns because James had been asking us for years when were we going to have a baby, and he was over the moon to think we'd listened to him.

The kids' response signalled the end to three months of waiting ... and waiting ... and waiting ... because we wanted to ensure everything was fine with the baby before we shared the news. The pregnancy has brought us all even closer, and Sara's rationale was that it was due to the collective realisation that we're going to have one 'piece' that'll be a part of all of us. Sara's desire to have a baby actually stemmed from being a stepmother to James and Holly. I think what best represents the depth of her feeling for them is the simple fact she never uses the word 'step' to describe her relationship with our kids. In the five years since we married, she's never once referred to them as *'your kids'* or introduced them to anyone as *'Glenn's kids'* because she believes to say anything other than *'our kids'* would betray the bond she and the kid's have established and share. I consider her view as not only important, but one that is quite moving. It's also heartening for me to know that as an only child herself, Sara was happy to think that if we should have a baby girl, she'll have Holly as her big sister. Sara views Holly as someone with a caring and special nature, and says she's exactly the type of person she would have loved to have as her big sister. Needless to say she's taken it, as have I, as a 'given' that James will be a protective big brother.

Becoming a dad again at 45 was yet another way in which my life bucked the path I figured it would follow. In 2003 I underwent a vasectomy after Holly was born, and while I consider being a father as perhaps my greatest achievement, at the time of the procedure I thought, That's it, I'll put the cue back in the rack. Even when I met and married Sara—something I vowed would never happen—my inclination was to not have another child. However, five years into our marriage, Sara and I thought becoming parents would be an expression, and an extension, of our love. I also believe that a child needs to be brought into the world through love and not as an emotional bandaid you sometimes hear of when people say 'we thought a child would be good for our relationship'.

While we had our plan to have a child, there was also a lot for us to consider. I'd turned 45, and that meant I'd be 66 at our 3rd child's 21st birthday party. I know there are people who say that doesn't matter, but it was something I figured required careful consideration. Ultimately, I came to the same conclusion: while I mightn't be in the backyard in 2030 playing a game of footy, I could at least ensure our youngest would be well loved and given good guidance. The idea of raising another child as I grew . . . *older* . . . didn't matter because, while some people say that's the stage of your life when you want time to look at sunsets and the like, the fact is Sara, Holly, James and I love doing things together as a family, and this adventure will be no different. However, there was the matter of the vasectomy I had 12 years earlier that needed to be dealt with first of all . . .

I went to the fertility doctor with no idea of what my part would be in the process. Being a father already, I was well aware of the absolute pain women endure to deliver a child, and when I heard the description of the procedure I'd undergo, I was quite certain it would bring tears to my eyes. Now it's been done—and I survived intact—I can honestly say that every bloke I've spoken to about it (and it hasn't been too many) has visibly winced as they heard me explain my side of the story . . .

The tests we underwent revealed good news: I had healthy sperm and Sara's eggs were viable. However, the doctors said there was no point in reversing my vasectomy because the chances of a natural conception were described as unlikely. The doctor explained that eight years after a bloke has a vasectomy, proteins that attach themselves to the sperm prevent fertilisation of the woman's eggs. Because my snip had occurred 12 years earlier, they said we had no chance of conceiving naturally. The only option available to us was IVF, and that meant Sara needed to take a concoction of hormones for over five months to allow for the 'harvesting' of the eggs that would eventually be fertilised by my sperm.

My role in the miracle of birth was 'simply' allowing a doctor to take a tissue sample from one of my testes to extract sperm and, mercifully, the process took all of five minutes. As Sara noted, it all happened while I was knocked out! However, we were keen that our desire to have a child wasn't played out in the media. We didn't need the kind of attention that had surrounded us when word leaked that Sara and I were engaged, and we were stalked by the paparazzi. So whenever we attended the IVF clinic, it was akin to undertaking a secret mission. Sara formulated a plan, which meant I wouldn't go to the clinic until the actual day of my procedure. Even then I'd have to wait until she'd left before entering. I also wasn't allowed to make eye contact with anyone in the waiting room because she figured someone might recognise me. (Well, that made me smile: I'm 196.5 centimetres tall and had played a bit of cricket for Australia, so I was going to be hard to miss.) In the end, Sara and I were extremely grateful—if anyone did notice me at the clinic, they had the good grace to respect our privacy, because we definitely didn't need the pressure that would most certainly have come with our fertility being a 'story'.

Our sperm and eggs were mixed to create embryos, and over the next few months Sara was constantly monitored to gauge when her body was ready to receive one. It was a difficult time for Sara; long after the pain in my testes had dissipated, her hormones were knocked out of alignment, and during our first attempt the embryo didn't 'take'. Thankfully, it was only a temporary setback. When we were successful at our second shot, we felt quite blessed because, as Sara and I appreciate, there are many couples who sadly don't experience that joy despite their courage, persistence and the love that's needed to endure years of attempting to produce a baby through IVF. Both of us know we're fortunate, and when the story about our pregnancy broke, a lot of people made a point of telling us they were just so happy to hear a positive outcome for a change. When people ask why we're having a baby, I like Sara's response: it was simply a matter of life . . . and love.

Being a father and husband means there are already three people in the world—James, Holly and Sara—whose lives I consider to be more important than my own, especially the kids because of the love and the sense of responsibility I have for them. They're the most important treasures in my life, particularly after all we've been through. I'm with Sara because I love her, and the kids are a part of who I am—it feels like they have been part of my life forever. James is 15 and Holly 13 at the time of writing this book—I can't imagine being without them. I was present when both of the kids were born and it was everything you'd expect: an emotional day and a time of wishing every blessing and wanting to do everything possible for the bundle of joy you cradle in your arms. Adding to the emotion of their arrivals was the fact that James and Holly were described as 'miracles', because they were born after doctors gave Jane and I no hope of conceiving as a result of the medication she required when she was fighting the breast cancer.

So, the medical experts were proven wrong, and together the kids brought a lot of joy into our lives. I remember the time I saw James and Holly have their first conversation, and while I'd give anything to remember what it was they were talking about, I remember well how I, feeling fascinated, watched them interact.

I loved playing cricket—it was 'living the dream', as some people say when they're happy with their profession—but all the time I spent away from home really did weigh heavily on my mind, whether I was on tour or on a training camp. Jane was the closest thing to being a single mother, without actually being one. While she tried hard to ensure I didn't miss the important moments of their lives by keeping detailed scrapbooks, taking photographs and videoing such things as birthday parties, it could never be a substitute for actually being there. Sometimes seeing what I was missing out on at home made it even tougher to be away . . . it reached the stage where it was a bit of a tug of war. The way I coped was to reconcile myself to the fact that cricket and touring was my job, and that was how I provided for us. I would be away for a while, but when I returned I made sure we always enjoyed quality time together. I thought to myself that the notion of 'quality time' made up for a lot, because in another life I could've had a 9 to 5 job and been stuck at the office working on a project while the kids were at home; I could get home tired, cranky; and maybe we could've had a bit of time together over the weekend before the grind would start all over again on Monday. It was a good way to deal with our situation when I spent a lot of time away, and I embraced it because I needed to believe it. It reached the stage where I'd say goodbye to Jane and the kids at home before I left for a tour, because I didn't like the airport farewells and the fact that those last few minutes before you'd be separated for weeks—and it's awful—were treated as fodder for photo-graphers or television news crews. Of course, once I joined the team I slipped straight into my role as fast bowler and team 'pest', annoying the guys by throwing things at them—and I really enjoyed their friendship and the sense of camaraderie we shared. But there was always a sadness when I heard the door shut behind me and the kids calling out 'bye' as I walked towards the taxi I'd catch to the airport.

During the drive to the airport, I would tell myself I loved playing cricket (but not as much as my family), that it provided good money for my family, and went over in my head whatever other thoughts might help. Ultimately, I realised I was spending too much time away from my family, and that was the deciding factor when I started to think perhaps the time was drawing near when I'd hang up the bowling boots.

In the build-up to the 2006–07 season, I spent eight months at home when Jane fell ill. It was actually a great time for me as a father, and I was pleased to be doing what's called the normal 'Dad' things. It opened my eyes to everything I'd been missing out on, so many good times and magic moments. Something I learnt during that time was that my family had its own routines, and there were times when I'd go to do something and the kids would say 'but we don't do it that way, Dad'. That was as much a shock to the system as it was an eye-opener. It also made me think about my own childhood. Apart from having my mum and dad around—well, until they divorced—my siblings Donna, Dale and I also had our grandparents nearby, so, without even realising it, there was always a sense of 'comfort' that we had people looking out for us. My kids didn't have that, because my parents and siblings lived almost 500 kilometres away in the Far West and Jane's family was on the other side of the world, and that played on my mind. In the eight months we were together, I formed a deep attachment with the kids: the love was always there, but being with them day in day out was great, and I learnt a lot from seeing the world through their eyes, too.

Holly has many of Jane's characteristics; Jane was creative—and I'm pleased Holly has inherited that streak—while James loved having his father around him. It made me think a lot about my relationship with my father. Dad was a hard worker, he provided for us and battled tough times. My term for him is 'good man', and he instilled in me a lot of positive principles. However, when he and Mum divorced, he moved away. It wasn't until I turned 25 and had broken up with my girlfriend at the time after I returned from the West Indies tour in 1995 that I went out west and spent three weeks with him on his farm. We reconnected and became close again. There was never an issue between us; Dad did his thing and I did mine, but that meant we could go for months without talking. The three weeks I spent out on the farm with Dad was probably the most time we'd spent together in the previous ten years, and the sense of 'reconnection' I felt then was the same I felt with my own children in that extended time at home, especially with James. Holly had me wrapped around her little finger, but I could see in James there was a need to have his dad around to kick the footy with or to play cricket, and to also be told by his dad what to do . . . they were the same needs I had when I was a boy.

When the day came for me to return to 'work' and leave for yet another tour, the looks on their faces broke my heart. It rammed home that I was spending way too much time away from home. When I asked myself if the time had come for me to call stumps, that look and that sense of *knowing* became the deciding factor. It was thinking about the life I could have with my family that made it quite easy for me to say goodbye to a sport that'd dominated my life for longer than I cared to remember.

Holly is growing into a special young lady and I feel an enormous sense of pride in that. And while she is creative, 'Doll' is also a great student and her school report cards acknowledge all of her positive traits from grades to manners. James is a real boy; he has lots of good mates and is into many sports. We do a lot together: one of our shared interests is scuba diving and free diving. It's something that we do together that I believe can only strengthen our bond. Sometimes I'm asked if I would like James to play cricket at a high level. All I ever say is if that's what my son wants, then I'll do all I can to help him, but if he doesn't, that's his choice.

I'm very proud of the people my kids have grown into, and are growing into. As proud of them as I am, and as much as I love them, I don't mind admitting it's scary to think what the world is like out there. It can be a mean place, but while it's a deep concern, I think we need to give our kids our trust and, as hard as it is, allow for them to make some mistakes. I believe that's how they'll learn who they really are. I've set myself the goal as my kids' father, and Sara backs me completely as their mother, to ensure they're raised to be people who care for others. That would make me, as their dad, very happy and proud.

4

PINK FIT

It's great to be back here at the SCG, which is my favourite ground in the world. To walk back on the hallowed turf is always something very special, but to think this is our seventh Sydney Pink Test we've been involved in is absolutely incredible. Through that time, through the Cricket Cares program with Cricket Australia, we've raised over $6.5 million dollars, which I think is absolutely amazing . . . I can't think of any other sporting event and charity/foundation that have teamed up and created something this special. To see everyone turn up in pink is amazing. To think the Australian and Indian teams have pink logos [is incredible] . . . I guess when I was a kid you wouldn't have anything pink near your cricket gear, to think what's been created here and how many Australian families have been supported just blows me away. We have come a long way in a relatively short space of time but we have a long way to go to achieve our goal, which is every Australian *family experiencing breast cancer has access to a breast care nurse where they live. That's still the driving force of the foundation, as is raising breast awareness, especially in younger women. We say in the foundation, together we can make a difference but I think it should be together we ARE making a difference . . . it's been amazing.*

—My thoughts to the media before the 2014–15 Pink Test

The most commonly asked question I field during the lead-up to the Pink Test at the SCG is what would Jane have made of her life being honoured in such a public way. The truth is this: she would have felt a mixture of shock, pride and humility, because she never believed the foundation—and definitely not breast cancer—was all about her. The third day of the SCG Test represents hope and enjoying life to promote the importance of educating people about breast cancer and ensuring that no woman, regardless of her background or where she lives, is condemned to go through her struggle alone. The McGrath Foundation provides specialised nurses who are trained to help in so many ways.

The Pink Test is a festive occasion and I guess that's helped by the fact that it falls in the Christmas–New Year period when people are happy and up for a good time. In that regard, my family is no different to anyone else. Jane McGrath Day means a lot to Holly and James, because when they see the SCG bathed in pink, because it's the colour most people wear to support the foundation, I think they realise the Pink Test is about hope and appreciating the gift that is life. It's also a sign for James and Holly that the legacy of their mother's fight with a disease that eventually took her life has become a rallying cry for so many people.

As was the case with the first Pink Test when I looked over the SCG with a sense of awe, I make it a point each year to take time out to soak in the scene and admire what has been created. The sight of the sea of pink around the ground—and the fact that people are prepared to help out and show their support for the cause—never ceases to amaze me.

The Pink Test is actually a joyous time for us, and Jane McGrath Day is one that I, James and Holly embrace. It's a day that reminds us, Sara included, that life isn't just about quantity, it *has* to centre around quality. I'm conscious of trying to hang onto what I learnt during that period of my life, and that is the importance of savouring the moments that count.

Cricket Australia acknowledged the importance of the foundation's work by naming the third day of the Sydney Test the Jane McGrath Day. While it was an extraordinary gesture, we didn't know what to expect going into it. Apart from anything else, I wondered whether the public would buy into it. I mean, it was after all a *Test*-cricket crowd, who value the sport's age-old traditions.

Kylie Tink was chief executive of the foundation at the time, and I thought she did an incredible job during the six years she was at the helm. I clearly remember the day we attended our first meeting with Channel Nine's head of sport, Steve Crawley. Every time we offered a suggestion that could help promote the foundation, Steve would shake his head before replying with a gruff, 'We can't do any of that.' I had no idea what to expect after we left that meeting; but on the third day of the Test I looked around my favourite cricket ground with what I can only describe as a sense of awe and disbelief. The signage around the ground was pink; the logos on the Aussie team's shirts were pink; the stumps were pink; and the Channel Nine commentators were dressed in pink. There were volunteers working tirelessly to collect money for the foundation, and the tradition-steeped Ladies Stand was named after Jane. Everyone from the prime minister to truckies and office workers were decked out in pink, and all I can remember thinking to myself was, How incredible is this? Channel Nine, Cricket Australia and the SCG Trust had exceeded the requests we'd put forward. I don't think I can ever hope to thank Cricket Australia's chief executive officer James Sutherland, Steve Crawley, the SCG Trust's Jamie Barkley and the crowd enough for their efforts, because that first Pink Test was the springboard for the tradition—and the warm spirit that I believe defines the day—in each of the summers that have followed.

That first day was a blur. I went from high teas to commentary booths to media interviews to mingling with the crowd to lunch, where the prime minister and other dignitaries were in attendance, to talk about the work of the foundation and to spell out our goals. I finished the day happy with what had been achieved. The success took everyone by surprise. I was elated for the foundation's sake, because apart from helping to raise the profile it was exciting to think of how many lives would change for the better.

These days Sara accompanies me to the SCG and her involvement is important to me. Her desire to support the work of the foundation means a lot to me. The foundation holds a special significance for Sara because her mother battled breast cancer. The Test is also a chance for her, now living on the other side of the world, to reflect on what she and her mother endured and the importance of their relationship. During the Pink Test the SCG is full of so many people with their own stories and emotions. I meet so many people throughout the course of those five days who, in one way or another, have been affected by cancer. Last summer a breast cancer patient named Jill Crozier was present for the Test against India because she wanted to be a part of the day, and I thought her story was more powerful than anything that happened out on the pitch. Jill travelled to Sydney from a sheep station nearly four hours from Broken Hill in outback New South Wales. She was exactly the kind of person we had in mind to help when we formed the foundation. You see, there was a five-month period after being diagnosed when she needed to endure a 1600-kilometre round trip from her property to Adelaide for chemo-therapy. What I can only imagine would've been a night-marish journey ended when the McGrath Foundation—in alliance with a valued sponsor, Elders—was able to fund a breast care nurse to be attached to the Royal Flying Doctor Service at Broken Hill in 2011. That nurse, named Jo Beven, is someone I have heard only wonderful things about over the years. Her posting means she's able to look after women like Jill, who live in remote areas in New South Wales, South Australia and Queensland. The care Jo provides patients goes beyond dispensing medication and offering advice. I was told that when Jill lost her hair, her eyelashes and eyebrows as a result of her chemotherapy treatment, Jo went to the trouble of taking a make-up artist along on a visit to show Jill the best way to apply make-up. Jo realised that was something that would allow Jill to feel good about herself. It's the human touch; and the reason I've mentioned Jill and Jo is because they put a face to the many, many stories behind the foundation. They are the people that the beefy blokes who dress up in pink and the women who normally wouldn't attend a cricket match in a pink fit are helping through their donations and support. Before the 2015 Test, when the foundation celebrated our 'decade of making a difference', we revealed our plan to try and increase our number of breast care nurses to 110, because we realised that would put us in a position to support another 10,000 families.

Normally Cricket Australia doesn't partner up with a charity for more than three years, but we have started talking about heading into our third term, and that is an honour. What also pleases me about the Pink Test is that we—Cricket Australia and the McGrath Foundation—have formed an alliance that is also giving back to cricket. It's my understanding that the pre-ticket sales for the Sydney Test, especially for the third day, are higher than at any other ground around Australia during the summer, and that's because there are more families and women coming along— and that pleases me. As I said on the eve of the 2014–15 Test, I can't think of too many charities or foundations that have partnered with a big sporting organisation with such success. The players have thrown their weight behind it; the sponsors are extremely generous; Channel Nine has certainly bent over backwards to help; the SCG Trust has been magnificent and they go to a lot of trouble to prepare the ground; while the crowd doesn't hold back its support. It's only getting bigger every year, and as a foundation we now have a far better understanding of what we need to do. And that's good, because after seven Pink Tests I'm not running around like a headless chook anymore.

We've had four prime ministers involved in the event since its inception—Kevin Rudd, Julia Gillard, Tony Abbott and Malcolm Turnbull. What I like is that, in the course of the day, the nation's leader could be found having a cup of tea with breast cancer patients or, as was the case for Mr Abbott last year, judging a cake-decorating competition, which included entries from his wife, Margie; celebrity cook Julie Goodwin; athletes Ellyse Perry and Candice Falzon; and Holly and me. Holly was the star of our team. It made me smile as the PM treated the matter as something of national importance when, dressed in his pink tie to support the cause, he stuck his finger deep into the icing, examined it closely and then, after some more consideration, declared the contest a dead heat. While he gave each team 18 points (and probably saved himself from a night in the doghouse at Kirribilli), my opinion still stands that Holly's effort was clearly the best!

Something I have noticed about the foundation is that everyone likes to have ownership of it, and I see that as very healthy. During the inaugural Pink Test, I took some time out and sat in the Cricket NSW box with two old friends. One was Brian Gainsford, who had a big impact on my cricket career when he picked me for the Tooheys Cup match that featured Doug Walters and the other first-class players in Parkes. The other was Brian Freedman who is a stalwart at the Bankstown Cricket Club and for New South Wales. As we watched, they commented that it was a pity they couldn't take a piece of the Pink Test to communities around Australia. It was from that off-the-cuff comment that the successful concept of the Pink Stumps Day was born. The Pink Stumps Day is an event where local communities raise funds for the McGrath Foundation by playing pink matches, and people really throw themselves into the spirit of the day.

There are other events run in conjunction with the Test, including the annual Pink Pigeon Race Day back at my hometown of Narromine. This event means a lot to me on a personal level. Some of the people I know from my school days and from playing local sport are out helping to raise funds and, at the same time, having a bit of fun at the expense of my nickname 'Pigeon'—a moniker bestowed upon me a lifetime ago because of my skinny legs. The race is held on Jane McGrath Day and the pigeons fly from Narromine to Trangie, which is about 30 kilometres away. The concept is the brainchild of the Trangie Hotel's big-hearted publican Steve Dalton, who is a pigeon racer. His idea has been a sure-fire success, raising well over $100,000. But I also really like that the race has become a genuine community event, with a three-person Ambrose at the Narromine Golf Club the day before, a sausage sizzle, and a Calcutta auction with the pigeons up for sale. They hold a Pink Lamb sale and on race day they have music and jumping castles for the kids. It makes me laugh that each of the pigeons are named after Channel Nine commentators, and sometimes the mind boggles when I wonder what characteristics they look for when they name a bird after Mark 'Tubby' Taylor, Shane Warne, Ian Chappell, Bill Lawry, Michael 'Slats' Slater, Ian Healy and the rest of the gang. In the true spirit of bushies helping out, the winnings from the race are split between the owner of the top placegetters and the foundation, and it helps a lot.

I have also found that the foundation can bring out the best in old foes. The visiting teams have always been happy to play a role in the day, but most surprising to me since my retirement is the way in which the Barmy Army have supported it. During my days patrolling the boundary I exchanged plenty of banter with them, but my attitude towards them has gone up a few notches in recent years. I'm not going to get mushy, but the way they've banded behind the Pink Test and the foundation tells me that maybe they're not such a bad mob after all; the last time they invaded the SCG they donated $35,000 to the kitty, which I consider a magnificent gesture. I think it says a lot about what they stand for: a group of people wanting to have a good time.

There was a time when I'd wonder how long the Pink Test would be a part of the cricket calendar, but it seems as though it's here to stay. I've heard the term 'iconic' associated with it in more recent times and I hope that is the popular view, because there is definitely a spirit about it, and there are plenty of people depending upon what the SCG Test and the generosity of so many people and organisations offer them.

Hope.

5

FOUNDATION OF HOPE AND DEVOTION

I just love cancer nursing, love it with a passion, because you just make a difference, that's why. No matter what part of the experience people are at, whether it's the beginning of their diagnosis, the middle or the end you can always make a difference.

—Bec Creeper, McGrath IGA breast care nurse

I'm humbled that the McGrath Foundation is considered by many people as one of Australia's most respected charities, all because it is seen as something the average person can relate to. People appreciate that our single goal is to help women suffering from breast cancer in the most practical way possible, and that's by providing highly trained nurses throughout the length and breadth of Australia, particularly in those rural areas where medical resources can be few and far between. After all these years—the foundation is ten years old—I still feel a thrill when I see someone wearing a McGrath Foundation cap as a show of support; or when I go to a refrigerator at a convenience store and see those rows of now familiar pink-capped Mount Franklin spring water bottles with our logo on the label; and I will forever feel an immense sense of pride when I hear our greatest treasures, the nurses, described by their patients—and the patients' families—as God-sent.

Despite my unabashed pride in what the foundation represents, the truth is I live for the day when we can shut it down . . . that day when we can lock the front doors of our office in the Sydney suburb of St Leonards and allow everyone involved in the organisation to move on and utilise their amazing talents, their compassion and creativity in other endeavours, other fields. The reason why I can't wait for that day is because it will mean the doctors and researchers who've devoted years of their lives trying to find a cure will have finally achieved what we've all been praying for—something to nullify an insidious disease that strikes one in eight Australian women and has brought far too much grief to the world. I firmly believe that day will come, but until it does we'll continue to do our bit to work hard and try to bring whatever comfort we can to sufferers, through the nurses and whatever else we might be able to provide them and their families.

In 2008 the McGrath Foundation had four nurses, but six years later—thanks to initiatives such as Cricket Australia's SCG Pink Test; to federal and state government support; and to grassroots community efforts hosting high teas, walkathons, bike rides, pink cricket matches or even footy games with big burly blokes decked out in pink—at last count there were 102 nurses throughout Australia, each of them helping to make a difference to so many lives.

The reason the growth of the foundation—and its impact—particularly pleases me is that when it was formed in 2005 we funded the cost of one specialist nurse at the St George Hospital. We were driven by the notion that if we could help just *one* person by providing them with treatment and the support of someone that would allow them to realise they weren't in the fight on their own, it would be worthwhile.

It wasn't easy because we had to raise $300,000 to fund the nurse. In the early days I would auction off gear I'd worn in Tests or one-day internationals to generate some money. However, as news of what we were trying to achieve became public, some of my sponsors offered their support and corporate clout. The general public also became involved, because I think people, especially Australians, like to back the underdog and they could see we were quite a small group who'd undertaken a massive fight. What it's grown into ten years later, and what it represents to so many people, is quite incredible. The foundation has helped over 33,000 families, and I'm regularly told about the effect the breast care nurses and support from our head office have had. When I meet people who are going through their breast cancer battle, or who are supporting someone suffering, I often hear that the nurses have had an amazing impact on their quality of life. It's something I always find moving, and those stories also help me to retain my focus. I was at the sprawling Miranda Westfield shopping centre one day recently when a woman walked towards me. I could see she had tears welling in her eyes. After stopping me, the lady gave me a big hug and a kiss on the cheek to thank me for the hope and the amazing care the foundation had given her when things in her life seemed quite bleak. Her reaction was a moment that really pinpointed the importance of the work that's being done by the foundation.

We have a team of over 30 people working at the McGrath Foundation office and it's a hive of activity. I'm impressed by the day-to-day running of an organisation that coordinates everything from helping to organise a ball, to raising funds in a country town, to running breakthrough initiatives to educate young people about breast cancer and how to deal with an illness that may be affecting their mother or a beloved aunt. My role these days is as the organisation's president, because it became too big for me to remain the chairman. The man who has assumed that position, John Conde, and our chief executive Petra Buchanan are marvels, and the success of the organisation can be attributed to the leadership and drive they provide. My role as president involves being on hand for the special events when we thank the people and corporations who have supported us over the years. I'm on the board and I make it a point to ensure I'm across everything that's happening in the organisation, and in my public speaking engagements I always talk about the foundation. It's very rare that a day has passed by in the last seven years when I haven't spoken about the work and goals of something that started with a mission to try and make a difference to one person's life. I have no doubt the reason why people hold the McGrath Foundation in high esteem is because they can see the *immediate* and tangible difference their donation is making to lives.

In recent years there have been a number of debates about the breast cancer charity dollar being funded into research programs that are trying to find a cure for the disease. Advocates for those groups say they should be given the donation over groups such as the McGrath Foundation that offer care. It's an argument I'm loath to buy into. I whole-heartedly agree research is crucial, but I also believe you can't overlook the plight of the people who are going through the illness *now*. I've seen their lives with my own eyes, I've heard their voices and they deserve help; they're entitled to dignity and they need to know that they matter—although I'm not suggesting for a moment that the research advocates don't also share that view. Breast cancer is far too big an issue to be simply boiled down to a battle between the labs and the lives. There should be enough generosity and goodwill in our society to ensure everyone can play their role in the battle and the quest, because ultimately we are all seeking the same outcome.

When $1.5 million was raised in donations after Jane passed away, it was thought that, if given the choice, she would have liked for that money to be set aside for an educational program. In time it provided the foundation with funding for a project called Curve Lurve, which is designed to teach teenage girls about their bodies and to not only gain an understanding of the telltale signs of breast cancer, but also to educate them about what they ought to do if they should discover a lump one day. It's an awareness program available to both sexes because breast cancer affects the whole family, and, despite what people might think, men aren't immune from the impact of this disease. It's important that people become familiar with their body and understand what their 'normal' is—and what's not. It's important for everyone to know themselves well enough to realise when something isn't right. One of the organisation's initiatives includes a so-called 'caravan of lurve' nicknamed 'Curvey' that travels around the nation. The young Aussie women who visit it are encouraged to observe the shape and appearance of their breasts and nipples in a mirror, firstly with their arms by their sides before lifting them above their heads to have another look. It's simply a part of teaching them to realise what their 'normal' is. They're instructed by a nurse on the correct way to feel their breasts and nipples and to keep an eye out for anything that appears to be out of the ordinary. Finally, those who visit the caravan are taught to appreciate that breasts come in different shapes and sizes. The most important message we want them to take away is that if there's something that seems abnormal they should head straight for the doctor, because early detection is vital. While I do have my reservations about social media, the foundation has developed a very useful app, which reinforces the Curve Lurve steps. It's an effective tool that not only encourages breast awareness but allows the user to personalise their profile, and also keeps them informed of the latest news; there is also a section where they can document anything they might find and they can even use the app to set a reminder each month so that they remember to self-examine.

The positive experience Jane and I had with her breast care nurse in 2003 gave us a focus to start the foundation boots and all. The nurse was someone who offered guidance and advice, but I learned she was also someone who Jane could vent her frustrations to, and someone who she could discuss her fears with without feeling as though she was being judged. These nurses provide comfort during the testing times.

The foundation identified the outback as an area that needed help. We realised there was no breast cancer support network for people living there. Fighting breast cancer, which is already traumatic enough, was made even tougher in the outback because patients had to pay to travel to their nearest city for treatment, which could mean time away from their families and a host of costs. After a lot of discussion it was decided we would pay the wage for a breast care nurse to be based in the bush. Then the numbers began to increase:

from one to two, and then from two to three. We then decided to try to gather an army of nurses in the outback; and there was no looking back.

Not just anyone can be a McGrath breast care nurse; it's a demanding job and requires a person who is giving, caring, compassionate and considerate. They also need to have completed their first unit of breast cancer nursing. The foundation has identified the importance of continually upskilling the nurses and providing them with an allowance so they can attend training every year to increase their knowledge. Above all I view our nurses as courageous people with big hearts. Every year we have a conference where we get as many of our nurses as possible to attend, and it's quite amazing—humbling, really—to see them in the one room. They definitely have a calling that's very special, but I'm afraid the reality is that what they go through during the course of their working week is tough. The job is incredibly stressful and it's a credit to their characters that each nurse continues, despite knowing it comes with the very real risk of heartache because not everyone survives. We are fully aware of the toll their important work can have on them and we offer support for our nurses, which is something that I not only rate as very important but as essential.

When I write about cricketers such as Sachin Tendulkar, Brian Lara, Shane Warne and Steve Waugh, I use the word 'great' to highlight they belong to the best of the best. The problem I'm always confronted by when I need to describe my thoughts about the McGrath Foundation's breast care nurses is that mere words don't do them justice. I think they're in a league of their own and to simply hail them as 'great' doesn't cut it. From talking to them and learning about their motives for embracing a life that isn't easy, I've come to the conclusion that perhaps the best tribute I can offer is to say these nurses—through their selflessness and a desire to provide a pillar of strength and a tender shoulder to cry on—set standards very few of us could ever hope to match.

MCGRATH BREAST CARE NURSES—THE FACTS

- Breast care nurses are registered nurses who are trained to act as patient advocates, who coordinate the care for women experiencing breast cancer, and support their families and their carers.
- They provide accurate information, support and referral to services.
- It costs about $380,000 to employ each full-time McGrath breast care nurse over a minimum three-year period.
- To become a McGrath breast care nurse, a candidate must have relevant postgraduate qualifications in either breast care nursing or cancer nursing.
- Most McGrath breast care nurses have a background in oncology, breast care, women's health and, in some cases, psychology.
- The McGrath Foundation currently offers four scholarships through the Australian College of

Nursing, which are open to registered nurses residing in Australia.

- The support of a McGrath breast care nurse can significantly help improve a patient's quality of care because they provide one main source of information and contact throughout the patient's treatment plan.
- Support from a McGrath breast care nurse can help to greatly minimise the stress and trauma of a breast cancer diagnosis for the patient and the patient's family.
- A McGrath breast care nurse is available to help a patient or family experiencing breast cancer at any point during diagnosis and treatment. If you or someone close to you hasn't been referred to a McGrath breast care nurse in your area, please make direct contact to receive help.
- The McGrath Foundation is working hard to achieve our goal of providing access to a McGrath breast care nurse for every Australian family battling breast cancer. Sadly, this is not currently achievable, but the foundation is determined to work towards realising that outcome.
- They are self-referable and a totally free service.

6

SELLING THE FARM

I love the fact I'm working with my hands and producing something, but you've got to be mentally fit to survive it . . .

Rural Victoria is slowly dying, communities are getting smaller, support is getting less. But every day the sun comes up. You just get back into it and do it.

—David Jochinke, Australian farmer

E ven though I left our family farm at breakneck speed in a cloud of dust to pursue a cricket career with Sutherland District Cricket Club 26 years ago, I had spent so much time out in the paddocks and working the land at Lagoona I doubt whether the dirt could ever be completely scrubbed from underneath my nails—and I wouldn't want it to be. While I now live on the shores of Gunnamatta Bay, 450 kilometres from the 485-hectare sheep and wheat farm I called home at Narromine, my affinity with the farmer still runs deep. I have a 13,750-hectare property 160 kilometres north-west of Burke in New South Wales that my brother Dale runs, and we have 4000 sheep, mainly Merino ewes with Dorset rams, and a few head of cattle.

I deeply admire the courage of the farmer. They're Australia's ultimate gamblers because they put *everything* on the line whenever they plant a crop. They're betting on the rain to come at the right time when they plant the seed, and they're banking on it not to rain at the crucial time of harvesting. I also value the strength of rural communities, and they need that foundation because it seems to help pull everyone through during the tough times; and such is the ebb and flow of life in the bush, there's plenty of tough times.

As much as I love the outback and its people, I'm fearful for their future. What has been a tough occupation—ever since a bright spark stuck a stick into the soil in 10,000 BC and threw some seeds into the furrows he'd scraped to grow grain—is getting even harder. And not just due to the traditional hardships of drought, flood, fire, frost and plagues that Mother Nature serves up from time to time. It's becoming harder to make a decent living in the Australian agricultural sector. Farmers are accused of whingeing when they complain that supermarkets are selling two litres of milk for two bucks as a ploy to lure customers in to buy other goods. But the farmer knows that that practice will eventually destroy the dairy industry.

My younger brother Dale is an exceptional farmer. He's hardworking and knowledgeable, and if ever a man was born to work the land, it's him. However, even he sometimes questions whether the hard yakka and heartache is worth his while. Sometimes it feels as though people in the city don't put too much thought into where their bread, butter, fruit and meat come from when they go to the shops—roll their eyes and say 'they're whingeing again' when farmers complain about the price of milk in supermarkets. Dale recently challenged me to name a profession where the workers would be happy to accept the same wage they received 20 years ago because, as he pointed out, that's what is happening to farmers—As the Australian Bureau of Statistics notes, a litre of milk was $1.03 in 1994. The country kids see what's happening to their parents and they're voting with their feet: they're leaving the farm to seek jobs in the city, and by doing so are joining the 89 per cent of the Australian population who live in urban areas.

In 2012 Sara and I were appointed ambassadors for The Year of the Farmer, which was an initiative to acknowledge the contribution the people on the land make to the national economy and the community. It was a very positive concept, which reiterated Aussie farmers produce almost 93 per cent of the nation's daily domestic food supply; 99 per cent of the 134,000 farm businesses in Australia were family owned and operated; that there were 307,000 people throughout Australia employed in agriculture; and that including the affiliated food and fibre industries the sector contributed 1.6 million jobs to the economy. We also learnt the average local farmer grows enough food to feed 600 people, 150 here in Australia and 450 overseas, and I reckon the bureaucrats described the situation perfectly as 'punching above our weight'.

The Year of the Farmer also highlighted the many challenges our farmers face. For instance, the average age of an Australian farmer was 52—a whopping 12 years above the national average for other occupations—while in the year leading up to 2012, some 18,000 people had abandoned the agricultural sector. To put that into context, that's five times the population of Narromine. Allied with the age-old curses of drought, crippling debt and frost, and with no relief on the horizon, farmers are buckling under the stress, and it cuts me deeply to think suicide is viewed by some as their only escape. In 2014 the federal politician Bob Katter said Australia's four big agricultural sectors of sheep, cattle, dairy and sugar cane were 'going straight down the chute at 100 miles an hour' and farmers, who he described as 'the toughest people this nation has ever produced', were crumbling. Katter claimed a farmer was committing suicide every four days. While that figure was questioned by critics who said it was based on data from the 1980s and '90s, the message that there's a serious problem unravelling beyond the city limits can't be ignored and it *must* be addressed. In 2006 the former Victorian premier Jeff Kennett, in his post-political capacity as chairman of beyondblue (a not-for-profit charity that has raised awareness for people with anxiety and/or depression), told the media during the midst of a terrible drought that he feared for the wellbeing of his nation's embattled farmers: 'My fear is that when under prolonged stress and, when they see their assets totally denuded of value, that we will see an increase [in suicides].' While Katter's figure was shot down by the academics, I think it's worth noting that studies by the Australian Institute for Suicide Research and Prevention found Queensland's agricultural workers and farmers were twice as likely as the general population to kill themselves. If that isn't a wake-up call to politicians and bureaucrats of the suffering and heartache that's occurring in the woolsheds, the wheat fields and sugarcane fields of their country, I don't know what on earth is.

The federal government released its *Agricultural Competitiveness White Paper* in July 2015, which included plans for tax changes, putting money away in farm management deposits, sending five new agricultural counsellors overseas to open up new markets for Australian food, setting aside money for roads and dams infrastructure, and encouraging investment in water infrastructure and fencing that will double as drought preparation. Despite this, I remain concerned that they continue to give the green light to foreign and local energy companies who, in their insatiable hunt for coal seam gas (CSG), will leave wastelands in areas with soil that's so rich in nutrients it should actually be fenced off and protected to help Australia feed a global market that demands 'clean' food.

Australia has shifted its economic focus from the primary industries to energy. Foreign companies are competing with local companies to drill holes, about the diameter of a dinner plate and up to a kilometre beneath the ground, in their hunt for CSG in some of the nation's richest agricultural areas. I've read about the many jobs it will supposedly create, and the billions of dollars the industry will inject into the economy, and I've heard talk that liquid gas fields will turn Central Queensland into Asia's answer to Saudi Arabia in terms of wealth, but at what cost? If prime agricultural sites around the nation are lost, we'll pay for it in the long run when we realise we sold out our opportunity to be the food bowl for Asia. The United Nations estimate that the current growing global demand for food and fibre means that by 2050 the world will require productivity to increase by 70 per cent in order to meet the global population's needs. I think Australia ought to protect prime agricultural land by putting fences around it to feed what's becoming an ever-increasingly hungry world. I'm not anti-mining, but I do oppose a policy that has us selling off the farm for a quick cash grab.

I don't know if this is a battle the farmer can win, and while I'm glad the government's *Agricultural Competitiveness White Paper* is addressing some issues in the outback, the populations in regional Australia are so small their voice is easily drowned out. Indeed, people should appreciate when they're eating their dinner or snacking on an apple at morning tea, that there are farmers just a few hundred kilometres away from them who have formed blockades around the gates of their properties to stop the CSG companies from just rolling in and taking over. A farmer only owns the first few inches of dirt on their property and anyone can buy the mining rights to that same property. It's a rule that has always been in place—and one that is being exploited today—and I don't think it's fair.

It's in the government's interest to invest in farming because there are analysts who maintain there will come a day when the vegetables grown in the backyard will be even more valuable than the car in the garage. Their message has certainly reached the rest of the world, because Indonesia, China, Qatar and the United States are among many countries buying up large chunks of Australian land to ensure they can feed their populations come the day when they struggle to meet demand with their locally grown produce. By buying properties here they're potentially cutting Australia out of the future economic benefits of controlling the production and processing elements required to take the food from paddock to plate. The government calls it foreign investment, but many say what's actually happening in the outback could be considered a takeover. There are a lot of North American and British superannuation companies buying up land for their investors out where I have my farm. They view it as a sure bet for the future, and I don't understand why Australian companies aren't flying the flag. While the ramifications of the mess that's unravelling in the Australian outback—CSG mining, free trade agreements, suicides, crippling debt, foreign ownership, a cringe-worthy 'she'll be right' approach—won't impact my generation, I know it will definitely hurt my kids and grandchildren. That concerns me, because I'd like to think people, especially those elected into office, would want to leave their nation in a better place than when they entered office.

The one positive is it's not too late to change the path we're treading as a nation. Farming is a great lifestyle, and I remember the time when Dale and I had to look after the farm while our father was driving road trains as the hardest work I've ever done but also rewarding. We have some brilliant young farmers, they have great passion, they're well educated in modern farming technology and they know how to apply the technology effectively. I have no doubt they can take the agricultural sector forward. However, I'd like to see it made a bit easier for them. If the government is not prepared to offer farmers subsidies like many of our trading partners do, maybe we could at least provide significant interest-free loans that would allow for people to set up a farm minus the stress that's currently killing many. It's a worthwhile investment, and I'm afraid that if we don't bite the bullet and do something to address the many problems people on the land are facing now, Australia will definitely pay for it in the future.

If you, or someone you know, are having problems and need help, I urge you to call Lifeline on 13 11 14 or beyondblue on 1300 22 4636.

7

A IS FOR ATTITUDE

Attitude is a little thing that makes a big difference.

—Winston Churchill, former British prime minister

I believe cricket is 70 per cent mental; that figure might even be higher, but the one thing I am certain of is that skill alone will take a player only so far. *Attitude* is what allows a player to progress from being the teenage cricket star who eventually dominates his team's annual presentation night to become a player who conquers the tough road towards the elite level.

Attitude is the element in your character that pushes you to attend training on a Friday night when you'd much rather be at a party or out on the town with your friends; it's what forces you to climb out of bed in the middle of winter to go on an early morning run while your rivals are snug in bed and sleeping; and, as a fast bowler, attitude is the inner-voice that demands you to steam in under a scorching sun and bowl yet *another* over against a batsman who may as well be a brick wall. Even when it'd be so much easier to chuck in the towel and lie down in the shade under a tree.

As a kid who was dismissed as never being good enough to be selected for junior talent squads, or given little—if any—hope by many people of going very far in cricket, I worked hard for everything I gained. The thought that people couldn't see that special quality in me as readily as they did in my teammates wasn't easy. While it hurt, I never allowed it to stop me from doing everything I thought I needed to do to try and make the grade. I was gutted the day I missed out on selection in the Country Colts' under-21s team when I played for Narromine in the annual Colts carnival. It cut deeply because I was *that* kid who, after spending a day at school and slaving my backside off on the farm would still pick up one of the scuffed cricket balls lying about behind Dad's machinery shed, mark my run-up and bowl at the battered old 44-gallon drum I used as a wicket. Not being picked went against everything I was taught to believe, which was that hard work and sacrifice was rewarded. But that line of thought was challenged every time a representative team was announced and I was left to deal with that awful sense of being overlooked. My attitude at the time was, rather than toss it in, I simply told myself 'Your time will come', and I truly believed it.

When Penrith sent a talent scout over the Blue Mountains and into the Narromine wheat belt, I was told that after he watched me perform he described the trip to his committee as a waste of time and petrol. In his opinion I was destined to be nothing more than just another good bush-basher. Hearing that as a 17-year-old, albeit second-hand, didn't do much for my confidence. If you allowed it, such a comment could rattle your self-belief—and attitude. In hindsight, I'm extremely grateful that I was born with the 'madness' Dennis Lillee says all fast bowlers require. I think that madness to not give in when the odds seemed stacked against me— and that's the reality of the paceman's lot, the odds can be against you—stemmed from my DNA, because my bloodline includes pioneers, farmers, soldiers and athletes. My brother Dale has that madness not to give in as a farmer. He and his family battle all the age-old adversaries people on the land are subjected to—drought, flood, bushfire and frost—with a steely determination and belief that, come hell or high water, they'll make good.

I honestly have no idea what I'd be doing now if my attitude had abandoned me in those crucial late-teenage years, when you can either follow your ambition or be like everyone else and put fun ahead of goals. Maybe I'd still be working in the bank, where I worked when I left school, or out on the farm. I will say that these days I remember that bumpy stretch of ground behind Dad's machinery shed as my field of dreams. I remember how, as the sun sank below the horizon, I'd pretend the great West Indies 'Master Blaster' Viv Richards was on strike and, with a shoe half-full of soil from the paddock, I'd run in after visualising Aussie skipper Allan Border tossing me the six-stitcher with orders to make the breakthrough Australia was desperate for.

Even in those sessions behind the machinery shed, I never lacked attitude's greatest ally—a healthy dose of self-belief. I think we're all born with self-belief, but it takes success to build it up to a stage where you back yourself in any situation. Throughout my international career I wanted to bowl every second over, because I believed that regardless of the circum-stance, regardless of who the batsman was or even the condition of the pitch, I could take wickets—I just needed the ball in my hand. I noticed there were (and still are) some bowlers who didn't handle a setback that could've been as minor as, say, bowling a poor delivery. It seemed as though one bad ball was enough for them to self-destruct, and their body language appeared to suggest, 'If I can bowl one bad ball, I can bowl more'. I was one of those bowlers, and there are a lot of us, who thought, 'I know I can bowl a good ball and I'll do everything I can to repeat it with every ball'. And that was how I played my entire career—I believed I was good enough to be there. There were times when I bowled 17-over spells, as I did in Barbados in 1999, but I never thought twice about it even if I was tired. I never once said to my captain, 'No more' or 'I've had enough, I can't bowl anymore'. Some might say that wasn't the smartest way to operate, but I viewed it as a sign that I was projecting a positive attitude and a commitment that I was ready to give my all for the team.

So, I could've taken the setback of missing out on a team, or being considered a player who simply made up the numbers, as a reason to quit. Think about it: who wants to spend their entire Saturday fielding at fine leg? If there is anything a young cricketer or a person with a dream that has a few obstacles in their way can take from my career, it's that you sometimes need to look for reasons to soldier on. More often than not I found that the motivation surrounds you. I realised early, from my life in the bush, that even in the worst of times a farmer has no chance of harvesting a crop if he doesn't plant seed. Yes, I know it sounds simplistic, but there's an unmistakable truth to it. That day I missed selection for the Country Colts squad, I embraced that philosophy of fighting on. I realised if I didn't continue to practise, I'd have no hope of proving everyone wrong, including Shane Horsborough, the captain of the first team I played for who believed a fishing pole had more talent than me. Hours after being told I'd missed the cut, I didn't follow everyone else to the pub; I was instead back behind the machinery shed and steaming in more determinedly than ever, because I realised if *I* stopped believing in myself I had no chance. My attitude was such that I wasn't going to allow a setback—as devastating as it seemed at the time—to dampen my desire to make it.

I maintain that success boils down to a few tangibles:
- a strong desire
- a willingness to sacrifice along the way
- mental strength.

Over the years I've seen plenty of cricketers who were blessed with incredible talent—they made everything look *so* disgustingly easy on the field—yet they failed to live up to expectations. In some ways I think those guys were cursed because anything to do with cricket came so easily to them, and seeing as though they never had to work too hard they lacked the mental capability to handle the tough times. Sometimes it isn't what's happening on the field that affects a player's form or their confidence; it could be other influences, such as relationships or alcohol, especially when they reach a certain age. I've seen plenty of blokes go off the rails around the 18–21 age bracket because their goals take second place to their mad pursuit of the so-called good life. You'll hear officials at any club in the cricketing world talk about 'so-and-so', who was always the best player in his age group and seemed destined to make the grade, but for whatever reason 'something' went terribly wrong.

I don't think I'm speaking out of school to say Ricky Ponting experienced some problems adjusting when he was a young player caught in the limelight that goes hand-in-hand with being viewed by the cricket-mad public as an athlete/celebrity. I spent time with Rick in the Australian Cricket Academy when he was a teenage prodigy. I remember freaking him out the day he walked into my room as I commando-rolled over my bed and with the precision of an assassin threw a knife military-style into the guts of a box of cereal that I'd positioned on my dressing table. I think I may have said something to him like, 'That's how we do it in the bush!' Rick was universally viewed as the 'next big thing' in cricket, but he was also seen by some as a bit of a hothead. While I liked him—I was impressed by his shocked reaction to my knife-throwing prowess—there were some who wondered if that perceived flaw could trip him up.

In 1999, as a 24-year-old, Rick went to the Bourbon and Beefsteak hotel in Sydney's notorious Kings Cross on his own after playing in a one-dayer against England. After a few drinks he became involved in a typical bar-room argument. It ended after he was punched in the face by a 130-kilogram bouncer, which left Rick with a badly blackened eye. He was photographed looking worse for wear by the paparazzi, and questions were asked about whether he had the attitude that was required to be a future Test captain. The first I learned about the drama was when he turned up for a team photograph and he didn't want to remove his sunglasses. Rick was suspended for three games as a result of his night on the tiles, but he was at least smart enough to realise he needed to curb his ways. He made a public apology for his actions, he worked hard, and his efforts in the nets, out on the training ground, on the field and in the public arena— as well as his determination to prove he was serious about gaining redemption—allowed for him to eventually regain the trust of the sport's hierarchy and that of the general public. His attitude was—so I thought—that of someone who realised he'd stuffed up and deeply regretted it. He was able to put his career back on course and fulfil his destiny to lead the Australian team and oversee the great rebuild of the Baggy Green after seven senior players retired from the national team in the space of two seasons.

I was offered my shot to come to Sydney after I played for Dubbo against Parkes in a 1988 Tooheys Country Cup match when I was 18. By that stage my hard work and self-belief was rewarded, because I'd been picked in a few representative teams for Far West and Western Districts. The format for the Country Cup was simple. Tooheys, who was a sponsor of NSW cricket at the time, would send some first-class cricketers to the outback where they played in day-nighters to allow fans in the bush to see their heroes in action for just three dollars a head. At the same time it gave a number of bush cricketers the opportunity to learn a few new tricks from playing alongside them. I remember thinking it was a great thrill to be picked to play alongside the Australian Test team's all-rounder Greg 'Mo' Matthews, future Test captain Mark Taylor and the state opener Steve Small. We played against the home team at Parkes's Pioneer Oval, which included Doug Walters—the king of the SCG 'Hill'—and Mark Waugh, who in a few short summers would be my teammate for New South Wales and Australia. I remember Mo taking me aside before the match and giving me a friendly tip to show Dougie the respect he deserved. Perhaps Mo sensed a mad streak in me, because he pointed out that Doug was 43 and his eyes weren't as sharp as the day he hooked Bob Willis's last delivery of the day for a six during the 1974–75 Ashes series to score his century. The truth is that while I listened to Greg talk about the honour of bowling to Doug, I had no intention of trying to rattle him, or even Mark Waugh for that matter, with a cheap shot. As kids from the outer yelled 'Bruce Reid' to me as I limbered up—because they saw a resemblance in my beanpole frame to the then Australian bowler's—my plan was to simply bowl a good line and length, and see how that worked for me. Well, I nearly had Doug out—caught—but it was too hot a chance for our gully to take, and I was denied a hat-trick when Mark Taylor, one of the game's greatest slips fieldsmen, fumbled a gift. In later years he'd blame the lights at Pioneer Oval, saying he needed a miner's helmet to see the ball. I remember the lighting as being pretty good. While I finished with 3–33, Tubby's fumble was one of four catches spilt off my bowling that night. But I made an impression on Doug because he phoned Steve Rixon, the former Australian wicketkeeper who coached Sutherland's first-grade team in Sydney, to say he'd found a player Steve ought to take a look at. I was thrilled to receive a phone call from a Sutherland committee member named Kevin Humphries. I needed a challenge because I think I was drifting a bit in life, and I guess Sutherland gave me a purpose. I was earmarked for the third XI, which was fine because I knew I'd have to earn my stripes. But after I went on a pre-season tour to Nowra with the team, first-, second- and third-graders, I performed well enough to start off with them. Far from living the high life in the big smoke, I lived in a caravan at Ramsgate on the shores of Botany Bay, which was midway between Caringbah Oval where we trained and the bank branch where I worked in Hurstville. Just as importantly, it was cheap accommodation.

Mum towed the caravan down to Sydney. It rained for every kilometre of the seven-hour journey from the gates at Lagoona to Grand Pines Tourist Park at Ramsgate Beach. She stayed to help me set everything up, but when she left the following day it struck me that I was alone for the first time in my life and that I'd need to fend for myself. It could have been scary if I allowed it to be. When I went back to the caravan, I surveyed what would be my home for the next 13 months. It was small and the only way I could stand upright was to stick my head through the vent in the ceiling. To shower, well, regardless of the hour or the weather, I needed to walk over to the ablution blocks a few hundred metres away. Not long after Mum started her long drive back to Narromine, my attitude kicked in and I welcomed the adventure. I realised it wasn't a time for self-doubt or fear or worrying about the cell-on-wheels I'd be living in or even the anticipated loneliness. *Oh, the loneliness.* While I made some good mates at Sutherland, my first year in Sydney was a pretty lonely time. I'd often go on long walks to the city—15 kilometres away—on a weekend just to break the monotony. However, my most vivid memory of that first day in the big smoke was ten minutes after Mum's car left, when I hammered a single cricket stump into the pitch at the cricket nets in the reserve across the road, and bowled the first few balls of my quest to make Sutherland's first-grade team. My attitude that day reinforced that I wasn't in Sydney for fun; I was a man on a mission.

While I steadily progressed through the grade ranks, I struggled to make ends meet. The reason I stayed at the caravan park was because the $90 a week for the plot was cheap by Sydney standards, but it was still a big chunk out of my meagre budget. I couldn't afford to eat properly, and I'd often have a packet of instant noodles or a chocolate bar for dinner—a far cry from what I was used to eating at the farm, where we wanted for nothing, and ate not just three meals a day, but morning and afternoon tea as well. I never told my mother about constantly feeling hungry, or even of the loneliness I experienced, because her marriage to my dad had broken up, and I knew Mum had enough problems of her own without being burdened with mine. That first 13 months in Sydney was my test. It was the period where I believe I was asked by the universe, How much did I want to chase my dream? I was being asked whether I was mentally strong enough to stick it out, and how much I was prepared to sacrifice. That time in the caravan—and *believe* me there were times when it was like self-inflicted solitary confinement—toughened me and gave me an edge. While my skill level was okay (I had good control and could land the ball on a good length), I knew if it was to be compared to that of other players, the difference would've been chalk and cheese. However, I had the attitude from those first few days that *nothing* was going to deny me. I had self-belief that I would be good enough, and I also knew how to deliver my game plan, just as I did that night of the Country Cup match against Parkes. My aim as a cricketer who had relocated from the bush to Sydney was to take wickets, because I knew wickets—and not whining about how hard life was—was what the club's selectors and officials would judge me on. So, I had a plan, I had self-belief and I had the attitude that nothing was going to stop me, even if that meant my evening's entertainment after a meal of instant noodles or a chocolate bar was bowling ball after ball after ball at a single stump in those nets across the road.

8

EATING PRESSURE

Pressure is a Messerschmitt up your arse . . .

— **Keith Miller, Australian cricket great and World War II fighter pilot**

I haven't worked out whether I was blessed or just plain lucky to have played my entire career unaware of the politics in cricket. My naivety meant I never worried about losing my place in the team. I never stressed about the selections nor did I ever fret that the selectors wouldn't consider me. I played with the belief that I was good enough to be in the Australian team, and I had that belief on the first day I was picked to represent Australia even though I was selected after only six first-class games for New South Wales. My goal from day one of my international career was to bowl the perfect game every match, and to take wickets from No. 1 to 11. I figured if I did what was expected of me—to take those wickets and contribute positively to the team's performance—then

I had no reason to ever second-guess myself or to worry about anything other than how I'd perform.

Throughout my career, and everyday life, my philosophy of 'control the controllables' means I'm not distracted by events that I can't directly influence. I accepted as a player that it was pointless for me to worry about the weather, the condition of the pitch, how a batsman had prepared for a series, or what may have been written about me that morning in a newspaper column. At the end of the day I realised there was nothing I could do to control any of those things. However, what I *could* control was how I prepared, how I focused and how I delivered the ball, and eight years after I retired it remains my opinion that to worry about anything outside of my control—as much as I may wish to be able to change it—is a waste of my energies.

Controlling the controllables also allowed me to (usually) keep my emotions in check and not get lost in the battle with the batsman. There were days when it didn't go so well, but they were caused by the frustration I may have felt at the way I was bowling. I had my share of critics, who said my behaviour was poor at times. On those occasions I wished I could have been more like the Swiss tennis player Roger Federer, because I admired how he kept his emotions in check regardless of what may've been going on in his head. While I didn't have the ice-cool water that runs through Federer's veins, the last thing I ever wanted to do was get so fired-up or frustrated with myself that I strayed from my game plan. So, my approach was to set myself high goals;

but outside of how I bowled, or fielded, or even batted, I accepted what else happened in the match was out of my hands. That didn't mean I wasn't absorbed in the contest, because I was always ready to seize the initiative or take action when a situation called for me to do or say something.

I'm often asked for my thoughts on the mental side of cricket, including how to deal with pressure. What I've realised from my corporate speaking experiences is that people in business are always looking for an edge. I provide them with insights on how I coped with my lot as a fast bowler, because while there's an old saying that a 'fast bowler's brains are in his boots', it's complete rubbish. The fast bowler has to be a thinker; he also needs the discipline to bowl to a plan; he must be smart enough to change tack if it isn't working; and he also needs to make mental notes about what he observes in the batsman's style and technique, and to store that away for use at a later date. The fast bowler also needs to push through the fatigue and exhaustion associated with the job, and he has to keep his head up when he suffers the inevitable setbacks of a dropped catch, an umpire making a wrong decision, or the age-old curse: sloppy fielding.

I've set out my thoughts on pressure and other matters of the mind, but I'll offer a disclaimer before you read any further: The observations that follow aren't from a psychologist, they're instead the simple offerings of a retired opening bowler who learnt a few things whenever he had the ball in his hand and a batsman at the other end of the wicket determined to nail his next delivery.

EMBRACING RESPONSIBILITY AND PRESSURE

For those 14 years I was in the national team, I constantly craved responsibility, because the more responsibility that was piled on me, the better I played; the more pressure that was on me to get a breakthrough or bowl at the so-called 'death' or end of a game, the better I played. I enjoyed performing under pressure and, yes, I've heard all the clichés—including 'Pressure produces diamonds' and 'Courage is grace under pressure'—and I can say from what I experienced, it's all true. However, I think most people misinterpret pressure to also mean probable failure, because over the years I saw how it crippled some otherwise good players. I was fortunate that I realised early in my career the only person who could put pressure on me was . . . *me*. In a pressure situation, such as the opposition needing four runs to win off the last over, the bowler needs to realise he has very little control over the situation. What he can control is his approach, his attitude or the ball/delivery he bowls. The way he thinks at this moment is crucial, and he has two choices: he either believes he can come through, or opts to underestimate his ability to cope. It's important to control what are called stress-creating thoughts. They're negative, and in that bowler's situation when he has to hold his nerve and starve the batsman of runs, the least helpful way to begin thinking is 'This *will* go for four'; 'If we *lose*, it'll be all my fault'; 'I'll be *hammered* if we lose this'; 'I *hate* these close finishes', or perhaps the most damning of all, 'Why me?'

I learnt to trust myself in tense situations because I knew what I needed to do, and I remembered that I'd trained for hundreds of hours for that one moment. I also realised the batsman was under just as much pressure, if not more, because everyone would have expected him to knock over the four runs required. While I was well aware the media, the fans and the selectors were all result-orientated, I always steadied myself for the job at hand by focusing on the *process* and not the *product*. Whereas people will describe how they were unable to watch the game on the television because they found it all too much to bear, I trained myself not to look at the game like that. I stripped back what I was about to do to its simplest form and focused solely on my next ball. I didn't think about what was at stake or what it could mean. Instead, I ran in, bowled the ball, and delivered it as well as I possibly could. After I did that, I got the ball and returned to my mark and focused on my next delivery. That done, I proceeded to do it all over again. If anything, it could be considered an example of living in the 'now', because all I ever thought about when I bowled was what I was doing, and not the result or the possible outcome. By adopting my approach to focus my entire being on that delivery, I accepted the result would take care of itself. It was an approach that, if it didn't empower me, it certainly helped me.

PRESSURE IS A TRUTHFUL GUIDE

I treated a pressure-packed situation as a great opportunity to see how good I really was, because it's a fact that most people can function well when things are calm. I remember when we were preparing to play India in the final of the 2003 World Cup in South Africa and we had our final training session at the Wanderers Stadium in Johannesburg. There was a lot of energy in the Australian squad; plenty of laughter and good spirit. As a group we were soaking up the experience and living in the moment. India trained straight after us, and what we immediately noticed was that they were at the opposite pole. They were tense, rigid, and they didn't look all that comfortable. There was no laughter, no obvious signs of enjoyment, and I think if someone had dropped a pin in the stadium during their session, it would've sounded like a bomb detonating. As their opponents, their manner told us that we held the upper hand before a ball was even bowled, and I was happy about that. I also accepted that India had plenty to deal with, including a population of a billion people who are fanatical about cricket and who demand success. It was obvious to me and all our boys that the Indian squad was feeling the weight of expectation that day, and they carried it into the final. I thought they allowed the pressure to suck the joy out of what should've been a career highlight and a wonderful experience. The history book will tell you who handled the stress best because Australia won that World Cup by 125 runs. I think the simple moral of the story is that you need to learn to control pressure and not allow it to control you.

During the Sydney Olympics I was one of millions of Aussies who was left in awe of Cathy Freeman's effort to win the gold medal in the 400-metre sprint; it was not only an amazing performance but it was a sporting achievement that unified the nation. I was fortunate to meet Cathy at a Sport Australia Hall of Fame dinner a few years ago. It enabled me to hear the answer to a question I'd wanted to ask her for many years: how did she perform when there was so much pressure and heavy expectation on her to win in front of a home crowd? Her response was perfect, and while it provided an insight into why she was a true champion, it also pleased me because I related to her answer. Cathy said she didn't feel any pressure because she'd invested 20 years of her life to be ready for that one moment, and when it dawned she had no intention of allowing it to slip away. I thought that spoke volumes about her inner strength, her mettle. She was ready for the challenge. She was ranked the world's No. 1 over that distance, and I guess the comfort that comes with being the world's best is that if you run the best you possibly can, no one is going to get close to you. Fifteen years after the Sydney Olympics, history notes that Cathy Freeman fulfilled what many considered her destiny, and I rate it as perhaps the finest individual performance by an Australian athlete. It's a great example of someone conquering the mountain called pressure and slaying the demon known as expectation.

BY FAILING TO PREPARE YOU ARE PREPARING TO FAIL

There is another saying that suggests 'The harder you work the luckier you are in life', but there should be a second line which states 'The better prepared you are for any situation the better you'll handle the expectation to come through'. It didn't happen all that often, but I would feel angry with myself if I ever went onto the field thinking I could've prepared better than I had. That could've been the result of not spending enough time in the gymnasium or the nets, failing to get enough rest or not eating properly. That mindset would frustrate me because I'd feel as though I was behind the eight ball from the start and from there it became a matter of always trying to catch up. It was easier to alleviate myself of that negativity by doing everything I could to prepare off the field, so when it came to the business of playing I was only focused on what I needed to do. That allowed me to relax and react, rather than to be out there beating myself up for not being able to tick off each box that indicated I was ready to roll.

BAD DAYS DO HAPPEN

There is a danger that if you dwell on your 'failure' or the 'disaster' that happened to you during a match, a day that would be better forgotten can manifest into something of far greater significance than it should. Rather than berate myself—and yes, sometimes I couldn't help but do that after a few of my efforts as a batsman—I learnt to resist the temptation to beat myself up. (Although the day I was dismissed against South Africa with just a few runs needed for victory, and I played a poor shot to be caught and bowled by Fanie de Villiers challenged that line of thinking because it was tough to get over.) In time I learnt to talk to myself about those kinds of things as I would want my coach to analyse my performance, or as I would talk to a teammate who sought a heart-to-heart to discuss how they were performing or about problems in their game. I found it was much more constructive in those situations to ask myself what I could have done differently. I learnt early in my career to identify the difference between a good and a bad game, and I put what I learnt into place fairly quickly.

My success came from knowing my game, knowing myself and being brutally honest with myself, because that's what gave me a foundation to build upon. Some people just don't like who they are, they don't know their game very well, and I'm afraid their inner struggle is quite often reflected in their performances. Sometimes they'll have a good game, some days they'll perform poorly, and what's characteristic about their career is that they're all over the place. You need to be honest with yourself; you need to work for consistency; and as for offering excuses, well, my tip is don't even try. Something that annoys me about the way of the world is that there's a tendency for some people not to take responsibility for their actions, and when something bad happens they either look for a scapegoat to pin the blame on or they cling to an excuse like a drowning man clinging to flotsam. If something happens to me that I'm not pleased about, I try to work out why the situation occurred and what I could've done to prevent it. Often the answers you need to be able to move on call for a tough dose of honesty and acceptance.

Whenever we lost a match, I was never upset with another teammate, even if they didn't perform well, because I couldn't control how they played. I'd sit back and think, Okay, we lost this game. What more could I have done to help prevent this or how could I have done more to help the team out? By taking responsibility I was assuming ownership of the situation. When I see people do the wrong thing or offer lame excuses for a poor performance, or, even worse, hear them blame others, I just think to myself, Come on mate, take responsibility, because people will respect *that*.

THE PAST IS GONE

I think the fact that I'm a person who lives for the 'now' has been beneficial, and it's something that has allowed me to push on. I'm certainly a firm believer that we should learn from the past—it's critical for personal growth and for developing an understanding of the way things are in life— but I've never lived in the past. If we had a big win, that was great and I celebrated, but as for bad performances, or those times when I acted poorly on the field and was fined for acting like a pork chop, I realised there was nothing that could be done to change it. I also accepted long ago that I am not perfect and I never tried to be. I am who I am. However, I definitely kept my mind open to learn from each moment. If I bowled a poor delivery and it was hit for a four, I felt really annoyed at myself, but I knew to just let it go. It was the same with losses: you can't rewrite history, regardless of how much you might want to or how many times you revisit that match in your mind. Sometimes when I see a bowler send down a bad ball, I notice that they rush back to commence their next delivery because they're so desperate to try and erase the result of their last one. More often than not, that catch-up ball will be poor and it risks compounding the bad place they're 'at'. My approach was to take my time, accept what had happened, refocus and commit to not bowling the same ball. I'd ask myself what I wanted to bowl next, and it wasn't until I'd made my decision that I'd start to run in. One thing for certain is I decided what I was going to deliver before I ran in. That would've been like the guy who goes into an important board meeting but doesn't think about what he's going to say until he's called upon—it's a sure-fire recipe for disaster.

SETTING BENCHMARKS

In the hours before I made my Test debut against New Zealand, Craig McDermott, who was the spearhead of Australia's bowling attack at the time and who took 291 Test wickets in his 71 Tests, asked whether I felt 'nervous'. Well, I was excited, because I still couldn't believe I'd been picked to play for Australia after only six first-class matches and nerves hadn't entered the equation. When I told Craig I wasn't worried, he smiled and said something like, 'Don't worry, it will get worse.' It took me quite a while to realise what he meant, because his comment had a few dimensions to it. One way you could have interpreted it was that the more you played for Australia, the more you stood to lose; but, as I've said, the concept of being dropped was never a concern for me. What I ultimately took his comment to mean was that the anticipation and the need to get yourself 'up' for the challenge is tough, as is having to constantly raise the expectations you place on yourself. The longer I represented Australia, the more I grew to appreciate that, in that respect, Craig was 100 per cent correct. It's an exhausting process, but the idea of raising my benchmark a notch higher after a good effort, such as taking 8–38 against England at Lord's, was one I actually enjoyed.

I also realised that if I wanted to be like everyone else, I'd simply do what everyone else did. However, if I wanted to be *better*, I needed to do things better. It meant I had to find different ways, like adjust my training. Plenty of people dismissed my regimen as being too tough, and believed that my personal trainer Kev Chevell pushed me too tough. Yet, they were more often than not the same people who praised my fitness, durability and longevity! I also noticed over the years that there were some players who, once they'd fulfilled their dream to represent their nation, thought that they'd 'made it'. After a while they stopped doing the things that had helped them reach the top. Their work ethic slowly but surely dropped off: they preferred to accept invitations to social engagements that came from being a member of the national team, rather than do their training; outside interests such as investments and portfolios suddenly became more important than their video analysis; and rather than getting to training a little bit early to prepare for the session like they used to, they'd be a few minutes late with an apology or story of how their new girlfriend needed a lift somewhere. They may have thought they were living the life, but the inevitable downward spiral was their not-so-nice wake-up call. I never judged them, but I learnt from them. I was the other extreme, and once I made the grade, nothing was going to affect me. My favourite saying belongs to Mark Twain, the famous American creator of Huckleberry Finn and Tom Sawyer. He said that, in 20 years from now, we'll have more regrets from the things we didn't do than from what we did. I've lived that philosophy. I was prepared to work hard when I could have rested. I set myself a series of tough goals, and I never dropped my quest to be the best. I figured if I gave everything I could give and still didn't make it, then I could live with that. I would've been devastated if I didn't make it because I'd stuffed up by partying and putting other things before my opportunities. That's why I haven't missed playing cricket since I retired. I put everything I possibly could into it, and I'm proud that at 45 I can honestly look at myself in the mirror and say I gave 100 per cent to every second I played. As a matter of fact, I think that was the reason I woke up one morning and thought, That's it, I'm done.

BODY LANGUAGE

It's no good dropping your head, slumping your shoulders or kicking the dirt when things don't go your way on the field, at home, in the classroom or at work. Do that and you may as well wave a white flag. What I learnt as a fast bowler was that all the batsman noticed when they saw poor body language was an opponent who had effectively surrendered, and there was no better sight for them than that. Batsmen judge your confidence and potency by the way in which you hold yourself throughout the game, and they're also good at observing how you look when things aren't going well—when you're either under pressure or bowling under the duress of an injury. Remember that perception means a lot. A sign portraying confidence during a tough period could be something as simple as a cheeky wink or a smile to the keeper after a delivery, because no one expects that from a bowler who should be upset at being down on his luck. It could be the strut in your walk as you head back to your mark or the way you steam in and follow the delivery through. Sometimes it's definitely a challenge to hold your head up and not slump your shoulders on those tough days, but mark my words: the moment a batsman realises that mentally you're on your knees, it'll only get tougher. Walk tall and proud, regardless of what's going on around you. No matter how grim things may have appeared, I always thought the worst thing that could happen to me on a bad day was to be taken out of the attack; the cold, hard reality of that meant there was no way I was ever going to bowl someone out while I was fielding at fine leg with the seagulls.

BEING CALLED ARROGANT ISN'T ALWAYS AN INSULT

In 1994 I was going out with a girl from South Africa. I remember the time I saw her a few years after we broke up, and she commented, 'My God, you've become so arrogant.' I treated her comment as a good moment. I replied that observation was perfect, because it meant when I was out on the field people could see I was confident in my own ability, and that was the perception I wanted to put out there. At the time, I'd started to play things out in the media, by answering the same old question on how I thought Australia would do in the upcoming series with responses like: 'We'll beat the Poms 5–0'; 'We'll smash the West Indies 3–0', or whatever the case may've been. I knew that the way those comments would go down with people was simply a matter of what side of the fence they sat on. Aussies (well, the majority of them) would like the confidence, but supporters of the country we were playing against probably dismissed me with a wave of their hand as an 'arrogant so-and-so'.

I also started targeting batsmen in the opposing team by declaring I was going to be their biggest nightmare during the series. I guess that was an exercise aimed at making me stand out, but it also meant I was putting pressure on myself and, to an extent, the team. I always assumed that, like me, my team members played better when we were under some pressure. I became aware in the early days, however, that there were a few of the boys in the squad who didn't appreciate me making my predictions; they didn't like being in the spotlight due to a teammate stating we'd win the series in a whitewash. In the end, they accepted it was just what I did—it was a reflection of my belief we couldn't lose—and they left me to either be hailed a genius at the end of the series for fulfilling my predictions or being portrayed as a blockhead who'd choked on his own words.

I thought targeting a batsman was a great psychological ploy, and I found declaring a certain player would be my bunny made them think about me, often to the detriment of their own preparation and performance. As it turned out, I was more often than not simply beating them at their own game. The tactic was something I picked up from watching the West Indians when I was a kid during the 1980s. They'd target the opposing team's captain, and once they cut him down the other batsmen normally followed cheaply and quickly. (Although, I might add, that's why I've long admired Allan Border. The way he stood up to the Windies—and the punishment he copped protecting his wicket—made him, in my opinion, one of the toughest blokes to have ever played the game.) My record shows that my ploy to publicly identify my 'most wanted' worked well, because during the '99 Test series against the West Indies when I said I'd be gunning for Brian Lara, I'd dismissed him three times (although he scored 213 in one of those innings) by the end of the series. In 2001–02 I pinpointed South Africa's Gary Kirsten as my No. 1 target, and I dismissed him in each Test. In my farewell Test series against England, I singled out Kevin Pietersen as the man I'd stop, and by the end of hostilities I'd also dismissed him three times. Once I'd made my declaration and bagged the target's wicket once or twice, the media would do the rest for me by turning the screws on them in a very public manner.

The one batsman who the records show couldn't handle being singled out for this attention was former England captain and opening batsman Mike Atherton, someone who I regarded as a great batsman. In our last series against one another, I dismissed him six times—and 19 throughout the course of our careers. His former batting partner, Graham Gooch, openly described the way he batted against me during the 1998–99 series as though Mike had some sort of problem, and it quickly took root as fact. My skipper, Mark Taylor, used it as a psychological weapon, and I embraced it by confirming to the media brigade that I considered him to be my bunny, just as Shane Warne tormented South Africa's Daryll Cullinan. By our final innings the contest had become too cruel. I wasn't bowling very well in that match at The Oval, and he kept playing and missing. I bowled a ball straight at his stumps and I couldn't believe it when Atherton nicked it to 'Warnie' in slips. It really wasn't fair, and while it proved I'd dominated him, watching Atherton trudge from the field was perhaps the only time I ever felt any semblance of sympathy for a batsman. Ever.

THE MIND HEALS

During an early tour of India, teammate Justin Langer gave me a book to read called *Zen in the Martial Arts*. It wasn't about karate or kung-fu, instead it had a lot of powerful messages that could be applied to everyday life to channel the mind as a source of inner strength and healing. There was one story that resonated with me about a guy who smashed his hand when he attempted to break a stack of bricks, and the doctor told him the damage was so bad he'd never use his hand again. However, before he went to sleep he used to imagine a workforce of little men going into his hand, like miners, to chip away all of the bad stuff. He considered them the night shift to complement all the rehab he'd done during the day, and when he woke of a morning he'd imagine a siren sounding to signal the end of their shift when he'd take over. The doctors described his recovery as a miracle, and the next time he tried to break those bricks he smashed right through them. I recruited those night shift workers when I had my ankle operation in 2004, and I'd like to think it helped out.

The book's author, Joe Hyams, also posed a question that made a deep impact. He asked: if you and another person each had a piece of string that was the same length, how would you make yours longer? Some people would cut it in half, but Hyams's answer was that you don't worry about the other person's piece, you make your own string longer and improve it the best you can. That philosophy struck a chord with me because that was always my approach as a bowler—to only worry about my own game and development. He also recalled the time when he visited an old master, who poured a cup of tea for him until it flowed over the cup's rim. Hyams yelled for him to stop because the cup was full and couldn't hold any more tea, but the grandmaster responded by saying the cup represented where his mind was. He told Hyams that his mind needed to be emptied to open himself to new training methods, to improve and grow. I could relate to that, because that notion of having an open mind and to keep growing was also my approach, and it's a message I'm passing on to young bowlers these days in my capacity as a coach.

PILLARS OF SUCCESS

I'm often asked for the secrets of my success. I'd love to be able to reveal something mind-blowing, but over the years I've narrowed the factors down to four things. While they're quite straightforward, you need to be true to them. In no particular order, they are:

1. **Self-belief:** Even when I had people in Narromine tell me that I was wasting my time going to Sydney to try my luck with Sutherland Cricket Club, I didn't allow for their negativity to rattle my confidence or sow seeds of doubt in my mind. I just thought they were wrong, and that perhaps it was because they weren't happy with their own lives that they weren't open

to someone else having a chance. Something I also realised growing up in the bush, as a kid who couldn't get a bowl for the Backwater XI, was that if I didn't believe in myself, why should anyone else? That was why I continued, day after day, bowling at that old 44-gallon drum. Some people are always looking for others to give them validation in life. They need to hear that they're special and talented. I never sought that, because even in the times that tested everything around me, if nothing else I always believed in myself.

2. **Work ethic:** As I've already said, the harder you work the luckier you become. I grew up on a farm, and that meant working out in the fields and being given other chores around the property that had to be done. One of my chores when I was very young was to take the food scraps to the chooks late at night when we got home from Dubbo, sometimes as late as midnight. As a kid it could be a real test because you never knew what was watching you in the dark, and that was scary enough to make me sprint back to the house. But it instilled a pretty strong work ethic in me. When I made the national team and trained under my personal trainer, Kev Chevell, there were those people who questioned my approach to training. They said I was pushing myself too hard, but it was those sessions when I'd often finish up by being physically ill that gave me the foundation I needed to survive the fast bowler's grind.

3. **Look to improve:** I never allowed myself to be content or happy with where I was. I wanted to master my skills and I set myself the goal to bowl the perfect game every game. I constantly searched for new deliveries that would allow me to achieve that. I applied that goal setting to my batting later in my career, and after two solid months of facing 500 balls a week from the bowling machine, I hit my highest Test score of 61 against New Zealand in my return match. That was a very rewarding day at the office.

4. **Have fun:** If you have a genuine passion for what it is you choose to do in life, you can't help but be successful because you'll live and breathe it; nothing will be too great a sacrifice. However, my one piece of advice is to ensure you take time to enjoy the journey because one thing I realised is the time went way too quickly.

9

THE PACEMAN'S AGE-OLD PROBLEM

I think the most obvious thing is age. If you look at history, I don't think there has been a young fast bowler under 23 or 24 who hasn't spent time on the sideline injured. That's the reality of what we do.

—Pat Cummins, aged 19, on fast bowlers breaking down

You only have to watch someone bowl to realise the human body is not designed for the rigours of such an unnatural action. Apart from the obvious strain fast bowling can place on an individual's lower back, it's been estimated that a force up to six or seven times their body weight is transmitted through the front foot of the delivery stride when it hits the ground. If you watch super-slow-motion footage of the impact—when the foot slams into the wicket—you see the force shudders through the ankle like a series of painful shockwaves. It's little wonder, due to the repetitive nature of the action and the constant pounding their joints and ligaments take during the season, that the pace brigade is considered cricket's most injury-prone players. However, rather than use that term, I'd prefer to say that they are the athletes who are prepared to put their bodies on the line for the team every time they commence their run-up.

Fast bowling also puts a person's back at risk of suffering a crippling injury. We've seen that with numerous pace bowlers in recent times, including young guns Pat Cummins and James Pattinson who've lost crucial time during their formative years in elite cricket as a result of stress fractures in their lower backs. There are many theories as to why stress fractures have crippled so many pacemen over the years. Some research suggests that the way the spine is positioned during the delivery stride is responsible for the stress that creates bone failure. Those fast bowlers who leap high to deliver the ball are considered a greater chance of developing lumbar (back) bone stress fractures or injury.

Some believe the workload required in the longer formats of the game—such as Tests or Sheffield Shield—can cause injuries through overuse. This theory proposes that young bowlers are at greater risk because their bones are yet to harden and that bowling-related injuries are typically due to technique errors such as a 'mixed bowling action', where a bowler has a half front-on, half side-on action.

Someone whose opinion on these matters I trusted when we worked together in the Australian team was Jock Campbell, the highly respected strength and conditioning coach. Jock suggested that the growth of Twenty20 competitions—more so the overseas ones—wasn't doing Australia's young fast bowlers too many favours, because the boys play outside of their Cricket Australia obligations and sign for big money to a franchise that's primarily concerned with winning the tournament. Jock also said that playing Twenty20 was nowhere near enough to prepare a fast bowler for Test cricket. He's a firm believer that it takes a pre-season of two or three months to build up both their bowling volumes and their speed. I believe fast bowlers need a break to recover after a tough slog. Jock also pointed out in 2013 that because many senior bowlers, such as Brett Lee, Dirk Nannes and Shaun Tait, had retired from first-class cricket to extend their careers in Twenty20, it meant younger players were shouldering more work. He also thought the expectation for a young fast bowler to bowl *every* ball flat out was both unrealistic and taking a terrible toll. I've read other theories that the back-to-back Tests increase a fast bowler's chance of injury by 87 per cent.

The art of fast bowling means there'll always be stresses, so a bowler must be mentally and physically tough to work through the grind. I'm working with my 15-year-old son, James, on his technique. I'm worried by it. He has already had a partial stress fracture, and that results from a combination of his technique and the fact he's growing so quickly.

When I was James's age I played cricket for fun—which is what he is doing—but my action was quite sound. When I watch James, I can see he's twisting a little bit too much, and that's something we'll need to work on. It's just a matter of refinement. As is the case for any bowler, as long as his shoulders match his hips when he bowls, James will be okay. Regardless of whether you're a front-on, side-on or semi bowler, if your hips and shoulders align, it alleviates the problems. It takes a long time to fix an injury caused by a mixed action. After healing, a bowler needs to start off on a one- or two-step action, and will then have to bowl thousands of deliveries to reprogram the body. To change a bowling action even a little bit takes a lot of work. The typical bowler wants to get back into bowling straight away after a lay-off and suffers because they don't work on it enough. It might appear fixed, but the injury is always there and will compound over time. It's a serious issue and I tell James he needs to hold the horses because he's here, there and everywhere. Despite his stress fractures, he'll do things like go surfing with his mates, then afterwards I hear him complain, 'Oh, my back.' James and I, we have some work to do!

His bowling action aside, James's back shouldn't be a problem if genes have any part to play. His great-grandparents on both sides of my family were in an osteoporosis survey (the medical condition in which bones become brittle and fragile from loss of tissue, typically as a result of hormonal changes, deficiency of calcium or vitamin D). My parents also participated in the survey, as well as Donna, Dale and I, and I imagine James, Holly and their cousins will be asked to do it, too. The survey showed that our family's bone density is quite high. When I had a scan three or four years ago, the person who conducted it said mine was the most perfect back she'd ever seen. I took that as a glowing endorsement that my action really was sound. She said the space between each of my vertebrae and the shape of my vertebrae was perfect. The fact that I'd opened the bowling for Australia for over 14 years made my back amazing, she said.

I think my core muscles also saved me from a lot of grief. My action meant that I was never going to bowl at 160 km/h, but it also spared me the stress fractures that plagued the likes of Dennis Lillee and Brett Lee. I guess I had a lot of things on my side. I didn't bowl a huge amount when I was younger, so my bones weren't affected. Those with a classic side-on action really engage their back muscles, but the worst thing you can do is mix your action because the violent twisting of your back exposes it to forces that lead to stress fractures. I had no idea of what my action looked like until I was videoed at the Australian Cricket Academy in 1990–91. All I knew until that point was that my action felt natural. I've bowled a few overs in charity games since my retirement and I discovered my shoulder is full of arthritis. It's only a problem if I bowl, which is something I don't intend to do all that often. The arthritis has prevented me from doing shoulder presses in the gymnasium, but that doesn't bother me. All things considered, I'm very lucky because my hips, knees and ankles are fine. My back has also been given a big tick, and that comes back to my action, to how hard I was prepared to work, and to my genetic make-up.

People ask how I enjoyed such longevity while other fast bowlers break down. All I can say is that it didn't come easily. In 1995 I returned from Australia's first Test-series triumph against the West Indies in 22 years. I was 25, and I'd finally cemented my place in the Australian team. I took my first five-wicket haul in the opening Test in Barbados and I felt as though I'd contributed something to the team. However, there was nothing to me. I weighed 77 kilograms—that's 25 kilograms less than I needed to be durable and to withstand the workload of a strike bowler—and I'd torn an area of my intercostal muscle, or the 'grunt' muscle, from where you generate your power as a fast bowler. I realised I needed to do something if I wanted to compete. While I was rehabilitating from my injury and thinking it was great to play international cricket, I also realised that if I didn't do something to toughen my body I'd have no longevity in the game. I asked around for the best fitness trainer in Sydney and one name kept popping up: Kev Chevell. He was known as 'Rambo', so I figured, based on that, he would have the right approach. He'd trained Mark Taylor in the lead-up to Tubby scoring his 334 not out against Pakistan in 1998. I also heard that quite a few first-grade rugby league players had been through his gymnasium, so I figured he knew his stuff. It turned out he also understood fast bowling. At 13 he had been a child prodigy. He had been selected to bowl fast and furious for

Bankstown in the 1970s when Jeff Thomson and Len Pascoe ruled the roost of what was then known as Memorial Oval. He had a break from cricket, then made his comeback in Western Australia a few years later when he clean-bowled the great South African batsman, Barry Richards, in a first-grade match after Richards had slaughtered Australia's pace attack.

After I told Kev I was prepared to do whatever was necessary to fulfil my goal to get fitter than ever, he promised to make me unbreakable—provided I could prove to him in a two-week trial that I was serious. He hammered me and there were times when I was physically ill, but Kev proved relentless. After the fortnight, he promised he could toughen me. However, he also made the point—and it stuck with me—that *my* attitude would determine how far I went. We trained so hard that I was happy when the cricket season started so I could escape his torture sessions. Kev's training philosophy, and it worked for me, was that my training sessions with him needed to be more brutal than anything I could ever experience out in the middle. He believed consistency and knowing you could conquer any challenge was what separated champions from the rest. For that reason he subjected me to drills that put me under duress, because he said that would program me to overcome pressure and stress. It worked that day in Barbados in 1999 when I bowled 17 overs straight. By the end of the spell, my teammates said I looked skeletal but, the truth is, I would've bowled an 18th, a 19th or even a 20th if it was necessary for my team. That was how Kev trained me, to be unbreakable in body and mind. He packed the muscle on me: during my career my playing weight ranged from 86 to 94 kilograms. Apart from the training, he introduced me to superfoods and insisted that rest was included in my daily program.

I'd stay with Kev and his wife Vee in Penrith for days at a time, and my training was punctuated by rest breaks and eating *five* meals a day. I'd be woken by him at 2 am to consume a concoction of eggs, banana, apple juice and oats, and would then go back to sleep, only to wake knowing it was another day of tough yakka. After the 2000 Sydney Olympics, where he worked with the German rowing team, Kev placed a lot of emphasis on the rowing machine. His rule was to use maximum effort from the first to the final pull! While I still carry the mental scars from that machine, his training regimen allowed me to bowl (according to the statistics) 41,759 balls in first-class cricket. In 2013 a newspaper report comparing fast bowlers' workloads discovered I'd bowled 1194 more deliveries than Ben Hilfenhaus had managed in 2012 as a result of Cricket Australia's rotation policy. The policy rested players in an effort to prevent them from either burn-out or injury. The report highlighted the difference in workloads when it said I played 37 internationals in 2002, while Peter Siddle played eight in 2012. I should point out that the injury situation of our quicks hasn't been as bad as it was a few years ago. It's pleasing that we seem to be seeing the likes of Cummins (aged 22), Pattinson (25), Hazlewood (24), Starc (25) and co. playing more games nowadays. I think that's as much a sign that their bones are getting harder as they grow older than anything else.

Kev Chevell fulfilled his promise to me. Through the work we did together I only missed one game due to an injury, apart from the ankle spurs I occasionally suffered from overbowling. Once I had those fixed I was fit and ready to roll for 95 per cent of my 124 Tests. Kev didn't train me specifically for fast bowling—his goal was to make me unbreakable. I know there's a school of thought in cricket that questions the value of gym work—Dennis Lillee and Len Pascoe are advocates of fast bowlers running and getting miles in their legs—but I placed a huge amount of importance on my work in the gymnasium. While my inclination is to advise fast bowlers that 'balance' is crucial, my gym routine was as important, perhaps even more so, than my bowling routine. I spent equally as much time in the gym as I did training in the nets and working on my deliveries, to help me be match-fit. I was never in the gymnasium to try and look like a body builder. I had a specific routine, which included the old-fashioned core-strengthening exercises Kev taught me; such classics as squats, deadlifts, dips, chin-ups, and clean-and-press reps. I was nicknamed Pigeon because of my skinny legs. I worked overtime to strengthen them because the legs, like the glutes, are of crucial importance for a fast bowler's ability to slog on.

Brett Lee hit the weights about five years ago, when his future in the national team had been placed under scrutiny because he was 33 and the critics were saying he was getting too old. He added six kilos to his frame and pumped up to 95 kilograms. He was photographed shirtless on Bondi Beach looking ripped and the image worked. He was lauded for looking fit. However, he used himself as a case study as to why young fast bowlers were better lean and loose, rather than bulky and chiselled. 'I felt strong but I felt as though I had to bowl around my chest or my bicep,' Lee said after describing his exercise program as 'cosmetic'. 'There wasn't the natural or smooth whippiness I was used to. And while that might work for an Andy Bichel or Michael Kasprowicz who bowled at 130 km/h, it was no good for someone who wanted to bowl 150-plus km/h,' Brett said. I think, at the end of the day, it's the job of the fast bowler to find out what it is that will make them unbreakable. My main tip is, whether it's working in the gym, bowling in the nets, running, or hitting the rowing machine, just work hard and train smart.

10

IN THE CRITIC'S CHAIR

Criticism, like rain, should be gentle enough to nourish a man's growth without destroying his roots.

—Frank A. Clark, US writer and cartoonist

I've never been a negative person. While I'll certainly speak up when there's something that needs to be said on a matter I'm passionate about, I do find it hard to offer criticism for criticism's sake. It's possible to take a negative or positive angle on any of life's subjects, but it seems controversy, negativity, slander and scandal is what sells in the modern world. I adopted the stance to be 'controversially positive' a long time ago—Australia will win the Ashes 5–0 is a good example of that—and while I copped a lot of stick for it over the years, there were plenty of people who understood my predictions were simple logic, because I was never going to say we'd lose a game, let alone a series.

I use an extension of being controversially positive when I'm commentating and watching a team that's being dominated by the opposition. It would be very easy to lash out at the blokes who are struggling—and every player of any standard has had one of those days—but I prefer to pay tribute to the dominant side and explain to the audience why they have the upper hand. I guess whether you appreciate that outlook depends on how you view life; I'm a glass half-full man rather than a half-empty one.

During my playing days, criticism never worried me unless I believed it was true. I was a player who knew his game. I was always very honest with myself and acknowledged how things were going. Because I also knew where I wanted to go and how I'd get there, I was very rarely bothered by what anyone may have written or said about me. I never took much notice nor was I ever concerned about which batsman I was up against on a particular day, because I'd realised early in my career that if I just focused on what it was I had to do—and did it well—everything would be fine.

With that as my outlook, there was very little chance an article or a couple of harsh words from a commentator would distract me. I will say there were times when I was often bemused (if not amused) by what I might read the morning after a game, and I would wonder if the correspondent had been at a different place to where I'd played. On the few occasions someone wrote or said something that I thought was off the mark, I'd have a quiet chat to them because I thought it was important that they at least be informed. I thought that approach was far more constructive than the cold shoulder that some other players preferred to serve; and while the chat was always amiable—on my part, at least—there were one or two journalists who handled being pulled up much worse than the way the players who copped their criticisms had! One thing I learnt from my time in the dressing room and out in the middle, that's carried over to my new life in the commentary box, is that it's crucial to be fair and consistent.

I remember the late Peter Roebuck wrote a piece for Fairfax Media about how he viewed the character of the Australian team—it was damning, comparing us to a 'pack of wild dogs'. Adam Gilchrist quizzed him about the article and asked why he didn't seek any opinions from the team members. Roebuck's response was that he preferred to draw his own opinion from his observations rather than being influenced by conversations with the players or officials, and that seemed fair enough. However, when he did a very favourable article on the Sri Lankans, he was asked by one or two of the boys about the detail in the story, and Roebuck told them he'd gained it by talking to members of the squad! I think, like most other sportsmen, I expected consistency; you want the media and the critics to be fair, and you'll expect that any opinion they express is based on fact. It shouldn't be too much to ask, because ultimately they are dealing with players' careers and creating perceptions.

I'm aware that whenever I make a public comment about a player, I could potentially have an impact on their life and their career. I never liked it as a player when the media seemed to gang up on a teammate and target him until he was either dropped or regained form. That targeted criticism is, rightly or wrongly, another mental side of the game. And while there are those players who thrive on the idea of 'proving them wrong', there are just as many who can't cope, and I have seen such criticism leave players feeling vulnerable and hurt.

From 2008 to 2011 I found it hard to watch the cricket when the Australian pace attack wasn't doing so well. The sight of our blokes bowling all over the place and from both sides of the wicket was tough to handle. The 2010–11 Ashes series won by England in Australia was hard to cop. However, I accepted we were in the throes of a rebuilding campaign, and despite the disappointment of the defeat I also appreciated the blokes playing were busting their guts. But I actually found I couldn't watch too much of it. I was contacted by journalists on numerous occasions throughout that 3–1 series loss to have a crack at the Aussie pacemen, but I never took the bait because I didn't want to become *that* former cricketer who appeared to have an axe to grind with the current players, because the truth is I didn't and I don't.

During the summer of 2014–15 I spent time commentating on Fairfax Radio Network alongside Ian Chappell, Dean Jones, Carl Rackemann, Damien Fleming, Greg Matthews and former England all-rounder John Emburey. While it was a great challenge and a rewarding experience, there are still those times when I can't believe I'm behind the microphone and describing to a national audience the way in which Indian skipper Virat Kohli has set his field. When I was a student at Narromine High, my fear of talking in front of a group was so deep-seated that it was one of the reasons I decided to finish school in Year 10. You see, I was terrified of being a part of the Year 12 graduation ceremony, where the students stood before a packed school auditorium and said a few words as they received an alumni certificate. If I had been given the choice back then to either deliver a speech or enter a lion's cage, I'd have asked for the keys to the cage. My shyness was so severe when I was in class that I refused to put my hand up to answer questions I knew the answers to. I was so conscious of what the other students *may* have thought of me. Unless you've suffered from that awful feeling of self-consciousness, you can't understand how terrible it is—praying not to be called upon to stand up in front of the class and recite a poem or read an essay, because you think people are laughing at you. It's socially crippling, which is why I'm pleased James and Holly get to practise public speaking at their schools, because it's a great tool for any kid. I think it empowers them to, at the very least, speak up and offer their thoughts on a subject. My attitude changed the day I made the NSW team. I came to the realisation that talking to people, being interviewed by the media and perhaps even public speaking was something I would have to do. I was given a wonderful tip at this time, which was that when you do speak in public, talk about what you know and be yourself. I found that helped because, in time, I overcame my fear.

I started commentating in 2012, a time when I had no clear direction in life. I was doing bits and pieces—I had corporate speaking engagements, the foundation kept me busy and I still worked with the sponsors who supported me throughout my career—but I had never had a set working week since I was employed at the bank for a four-year stretch more than 20 years ago. When I received an offer to commentate on Channel Nine, my first reaction was to wonder how I could possibly get excited watching a batsman hit a four when I had deplored that as a bowler. Anyway, I tried it and found I enjoyed the experience. But my views on commentary and criticism means there have been a few times when I've squirmed in the hot seat and wished to goodness I was just about anywhere else, away from the microphone and the public expectation to say *something.*

I was in the Channel Nine commentary box at the Gabba in 2012—just three days into my new gig—when my old skipper Ricky Ponting was dismissed for a duck by South African quick Morné Morkel. It had been a tough time for Rick, who I had befriended in 1992 when he was only 17 and we attended the Australian Cricket Academy together. I really wanted him to succeed that day because he hadn't been playing very well, but he fell for his third duck in four innings against what was regarded at the time as the world's premium pace attack. Even though he'd scored eight centuries and 11 half-centuries at an average of 51 across the 24 Tests he'd played against the South Africans, on this day he played a poor shot. Rick was then aged 37, he'd lost the captaincy to Michael Clarke, and at that time there would've been people sharpening their knives to finish him off. I was well aware that despite his disappointing efforts at the wicket, he was working hard in the nets and probably living with constant pressure. I know no player—especially Ricky Ponting—goes out and plays a poor shot, delivers a bad ball or spills a catch on purpose; but when it happens, the last thing you need to hear is criticism from one of your old teammates sitting in the comfort of an air-conditioned commentary box and hammering what would feel like yet another nail into your career's coffin.

So, there I was, the glowing red light showing the camera was on and my microphone demanding I offer something to relay that the besieged Ponting was out for a duck. While I had to say *something*, my initial thought was, Is a 20-year-old friendship going to come down to the next few words that leave my mouth? I didn't want to slate him; all I could do was mumble he'd played a poor shot. That was fact, and the reason I took comfort from that was because I knew from my own experience as a player that while it might sting, it's hard to hold a grudge about a truthful observation. Regardless, as I watched Rick make his long walk back to the pavilion with his place in the team on the line, I thought to myself, It's only my third day of commentating and I *hate* this. I realised that I was perhaps still a little bit too close, if not to the Australian team, then definitely to some of the players.

After stumps, I went back to my hotel and asked some tough questions of myself, the main one being, Can you do this? I realised I'd feel pretty lousy about myself if I ever got behind the microphone and just mouthed off to be controversial or colourful, but Rick's dismissal that day actually proved to be a breakthrough of sorts for me as a commentator. I realised I needed to have fun; I had to let go of my tight grip on the rope and enjoy it. Some commentators might disagree with me, but I found it hard to say negative things about my teammates—it just doesn't sit well with me—and that is why commentating is getting easier for me every time a Rick Ponting or a Brett Lee retires.

One of the real thrills about commentating for Channel Nine was the opportunity to get a glimpse of the late great Richie Benaud in action. He was such a great commentator—the doyen—and such was his fame for his work behind the microphone that I'm sure there'd have been plenty of young viewers who were unaware of the fact Richie was also one of Australia's greatest cricketers. Not only was he a top leg spinner who became the first Test all-rounder to take 200 wickets and score 2000 runs, but he was also a great captain, who was regarded as being both innovative and one who led by example.

As I say, I only had a glimpse of what made him such an outstanding broadcaster, but first and foremost I believe the key to Richie's success was his 'feel' and his obvious love for the game—that was the foundation that made him quite special.

When I was given my chance in the hot seat, Richie was 82 and he didn't say as much as he used to. Nevertheless, he would still offer his unique pearls of wisdom because that's what he did, it's the way it was. And for my part, those few times I was in his presence I just watched, listened and tried to learn. He mastered the pregnant pauses better than anyone else (and plenty mastered impersonating his voice); he possessed a dry sense of humour; and while he was witty, Richie Benaud was wise enough to allow the players to tell the viewers the story of what was happening out in the middle and he'd pick his words carefully to enhance the scene. Everyone hung off each of his words. When Richie passed away in April 2015, the game mourned the passing of a true legend. In the spirit of the great performers, he left his audience wanting more.

11

LEARNING TO COACH

The philosophy of the school room in one generation will be the philosophy of government in the next.

— Abraham Lincoln, 16th US President

When I retired from cricket, there were two fields I told my manager Warren Craig I didn't want to pursue: one was commentating and the other was coaching. At the time I needed to get cricket out of my system. The sport had dominated the previous 20 years of my life and while I enjoyed 'the life', I wanted to spend time with my family. After missing too many of the moments that mattered while I was away on tour, I welcomed the chance to do the fatherly things with Holly and James that most kids took for granted. However, eight years since my last match I'm doing both, and absolutely *loving* it. Based purely on how much I'm enjoying my role as a fast-bowling coach, it seems strange to admit my initial reaction was to panic and doubt my ability to do the job. When my childhood hero Dennis Lillee suggested I take the reins from him as a coaching director of the renowned MRF Pace Foundation in Chennai, India, that's exactly what I felt—panic. Dennis is one of the world's foremost fast-bowling coaches. He has the ability to immediately work out what issues are troubling a bowler simply by looking at them run in. That's a unique talent. My approach to taking something on is to give it my best, and the first thought that came into my head was 'no' because I wasn't sure if I'd be any good. I now understand why I needed time to consider what I'd be getting into if I accepted Dennis's generous invitation. Firstly, I had never thought about coaching as a career because all I ever did when I bowled was what came naturally to me. I assumed everyone else was the same. Secondly, I was worried that some Australians would question my decision to help produce another nation's players.

The MRF Pace Foundation is based in the grounds of the Madras Christian College Higher Secondary School in the Chennai's Chetpet district. The foundation was the brainchild of the late Ravi Mammen, who established what could be described as a factory of pace in conjunction with Dennis. Mammen backed it with funds from his family's company, the tyre group MRF Ltd—a company that started by making balloons in a tin shed in 1946 but evolved into one of India's great corporate success stories. The foundation was borne from a sense of frustration with the state of the Indian cricket team's pace line-up. As Vinoo Mammen, the chairman and managing director of MRF, said in an interview a few years ago, it seemed an insult to the nation's pacemen that there were times that India's famous opening batsman, Sunil Gavaskar, would open the bowling. While Kapil Dev emerged as a feared pace bowler in the 1970s, it was clear India did not have a depth of talent in the fast-bowling department. Ravi Mammen—who sadly passed away from a heart attack aged 39 and just two years after the foundation's inception—took action by presenting Lillee with his blueprint and selling him his vision.

I attended the foundation as a student in 1992. It gave me my first insight into the subcontinent's conditions—and it's no scoop to reveal they're tough. The pitches do the pacemen few favours, the heat and humidity is mind-numbing, and any success is through a wild-eyed persistence. That's why the foundation is so important—it helps to give the fast bowler a fighting chance. The facilities are brilliant: there's a world-class gymnasium, an Olympic-size swimming pool, four different turf pitches, residential facilities and its own cricket stadium. The ethos is 'service' to fast bowlers and it's impressive to learn that the MRF Pace Foundation helps pay the fees of emerging fast bowlers selected to be tutored there. The success rate has been staggering with 55 trainees progressing from their nets to represent India. Among the foundation's roll of honour are the likes of

Shanthakumaran Sreesanth, Zaheer Khan and Irfan Pathan. Since the foundation opened its doors to foreign players in 1992, the likes of Brett Lee, Mitchell Johnson, Chaminda Vaas, Mohammad Asif, Dilhara Fernando and myself have all been fortunate to benefit from what's on offer.

So, there was Dennis on the other end of the phone offering me what anyone else would have considered a brilliant opportunity, and all I could do was 'umm' and 'ahh', while my mind was bombarded with doubt after doubt, questioning how could *I* possibly coach. My greatest strength as a bowler was the mental side of the craft. I understood my mindset; I ensured I understood my role in the game plan; and whether it was stretching or working on a particular delivery in the nets during team training or in my own time, I prided myself on the fact I went about my job professionally. I think I had a fairly decent action, and the reality is that was the result of being left to my own devices. As a kid I was rarely called upon to roll my arm over for my junior team, the Backwater XI. I was banished to the role of specialist fine leg, all because my captain believed a fishing pole had more ability to bowl a yorker than me! Most of the people at the club thought I ought to focus on shooting hoops in the burgeoning bush basketball league, so no one at the cricket club gave me a second thought. I guess they figured it'd be a waste of time. In hindsight they did me a massive favour, because that perception prevented someone from tinkering with what my body found to be the most natural action and inner rhythm. I have no doubt that's what allowed me to enjoy my longevity in the game. Back in 1992 I was sent to the MRF to work under Dennis after I'd spent time with him at the Cricket Academy. After he had watched me there for a while he told me that I had a 'sound action'. The Cricket Academy sent us to India to get familiar with subcontinent conditions and to have Dennis monitor our progress. He liked that my hips and shoulders were aligned when I bowled, because he noted that restricted the risk of the career-threatening injuries he had endured. Rather than commit to an overhaul on me, his priority was to work on what he called 'refinement'.

The more I think of it, the more I believe I am a coach— my first student was my 15-year-old self. But I wasn't thinking so clearly when Dennis was on the other end of the phone and offering me a challenge. The waves of reluctance continued. It struck me that despite the fact I'd played in 124 Tests and 250 one-day Internationals, *technically* speaking I couldn't articulate how I did what I did. I'd tell people the secret to my success was controlling the controllables, keeping it simple and bowling a nagging line and length to force the batsmen into a mistake. But the thought of actually sitting down, dissecting an aspiring bowler's action and going through the process of teaching *how* to bowl was quite daunting as I struggled to pinpoint where to even start. I asked Dennis the inevitable question of 'Why me?' as we spoke on the phone. He explained that when he joined the MRF Pace Foundation in 1987, the people who ran it wanted the best retired fast bowler in the world as their coaching director, and few could disagree Dennis Lillee definitely fitted the bill. Now, 25 years later, he was charged with the duty of recruiting his replacement. He identified me as the man for the role. While I hesitated, Dennis pointed out that my 563 Test wickets carried some clout. Though I considered the phone call as much a massive compliment as it was a vote of confidence, I still couldn't help but hesitate. Thankfully Dennis had faith in what he thought I would bring to the table. When he sensed my reluctance was due to self-doubt rather than a lack of interest or enthusiasm, he suggested I simply think about it. That advice sat well with me because, while I didn't want to make a rash decision I also didn't want to slam the door shut without giving his offer the consideration it deserved.

Sara saw the phone call as an opportunity for me to give back to cricket, by passing on some knowledge that might help a couple of kids fulfil their dreams; and her view made great sense. However, while I know it may sound ridiculous now, I also struggled with the notion that people who'd supported me might brand me a traitor for seemingly turning my back on Australia for Indian money. I also thought long and hard about how I would handle the idea of a young Indian kid tearing through an Australian line-up, and then thanking me for helping him. It's ridiculous, because you'd find few more patriotic Aussies than Dennis, or me for that matter. I'd also been asked by a couple of international teams to help coach their bowlers, but I baulked because I had played for Australia. I'm still close to the national team and

I want to see it continue to do well. The concept of passing on the tricks of the trade that I had learnt through the Aussie system didn't sit well with me. I also know my character, and it worried me to think that if I was working with England, South Africa, India or Sri Lanka I'd give them my all and would want to see them do well, even against Australia.

While Dennis's offer was a great opportunity, it certainly threw up its challenges. Ultimately, I was swayed by the idea that former players have a duty to share our knowledge to the new breed as generously as Dennis did with me throughout my career. He, of course, wasn't the only pace bowler to 'gift' me with the insights of a champion. It's now a treasured memory for me to think about a conversation I had with Ray Lindwall not long before he died of a stroke in 1996. Ray, who was the strike weapon of Bradman's 1948 Invincibles, sat in the change sheds with me at Hobart's Bellerive Oval after a match to talk about the 'art'. Lindwall was in his seventies and he asked for my thoughts on such things as reverse swing. While I was well aware of his status as one of cricket's greatest pacemen—one who mixed his outswinger with a brutal yorker and a frightening bouncer, all delivered at a frightening speed—it's only as I've grown older that I can fully appreciate why Lindwall wanted to share what he could with a youngster. It was his duty to pass the wisdom down. He was a kid who grew up bowling to his mates at a paraffin-tin wicket in a suburban street in Sydney. It just so happened that this street was where the great Australian spin bowler Bill 'Tiger' O'Reilly walked home from work every day. When Lindwall came under O'Reilly's wing in the St George grade team, O'Reilly mentored him, passing on insights and wisdom about the game. Lindwall, in turn, passed on his knowledge to the great left-armer Alan Davidson when he was a rookie in the fifties, a young Lillee in the seventies and, late in his life, to me.

When Dennis heard my concerns about appearing un-patriotic, he pointed out that young Australian players also attended the foundation—just as I had 22 years earlier—under a reciprocal agreement between Cricket Australia and the foundation. In my first stint as a coach there I had a handful of Australian cricketers, including Josh Hazlewood and Gurinder Sandhu, for two weeks, and they've since gone on to earn their international spurs. In my last visit, a few quicks from the National Performance Squad, including Liam Hatcher, Billy Stanlake and David Grant, came to the foundation for their first taste of the subcontinent's conditions. I have no doubt what they experienced over that fortnight will give them a head start should they be picked to tour India in the future. My view on having an involvement with foreign teams is a lot more relaxed now. I note that former NSW coach Trevor Bayliss is the head coach of England, Dav Whatmore coaches Zimbabwe, and in the past Greg Chappell coached India. Geoff Lawson coached Pakistan, Trent Woodhill coached New Zealand and John Dyson, Sri Lanka. When my old Sutherland and NSW coach Steve Rixon coached the Kiwis, he even told their batsmen to try and unsettle me by charging me! In more recent times my old teammates have done the same: Michael Hussey was involved with South Africa's last World Cup campaign and Brett Lee helped Ireland. My view is that apart from putting bread and butter on the table, they're helping the game by sharing their knowledge. I'll always want Australia to do well, but at the end of the day, when a team is out in the middle, it's up to them. As a cricket lover you want to see the players perform at their best and for the best team to win. With my original doubts quelled, I asked Dennis if I could travel to Chennai with him and watch how he operated. I wanted to get a feel for what was required in the job and to see if I could do it.

As has always been the case, whenever I've been in Dennis's company, I absorbed what he said and watched what he did. It was inspiring—he simply reinforced to me that he really is a great teacher. I took mental notes when I heard him say that his attitude to an individual's bowling action is that unless it is grossly wrong or prone to injury he doesn't change it, he preferred instead to refine—or hone it—with what he called 'slight modifications', as he did with my action. My own belief is that the body works out the action best suited to it, so his view not to make change for the sake of change resonated with me. He is also a believer in fast bowlers 'knowing' their body in this age of stress fractures and serious injuries. He says that while a bowler's workload needs to be managed, the bowler must also have some accountability and know how much is too much. It was just common sense stuff, and I found that the more

Dennis spoke, the more I started to think I could follow his lead; although he's a tough act to follow.

I also liked the feel of the academy—it has a rock solid foundation of goodness. It speaks volumes that in the 25 years Dennis worked there, he never signed a contract because he said the relationship was built on a cornerstone of trust and faith. The foundation trusted he'd give his heart and soul to the trainees, and he had faith that they would fulfil their promise to look after him. I saw it was a great relationship, and that helped me warm to the idea of committing to the job. I was just as impressed by the facility's chief coach Myluahanan 'Senthil' Senthilnathan, who once captained India's under-19s team and represented the Rest of India. While he was a batsman, he's technically a brilliant bowling coach. Though we're the same age, Senthil had worked alongside Dennis for 23 years and this has armed him with tremendous knowledge. I also liked that his manner suggested from the moment I arrived that if I took on the role, he'd want me to succeed. All of the doubts that clouded my mind were brushed away when I arrived in India by the excitement of believing I could make a fist of coaching. Almost three years after taking on the job I've never looked back.

My role involves spending three stints a year—each of them a two-week duration—in Chennai, and I'm continuing to learn a lot. Now, with a few years' experience under my belt, I look for someone who can bowl quick; the faster he is, the more unique he is, so I aim to ensure we don't do anything that will make him lose that. However, I'm also looking for those young bowlers who have the attitude to work hard without complaining, because I think where you can marry blistering speed with a good work ethic, you'll have a world-beater. I can look at someone's action now and pick up any flaw straight away. The reaction from the bowler when they fine-tune the fault—it's as though you have helped them solve one of the world's great mysteries—is very rewarding. Their reactions have helped me understand why Dennis said that receiving a letter from Chaminda Vaas—who took 355 Test wickets for Sri Lanka—to thank him for his help early in his career was very humbling and meant a lot.

I wish I had known when I played what I've learnt since taking on the role at the foundation. I think I could've done more with my action and perhaps bowled a little bit quicker. When I look back on my action, there were times when I jumped into the wicket and I was too close to the stumps. I jumped in and came around myself. I didn't fall away too much despite doing that because I had a strong core. That allowed me to hold myself quite well and drive through the crease. I would have preferred to go through the crease straighter, which would've allowed me to finish better and probably even swing the ball more. However, the quandary for me as a coach is this: if I was to look at that action, I'd realise that jumping in allowed me to come across myself, which then allowed for the ball to hit the wicket and seam away from the left-hander. This action earned me a lot of wickets. I think it highlights that coaches need to realise there's a bit of give and take. While I'll push and push a young bowler to strive for perfection, I'm too long retired to hit the nets myself to see whether tinkering with my own action would've made me even more successful.

I enjoy working with the Indian boys that are sent by their state association to trial at the foundation. We spend time videoing them so that we can do a thorough analysis of their action and then offer directions on how they can improve. A lot of work is done on the centre wicket, because we've realised a lot of bowlers look different in a match situation compared to how they might perform in the nets. Something I've learnt to think about when I watch a young bloke bowl is injury prevention. Efficiency is the key. I'm trying to impart that to the bowlers, just as I'm instilling in them the importance of the thought process and how that can help them get wickets. There are some quality bowlers coming through, but the hunt for that kid who can bowl in excess of 150 km/h continues. I don't know if it's due to diet or genes, but it's a mystery why India struggles to produce those pacemen with the X-factor. You look across the border into Pakistan and they develop express quicks. I know the people in the north are taller than most people in India, and I imagine that's an area the foundation will again target. I have seen a lot of positives at the foundation that suggests to me that India will improve its depth of quality quicks. Their fast bowlers aren't scared to work hard, they respond well to advice, they're hungry to succeed and they have an obvious passion to want to help India dominate world cricket—I see that in their actions. While I'm starting to get a good feel for coaching, I realise it'll take time and much more experience before I'm confident that everything is in order. At the moment I am drawing upon my own experiences and sometimes I hear myself reciting what I set out as my ten golden rules in my first book *The Pacemaker: The inner thoughts of Glenn McGrath*. I've found they're as applicable to my new role as a coach as when I played:

1. Keep everything simple, don't complicate things for the sake of it.
2. Work hard off the paddock to improve your skills and fitness.
3. Exercise patience and control over haste and aggression.
4. Always strive to improve. No matter how you progress in cricket—or life—there is always something new to learn.
5. Enjoy life, and be sure the main reason for playing cricket is because you enjoy it.
6. In life—and cricket—don't worry about things you have no control over. That is wasted energy and does nothing to change a situation.
7. Be a team player and try to ensure your individual actions in batting, bowling and fielding count for the good of the team.

8. Never give up. As a fast bowler I always remember it only takes one ball to dismiss a batsman no matter how good he may be.

9. Don't ever let your fieldsmen see you drop your head when you're doing it tough. Let them know by walking tall that you're not going to wave the white flag because that will inspire them to also give their all.

10. Always remember your teammates and umpires are human. Umpires will sometimes make mistakes and fielders will drop the occasional catch.

I have no doubt I'll add a few more golden rules over the coming years as I gain more insight as a coach. I'm a long way from being like Dennis—able to sum up the problems of a fast bowler with a quick glance at his run-up and delivery. But I'm getting a lot better at reading the telltale signs of a bowler with problems. I am relying heavily on slow-motion vision at the moment, but I'm learning, and I am glad the recommendations I'm making are helping the bowlers.

What I learnt from procrastinating over the offer to try something new at the MRF Pace Foundation is that there is paralysis through analysis. Despite my initial fears, I'm loving my role as a coach. I realise I have a lot to offer and I've already seen where I've been able to help a few bowlers improve, and it's rewarding. I'm looking forward to undertaking courses such as my Level 3 coaching certificate through Cricket Australia. This will ensure I have the textbook side of coaching up to scratch. But the greatest indication that I'm doing okay has come from my son James, as I've helped him to work on his fast-bowling action to avoid the stress fractures he's suffered in the past. It pleases me to say that since I started at the foundation, he hasn't once said 'What would you know about bowling, anyway?' when I've offered him my advice.

12

GAMESMANSHIP NOT SLEDGING

Send-offs are send-offs. It's not something we're necessarily concerned about. The focus should be on how well Australia played rather than those minor issues. I don't want to go too deep into that.

—New Zealand captain Brendon McCullum on the send-offs his players received in the 2015 World Cup

The Australians proved to be the dominant team in the 2015 World Cup by defeating New Zealand—installed by many as the favourites based on their form going into the decider—in what turned out to be a one-sided final at the MCG. It was a great victory, but Michael Clarke's men were condemned in the court of public opinion for being too aggressive and for displaying their obvious will to win. That was a reaction I found quite strange.

Wicketkeeper Brad Haddin was hammered because he told a Sydney radio station (after a big night celebrating) that the reason he gave some of the Kiwis send-offs—including their outgoing skipper Daniel Vettori (one of cricket's loveliest blokes)—was because he felt 'uncomfortable' about the way the Aussies were treated in New Zealand prior to their pool match against the home team. He told the radio station that the Kiwi hosts were 'too nice' in the lead-up to Australia's loss, and he apparently declared in the team meeting after that defeat that he'd 'go' at them as hard as he possibly could if the two teams met in the final. And true to his word, Brad did.

I haven't spoken to Brad about that incident, but what I'll say is that I've always found 'Hadds' to be a decent bloke. While he retired after the 2015 Ashes series, he'll be remembered as an old-school competitor, a champion keeper and also a great leader. Maybe he thought the Australians needed to play with more intensity in the final than they did in the pool game, but I really don't know.

What I do know is that how a player behaves on the field is up to him, and guys go about things differently. Some will expose their soul, warts and all, while others prefer to keep to themselves. There's an old saying in sport that nice guys finish second, and I've found in the majority of cases that rings true. However, I also learnt that sledging doesn't win games; it's how players perform under pressure that does. When the Australians qualified for the final against New Zealand they were never going to give the Kiwis an easy ride, because if Michael Clarke's men knew one thing, it was how to win.

Despite the collective wringing of hands in Australia after the World Cup final, I found it very interesting that India's captain Virat Kohli was quoted in an article on Indianexpress.com saying he envied aspects of the Australian game. He said that he even wanted to include some of those aspects in India's game so they could dominate world cricket for the next five years. I respect Kohli—from what I've seen of him he's a player with a winning attitude and he seems to have the gumption to get through the tough times and to also dish 'it' out. Sometimes it seems to me he might even get the first barb in. However, I felt pleased to learn he saw good things in the Australian game. He was quoted as saying: 'On the field you see them [Australia] play and you think like, damn, that's a unit, we have to play our bloody best to beat these guys. I want that to happen to Indian cricket.' Based on that, I guess the message from India is it's really not all bad.

While the world's media seems to focus on the Aussie team's sledging I'm very proud of the current team for a few reasons. The way in which they rebuilt so quickly to fill the holes left by a number of retirements was incredible. Many people predicted they'd be the whipping boys of cricket as the new blokes found their feet in the team, but that proved not to be the case. We've had world-class bowlers such as Mitchell Starc, Josh Hazlewood and Pat Cummins emerge to complement Mitchell Johnson and the recently retired Ryan Harris. Steve Smith continues to go from strength to strength. Adam Voges, at 35, made a century on his debut in the West Indies during the 2015 tour. Michael Clarke and Brad Haddin provided a tough lustre before their retirements. And there's a lot to be confident about in the team's future when you realise we have guys such as Peter Nevill, Mitchell Marsh, Jordan Silk, Nic Maddinson and Sean Abbott all making good noises at first-class level. However, time changes everything and I reckon the culture of the Australian team is altering ever so slightly. While the ties that bind the team remain tight, I've noticed that the players aren't in the dressing sheds until 2 am after a match like we were back in the day. Although I heard they were in the dressing room for a few hours after destroying England in the Second Test at Lord's in 2015. I'm not suggesting a team's harmony or its strength should be judged on something like that, but I do think some issues from recent times ought to have remained in-house and should never have been played out in public, such as the supposed problems between Shane Watson and Clarke.

The revelation that there was a rift shocked a lot of observers because they don't expect that from the Australian cricket team. Even though the team had some big personalities when I played, there were never too many 'issues'. Everyone pulled together because it was all about the end goal, and we wanted to do as well for each other as much as we desired personal success. I'm sure it's the same for the current players, but one of the biggest issues they need to contend with is social media. It can turn a sniff of a rumour into an ironclad fact, and no one seems accountable for what they might post, even if it's proven to be completely wrong and hurtful.

Something I believe was a real boon for Australia after the Mickey Arthur era—where an embarrassing lowlight was the instance of Shane Watson, James Pattinson, Usman Khawaja and Mitchell Johnson being stood down from the third Test during the 2013 tour of India for not doing their homework—was the appointment of my old teammate Darren Lehmann as head coach. 'Boof' was always a person who'd understand the team and what was needed for them to perform at their best. He's provided an environment where his players can be successful because they're allowed to relax and are free to enjoy themselves and the experience.

I think it's fair to say that the Australian team was in a state of disarray when Darren signed on, but since his arrival it's as though the weight has been taken off the team's collective shoulders—Michael Clarke appeared more relaxed, while the team seems overall to be happier and are back to playing their 'normal' game. That's not to suggest Mickey Arthur isn't a good coach—under his stewardship South Africa became the world's No. 1 one-day international team in 2006 and enjoyed an unbeaten streak of nine Test series—but sometimes, for whatever reason, personalities and teams just don't gel. In Lehmann, Australia has a coach who can handle pressure, who stands by his decisions, who can deliver bad news but at the same time enjoy the respect of his players; and the team's performances reflect that.

I rated Michael Clarke's captaincy very highly. 'Pup' is someone I class as a mate, and I can say without fear of contradiction that he's never been short on confidence. I think you can see the obvious influence Shane Warne has had on him, because Warnie took him under his wing early in his career and I reckon that's been a real positive for him. Apart from his feats for Australia, you only need to see what Shane achieved while he was at the English County team, Hampshire, to appreciate how well he understood the tactics of cricket, the psychology of the game and the personalities of his players. I think he passed on some great advice to Michael, but that's not to suggest Pup wasn't his own man. He's a great leader, he has strong views, is a good cricket brain, and, in the spirit of the likes of Border, Taylor, Waugh and Ponting, he too leads by example.

It's clear Steve Smith's appointment as captain sits well with me. I've known 'Smithy' for quite a while because, apart from being looked after by my manager Warren Craig, he also plays for my old first-grade club, Sutherland. He was identified as a rare talent a decade ago and was given a taste of captaining a senior team when he was named the leader of Sutherland's first-grade team at 19 years of age. He's a lot more introverted than Pup, and had the pair been playing during my era, when the national team was divided into two factions, I have no doubt Michael would've been the skipper of the 'Julio's' (they're called 'metrosexuals' these days), while Smithy would've been leader of my crowd, the 'Nerds'—guys who might've taken their fashion tips from Jethro Bodine of *The Beverly Hillbillies* fame. I'm certain Steve will be an excellent skipper, and from what I've seen he'll have a 'team first' approach. I believe his biggest challenge is avoiding being one of the boys. It's nice to be liked by the blokes, but as captain he'll assume a lot of responsibility and it will mean he has to rise above things he might once have enjoyed being a part of. But that's the price of the title and I know he'll handle it well. Actually, he'll be outstanding. He plays with a lot of passion and flair—as his 215 at Lord's highlighted during the 2015 Ashes series—but I suspect there'll be some tough times. I think his biggest test as a captain could be the impact on his own form of the team not performing well. But, mark my words, he has plenty going for him: he's level-headed, he's well grounded, and, despite being one of the world's best cricketers at such a young age, he's quite humble. I was at Lord's when Steve scored his 215, and I bumped into the former Australian fast bowler Merv Hughes, who was a national selector when Steve was first called up to the Aussie team in 2010. Steve was picked then as a leg-spinner. It made me laugh to hear that, when his batting technique was discussed at the selection table, the common consensus was he'd never bat above No. 6. As Merv said that day in London: 'How wrong were we?'

I have no doubt one issue Steve will need to contend with is the continued criticism of the Australian team's reputation as sledgers. 'Sledging', in case you don't know, is making comments to unsettle an opposition's batsmen. It is just banter, a bit of a chat, and while some people call it gamesmanship, Steve Waugh described it as mental disintegration. I see both terms as a more apt description than 'sledging'. I didn't really want to talk about sledging, but I'm told it's not a cricket book these days unless it's discussed. Whenever I hear commentators from other countries dredge up Australia's reputation as sledgers, I can't help but think it sounds a bit old and tired, because I feel it's as though they are doing their best to give the other teams an edge. I think Australian teams were characterised by sledging a few years ago because the more we won, the harder people searched for an angle to attack us from. Regardless, it was seen by many critics as something they could nail us on. Look, there's no doubt some of the boys didn't mind a bit of a 'chat' out in the middle (at least when I played), and while there were other teams who were just as verbal and as cutting in their comments, the media treated it as if we were the only ones who did it. I formed my own views on why that was the case. My first theory is, as I've said, we were the world's dominant team and people needed to find something about us to attack. Secondly, Aussies, as a rule, are upfront about the way we go about our business. I think the one common thread that binds all of Australia's sporting teams— be it swimming, soccer, rugby league and rugby union, hockey and netball—is that we don't try and hide the fact that we're out there to win. We'll play aggressively, and we'll back ourselves, regardless of whether we're given any hope against a superior team or not—because we're expected from a young age to play hard. Look at the Matildas women's soccer team when they beat Brazil in the 2015 Women's World Cup as an example of that. I think that this is a result of Australians being brought up to be honest, and to also cop whatever happens during the contest on the chin.

I'm tired of talking about sledging, because the constant reference seems to overshadow what we've achieved as a cricketing nation. Sure, there were some funny sledges and the quick-witted responses to them have kept dozens of old cricketers employed in after-dinner speaking gigs. For instance, there was the time when Merv Hughes was said to have been so frustrated by the English skipper Graham Gooch continually playing and missing, that he asked after bowling a delivery: 'Would you like me to bowl a piano to see if you can play that?' During a duel between big Merv and Pakistan's Javed Miandad, it was claimed Miandad said to Merv, 'You're a big, fat bus conductor.' Merv's immediate response was simply to grin, but a few balls later when he dismissed Miandad, he ran past the batsman and yelled 'Tickets please!' Then there's the famous story of when an English County fast bowler whizzed a few deliveries past Viv Richards' bat and, feeling confident, sidled up to the Master Blaster and growled, 'It's red and it's round. Now hit it!' Of course it was a silly challenge because Viv not only belted the next delivery out of the ground, but, to add salt to the wound yelled down the pitch: 'You know what it looks like, now go and get it.' I don't know if any of those anecdotes are true, but they've been passed down over the years and are accepted as fact. I suppose that's one of my concerns—the stories about sledging are accepted as truth. My blood still boils to remember how, in 1996 when the World Cup was hosted in Sri Lanka, India and Pakistan, my short bio in the official program stated that I'd called Sri Lanka's star batsman Sanath Jayasuriya a 'black monkey'. I was ropeable when I saw it; the story behind it stemmed from a false accusation Jayasuriya made during the one-day international final at the SCG in 1995–96. Of course there was no substance to it—I'm not a bigot—and to read that rubbish infuriated me. But what really grates is that it's a lie that has become ingrained in Sri Lankan cricket as fact, because their national team's former opener, Roshan Mahanama, repeated the claim in his biography in 2001. He didn't even play in the match and he certainly didn't seek comment from me. I actually sought legal advice because he'd branded me a racist.

While I know there have been reports of inappropriate comments made by some players in the past, none ever left my mouth because I've never judged people by their skin colour, just as I'd expect they don't judge me by mine. If you think other teams don't have a go at the Australians, well, you're wrong. We copped it over the years on the field from rivals and from spectators overseas, but we didn't run to the authorities and we didn't whinge about it.

If I'm discussing sledging, I'm obliged to address a moment that I'm still embarrassed about. It was not the result of the Australian team's supposed culture of arrogance but was more a reflection of where my mind was at the time. In the minutes that followed my blow-up at West Indies batsman Ramnaresh Sarwan during the Caribbean tour in 2003, commentators tried to work out the cause of the heated exchange of words between us. They concluded that it may have been because I made him run around me as he ran for a single. It was instead a split second of rage, ignited by the pressure of what was happening back at home. I had returned to Sydney from London on our way to the Carribbean when Jane was diagnosed with secondary cancer, but I linked up with the team at her insistence because she believed things were normal when I was playing cricket. But they weren't. It was a hot day in Antigua, and while I was in the outfield as the Windies were chasing down a record 418 runs to win, I was thinking I really ought to be at home. I was never a good sledger and my offering to Sarwan that day was pretty lame; stupid really. He mentioned Jane in his response, and I snapped, pointing my finger in his face, and made a series of threats. When Sarwan heard about Jane's health battle he apologised to me when we shared a drink after hostilities; but I made it clear that what happened was my fault and I was sorry for my comment and reaction. It was a reaction many people at home said made them feel ashamed to be Australian. I appreciated that Sarwan was happy to let the matter drop with a handshake, but it was a different story at Cricket Australia's HQ in Melbourne. James Sutherland, the chief executive officer of Cricket Australia, ordered Steve Waugh to control his team and to look at the way we behaved when things didn't go our way. Sutherland didn't need to do that. My actions had nothing to do with

Steve's captaincy or his control over his players—it wasn't a reaction to anything that happened in the game. It was simply the frustration of a bloke under personal pressure which had come to the surface, and that's not an excuse, it's a fact. Nevertheless, it remains the lowlight of my career, and in the aftermath I felt bitterly disappointed in myself. Even after all these years it still embarrasses me to think about it.

I believe one positive of the IPL, the Big Bash League and other Twenty20 competitions around the world, is that players are being brought together in franchises, and as a result friendships are being forged. In some cases, people are finding that the image they may have built up in their mind about a rival competitor is way off the mark and that has to be a good thing. What you learn when you spend time with players from other countries or rival teams is that at the end of the day we're all the same: we want to do our best, and we all have our strengths and vulnerabilities. Since retiring I've worked with some old foes such as Brian Lara, Michael Vaughan and Kevin Pietersen. What I've learnt retrospectively is that even during our toughest on-field battles, we were probably a lot closer than we ever realised. Perhaps it's the relationship building that's happening around the cricket world at the moment through the numerous Twenty20 competitions that will eventually bring an end to the sledge as we know it.

13

ALL BLACKS IN BAGGY GREEN CAPS

If it's difficult, I'll do it now.

If it's impossible I'll do it presently.

—Don Bradman quote inside the SCG's home dressing room

Back in the 1990s the Australian team set itself the goal of becoming to cricket what the All Blacks were to rugby union. We wanted to be relentless, we wanted to have the opposition beaten in their minds before they left the dressing room, we wanted to be the team that defined what it took to be the best in the game, we wanted to be tough and to conquer the world. And in the 14 years that I was a member of the Baggy Greens—under the reign of four different captains in Allan Border, Mark Taylor, Steve Waugh and Ricky Ponting—every player on the team bought into the plan.

We fulfilled our objective—not only were we ranked No. 1 for most of that time, but I was involved in only three losing series, something which I still find quite amazing. In 2001 we received global acclaim for our prowess at the prestigious Laureus World Sports Awards held in Monaco. It honours the year's most outstanding sporting performances and is described by many as the Oscars of the sporting world. We were voted in ahead of the Los Angeles Lakers, the Ferrari Formula One team and the French soccer team as the team of the year. The statuette was presented to Steve Waugh on behalf of his men on the back of a massive year in which we'd won the inaugural International Cricket Council (ICC) World Test Championship and extended our winning run to a record 16 Tests. Steve summed up our collective effort and what drove us to be the best by simply saying: 'It's a great achievement, we've worked hard for it.'

I think businesses or corporations could study what made the Australian team great and learn from it. We were an example of how a team with dynamic leadership, a common goal and people who put the greater good before self, really can take on the world and win. We also had a tremendous support staff—people who knew their roles and who could be trusted on every level. The end result was, apart from adding a successful chapter to Australian cricket's history book, we're also acknowledged on a prestigious sports honour roll which, since its inception, has included the Brazilian and Italian soccer teams, Manchester United, the Chinese Olympic team and the European Ryder Cup (golf) team as the best of the best.

Some people criticised us, saying we were too aggressive and too over the top, but my experience as an Australian player was overwhelmingly positive because it allowed for me to see the world, to meet great people, to pit myself against the game's best players and to constantly set goals and challenge myself. People often ask for my thoughts on what made us so successful. Rather than just say 'train hard', I've broken it down to give a few insights into what I think made it all so special.

THE BAGGY GREEN CAP

I'm Australia's 358th Test player, an honour that at the time of this book's publication had only been extended to 443 of us since the first Test was played between Australia and England in 1877. My baggy green cap means I'm a member of a club that includes household names such as Don Bradman, Dennis Lillee, Victor Trumper, Bill O'Reilly, Alan Davidson and Ray Lindwall. But it also binds me to other great Australians who may not be as well known, including Albert 'Tibby' Cotter, the fast bowler who was killed in World War I during the last great cavalry charge at Beersheba, near Palestine, and Roy Park, a talented enough Aussie Rules player whose entire Test career in 1920–21 consisted of a first-ball duck. It's said his wife missed his entire Test career because he was dismissed the moment she bent to pick up the knitting she dropped just before he faced his first delivery. It's also been said that on the eve of his debut, Park, who was a doctor, was called to help a woman who was having difficulty giving birth, and so he was up all night trying to save the baby. The cap also ties me to Samuel Morris, the first player of West Indian extraction to play Test cricket for Australia, until Andrew Symonds hit the scene. And then there's Tony Dell, who opened the bowling for Australia in 1970–71 after fighting in the jungles of Vietnam two years before his selection. These days he's a great advocate for veterans who are coping with Post Traumatic Stress through his group Standtall4pts. The cap represents a lot, particularly the character of the 443 players who've worn it, as each has, in their own way, helped to give cricket the special role it has in Australia's cultural identity.

I credit the former opener David Boon as being the person who made me appreciate what the Australian cap represented. Originally, I was like a lot of other players—I wore a floppy white hat in the field. That was until he told me what the baggy green represented. 'Boonie' spoke of the tradition, of the men who'd worn it over the years, and also those who were devastated to never get their chance to wear one. He also said it symbolised all that was good about Australian cricket, because regardless of our backgrounds there was 'honour' stitched into the cap. When I heard the unmistakable passion in his voice, I made a point of wearing my baggy green cap in every game after that chat. I agreed with Boonie: it's important to pay homage to those who preceded us, and to acknowledge how the history they helped to forge shaped us as a team.

THE INNER SANCTUM

I was 23 and had played only six games for New South Wales when I was selected for the Australian team that took on New Zealand in the 1993 Test in Perth. I was picked because Merv Hughes had a knee injury, Bruce Reid was also recuperating from a health problem, Jo Angel was sidelined, Carl Rackemann had had a poor game for Queensland against New South Wales, and according to the critics my Blues teammate Wayne Holdsworth hadn't lived up to expectations during the 1993 Ashes tour. When I entered the dressing room I needed to introduce myself to most of the blokes, and while joining a team can be overwhelming for anyone, I still hadn't completely conquered the terrible shyness that tormented me throughout my school days. I was pleased my self-consciousness quickly disappeared as I was warmly greeted by guys such as Shane Warne. I had no idea how Allan Border would welcome me, because the only time we'd previously 'met' was during a Shield match against Queensland at the Gabba, and he had torn into me. He'd noticed that my trousers came up to my shins, and I remember how he smirked before asking stuff like, 'Why are your pants so high? Expecting a flood, mate?' and

'Do you like to dress like Jethro from the *The Beverly Hillbillies?'* (I could've answered 'yes' quite honestly back then). He seemed surprised that regardless of what he said, I didn't retaliate. I just turned my back and returned to my mark, which I think puzzled him. After I bowled a bouncer and failed to respond to yet *another* wisecrack, he asked: 'I know you can grunt, but can you speak?' I was bowling as hard as I could and I wanted to get his wicket—I bagged it in the second innings—but the truth is, I respected him too much to say anything. Allan Border was, after all, the guy I had imagined throwing me the ball and sooling me onto the West Indies when I 'played' for Australia behind the old machinery shed back home. He'd earned his stripes against the West Indies pace attack; I was just a rookie trying to make his mark. Anyway, I was now in his Aussie team and he was my skipper. I imagined that Shield encounter was probably forgotten because, while he left me be as I familiarised myself with the team, he also made it clear I was welcome. Although I still sometimes wonder if he had a joke at my expense, because the team blazer I was presented with was way too small. The management had apparently based it on Reid's measurements. As I spent that first night at an official team function looking like a hillbilly in the big smoke, I'm pretty certain I heard Allan refer to me as 'Jethro' as he spoke to someone during the meal!

Throughout the era that I was in the national Test and one-day teams, the one constant was that regardless of how long you had been in the squad, each captain encouraged everyone to have a voice and to express their thoughts. While I'd have needed to be prodded with a pitchfork to say something in my early days, I saw that this allowed a newcomer to feel as though he could offer something to the team. I considered that to be a mark of good leadership because it made everyone feel as though they belonged and that they were valued. I was focused on what I needed to do in Perth, but I also absorbed everything that was said and watched how guys like Craig McDermott and Paul Reiffel prepared themselves for the game. Over the years I treated the dressing room as a special place, because once the door was shut you were locked away from the outside world; it was just you and the team. It was a place of superstition, some of them weird, including the one that decreed players weren't allowed to leave their seat during an innings, for fear it would somehow unsettle the universe and get one of the batsmen out as a result of a comet being knocked a millimetre off course because someone wanted a drink. It was a place where players privately summoned whatever it was that inspired them before a game. And it was a sanctuary where the team could take stock of a great win or a disappointing loss. When I visited the Australian dressing room at the SCG during the McGrath Foundation Test against India in the 2014–15 season, it reinforced that while I really didn't miss playing at all, the one thing I definitely missed was the camaraderie I'd enjoyed with my teammates.

CAMARADERIE

It sounds clichéd but I'm going to say it anyway because I believe it: for 14 years the Australian team was my second family. I loved the blokes and I never had any trouble in trusting that when everything was on the line, they'd do whatever they possibly could to ensure the team succeeded. Our former opening batsman, Justin Langer, was prepared to defy doctor's orders not to go out and bat after he was badly concussed by a Makhaya Ntini bouncer in the Third Test of the series against South Africa in 2006—that epitomises the level of commitment in our team. I wasn't there, but I know there's no way on earth that his skipper Ricky Ponting would've allowed for Justin to bat after doctors warned he'd risk being killed if he was struck on the head again. However, when Australia looked to be in trouble with victory within reach, 'J.L.' was found in the dressing room at the Wanderers ground dressed in his whites, padded up, and running up and down the length of the room in an effort to prove to himself he was okay to bat. Apparently he looked unsteady on his feet and had been physically ill. While it said a lot about his commitment to his team, it was a good thing that Brett Lee hit the winning runs to avoid what I imagine would've been a battle between a player who didn't want to let Australia down, and a skipper who would have been more concerned about the welfare of his player than the result. There are other examples of players defying terrible injuries to help out the team; while on the other side of the coin there are also stories of injured players who made the tough decision to rule themselves out of a Test—knowing they would be presenting someone with the chance to take their place—for the good of the team.

Something I *really* enjoyed was the laughs we had. More often than not they were over silly things, such as the time we attended a store in Colombo as part of a sponsorship agreement to meet customers and sign autographs. The shop was like a sauna, and once we finished everyone raced upstairs to raid the fridge for cold bottles of water. When Mark Taylor and Mark Waugh both reached for the last remaining bottle I thought it was quite generous of our skipper to allow 'Junior' to take it. Waugh was so thirsty he ripped the lid off and took a swig, but after the first mouthful he spat the liquid out, because he was sculling vinegar! The always attentive Taylor had noticed the label before he backed off, and poor old Junior's pretty awful situation was magnified by the sound of everyone laughing at his expense.

Andrew Symonds was someone who I loved playing and touring with. He was perhaps the most natural talent to grace a cricket field. He could bowl fast, bowl spin, move like a gazelle around the field because he was so quick and agile, and when it came to batting, well, he was tremendous. No matter how you look at it, he ticked every box as a bloke you wanted on your team. He also has a sense of humour and that's why I'm sure he won't mind me saying that the only time he ever got himself into strife was when he had to think. There are plenty of stories about him that are legendary and, as is the case with big personalities, some are true but most aren't. One such case was the day in Adelaide when he bought a raffle ticket, and upon being told that it would be drawn on the 31st, he supposedly replied: 'Well, I'll expect a call on the 32nd.' On another occasion he was said to have been heard ranting about the movie selection on offer at a particular hotel we were staying at. 'Disgusting,' he fumed. When he was asked what was wrong, it's claimed that the 'Symo' rant went like this: 'It's disgusting! There's new releases, action, comedy, family movies, drama, adult movies and . . . *disabled adult movies!*' He needed to be told that it was not a pornographic channel for people with a particular bent, but was instead the instructions on how to disable the adult movies to prevent kids accessing them. I love the bloke to bits, and when I think about what made playing for Australia so special, it was because of the bond I shared with guys like 'Symo', 'Tugger', 'J.L.', 'Punter', 'Junior', 'Binga', 'Gilly'—the whole box and dice. If it was at all possible, I'd do it all over again in a heartbeat.

LEADERSHIP

Captaining the Australian cricket team has long been described as the second most important job in the nation after the prime minister's. Actually, former prime minister John Howard even described it as *the* most important in the nation. I'd argue that being a fast bowler for the national team is, but I guess that's a discussion for another day. Nevertheless, the captains, and their decisions, are heavily scrutinised—sometimes more so than the actions of our political leaders in Canberra. I see that as being a result of how much everyone loves cricket in Australia. I feel very fortunate that at a time when people lament a lack of leadership in the world—be it in business, commerce, sports administration, schools and, in some cases, even the family home—I was led by four national captains who were all very strong leaders in terms of their characters and decision-making abilities.

When I look back on the teams I played in over the years, there were some big egos; but they were kept in check by good managers. I also think the fact that I was asked to volunteer my opinion at that first team meeting in 1993 sent out a positive message that defined my time in the team. It told me that everyone was entitled to have their say, but that ultimately the final decision rested with the skipper, because it was his call, and in professional sport he lived or died by the outcome. It was a transparent structure and by being empowered to offer my thoughts, it gave me a sense of ownership over what happened out in the middle.

I also liked that my leaders were blokes who led by example and who never demanded their men do things that they didn't have the stomach for. For instance, I remember during the 2001 Ashes series when Steve Waugh was stretchered off The Oval during the Trent Bridge Test with a badly torn calf muscle. Rather than ease up and relax because we'd already won the urn, he put himself through a tough 19-day recovery program and managed to play in the final Test, although he was hobbling after being at the crease for a while. Australia was in a dominant position when he took strike. We were 3–489, and there wouldn't have been any shame if he retired hurt because it was obvious he was in pain. Steve instead stood his ground and clubbed 21 fours and a six, and batted until he finished the innings with an unbeaten 157. Rather than retire hurt he declared when Australia reached 4–641. I interpreted his actions that day as a statement of what Steve expected from his men. It also sent a message to England that even though we had our foot on their throat (we won the series 4–1), he refused to take the easy option. It was an effort that proved to many people that he was first and foremost a fighter.

Steve was the same as every captain I played under. Each had inherited the team at different stages of its development and they took it upon themselves to push it further, so when it came time to hand it to their successor, the team was in better shape than how they found it. I think the fact that Border, Taylor, Waugh and Ponting all led Australia to World Cup victories spoke volumes for the Australian cricket team's succession plan. Business could learn a lot from studying the mechanics of the way in which the team operated.

Each captain had a different approach to how he led and it worked. While Allan Border took Australia from being a pretty ordinary team to world champions, his aim was to get us into a position to win before we went for it. Mark Taylor inherited a very good team and his aim was to win from ball one. I enjoyed that approach. Something

I remember about Mark's leadership was that even though his form during the 1997 Ashes was described as scratchy, he had the mental strength to put that criticism aside and make great decisions.

Steve Waugh led the best team in the world but he didn't merely want to win from ball one, he wanted us to *crush* the opposition from ball one. His favourite word was 'ruthless' and he gave the opposition no chance at all. He liked mind games and even changed the word 'sledging' to 'gamesmanship' because he thought it sounded better.

While Ricky Ponting fulfilled the predictions that he'd one day captain Australia, within two years of his appointment he lost *seven* senior players. If a team loses just two players at one time it can potentially destroy it, but Rick was tough and he oversaw the rebuilding of the side. I think the way in which he handled that transition proved his leadership calibre. He won two World Cups, but the achievement that resonates most with me was how in 2004–05 he ended Australia's 35-year drought by winning a Test series in India.

The reason why our captains enjoyed success was straightforward. They knew their team and how to get the best out of the players. I think what makes a great team is the ability to adapt to change and to learn from disappointment. I remember in 2005, when England took the Ashes urn for the first time since 1987, we returned to Australia very focused. We were hurting but were determined to redeem ourselves. We became more specific in our game plan, and when England toured Australia in 2006–07 they didn't stand a chance, because we put our plan into action and defeated them 5–0. What I learnt that summer was that while winning is great, the lessons are often forgotten amid the euphoria. I appreciated that people could learn from their defeats and setbacks, because no matter how you look at losses they sting.

14

THE PIGEON'S TEST SQUAD

The role of chairman draws a lot of public and media scrutiny and seldom receives the recognition it deserves.

—Cricket Australia statement when Trevor Hohns resigned as chairman of selectors in 2006

I've never thought much about picking my best-ever Australian Test team because in my opinion whatever team I was selected for, be it for a Test match or World Cup game, I believed it was the best national side possible for that particular game. I always believed the Australian team was selected on form, and, now I have had a chance to think long and hard about it, I realise I was fortunate to have played in a talent-rich era. The guys I played alongside from 1993–07 included the likes of Michael Slater, Mark Taylor,

Damien Martyn, Michael Bevan, Damien Fleming, Greg Blewett, Stuart MacGill, Darren Lehmann, Michael Clarke, Simon Katich, Andrew Symonds, Shaun Tait, Michael Hussey and Shane Watson—all of who should feel entitled to be named in many of these 'best-ever' teams.

When I sat down to select my team during a lull in my commitments at the MRF Pace Foundation, I really wrestled with this job because I think it is an exercise that can risk bruising the egos of the friends I leave out. Nevertheless, I've bitten the bullet and among the criteria I've used to select my crew is consistency, character, ability to perform under pressure, and effort. It's taken me the better part of a week, but after much deliberation and scribbling on hundreds of pages, I have come up with a 13-man squad to take on the world. It is as follows: Matthew Hayden, Justin Langer, Ricky Ponting, Mark Waugh, Steve Waugh, Allan Border (captain), Adam Gilchrist, Brett Lee, Shane Warne, Craig McDermott, Jason Gillespie, Andy Bichel and Michael Kasprowicz.

I'd like to think the selections are seen by even the harshest critic as 'givens'. After all, Langer and Hayden formed one of cricket's most successful opening combinations. Rick Ponting is the second most successful run-scorer in Test cricket history. Twins Steve and Mark Waugh were so different in their approaches to the game, but they brought unique and invaluable traits to their teams. Allan Border was perhaps the bravest player to ever wear the baggy green cap because he was targeted by the opposing pace attacks. Adam Gilchrist is arguably the greatest batsman-keeper cricket has ever seen. Brett Lee's longevity as a genuine pace bowler—he was still bowling in the high 140s at 38 years of age—puts him in a league of his own. Do I really need to justify Shane Warne as a walk-up starter? Craig McDermott carried the burden as Australian cricket's great spearhead after Lillee and Thomson retired and he did an outstanding job. Jason Gillespie was a quality bowler who I was fortunate to have partner me in many tough battles. My 12th and 13th men, the big-hearted Queenslanders Andy Bichel and Michael Kasprowicz, were two of the greatest team men you could have wanted on tour or in the dressing room because they threw themselves into their roles.

I think it's a well-balanced team and while there are three captains in my squad, four if you include Adam Gilchrist who led the team on a couple of occasions, I am certain that both Steve and Rick would have no objections to my decision to bestow the title on Allan Border. I have named him as my skipper because of the job he did to single-handedly drag Australian cricket from an era where it had struggled—after being gutted by the impact of the World Series Cricket war and then rebel tours to South Africa robbing the establishment of its experienced and best performers—to reach the top of the world; an effort that was realised in the 1987 World Cup victory over England in India.

So, it's been a long process and without any further ado it's my pleasure to introduce the Pigeon's Australian XIII to take on all comers . . .

NB: * denotes not out

MATTHEW HAYDEN

You never want an Australian with his back against the wall. Put any 12 blokes together and you'll get a job done. Whether it's getting a bogged four-wheel-drive off the beach or standing in front of a cricket wicket and making sure we're in a dominant position. It's the same dog, different leg action, so to speak.

—'HAYDOS' ON THE AUSSIE SPIRIT

Full name: Matthew Lawrence Hayden

Nickname: Haydos

Birthdate: 29 October 1971

Birthplace: Kingaroy, Queensland

Major teams: Australia, Queensland, Brisbane Heat, Chennai Super Kings, Hampshire, ICC World XI, Northamptonshire

Role: Opening batsman

Batting style: Left-hand bat

Bowling style: Right-arm medium

TESTS: 103

Test debut: v South Africa at Johannesburg, 4–8 March 1994

Last Test: v South Africa at Sydney, 3–7 January 2009

Test runs: 8625

Highest score: 380

Average: 50.73

Strike rate: 60.10

Test centuries: 30

Catches: 128

ONE-DAY INTERNATIONALS: 161

Runs:	6133
Highest score:	181*
Average:	43.80
Strike rate:	78.96
ODI centuries:	10
Catches:	68

Few batsmen went out of their way to impose themselves on the opposition's bowling attack quite like Matthew Hayden. Tall, powerfully built and boasting a chest that always seemed to make his shirts appear a size too small, Matt had a formidable physique. Over the years his menacing presence (and ability to murder the attack) resulted in him being described by sportswriters and commentators as a 'bully and a brute'. As I say, he differed to other batsmen because he was happy to get to the crease, scratch around like an old chook, squat and stretch, and before the first ball was bowled he'd get stuck into the bowlers by shouting out to them that they were 'rubbish'. While some might consider that an act of lunacy, Haydos did it to fire himself up, and just for good measure he targeted the biggest and the best in the opposition's attack. For instance, when we played against Pakistan Matt would go out of his way to pick out their express bowler Shoaib Akhtar and let him know that he didn't have too high an opinion of the way he bowled, and it lit the fuse for a duel. I view Matt's approach to psyching himself up as the ultimate sign of a batsman backing himself, because getting into the bowler's face was a *different* approach to that of the vast majority of batsmen who liked to overcome the opening bombardment and ease themselves into their innings.

The record book shows how good a batsman he was— only nine batsmen in the history of Test cricket scored more than his 30 centuries and the list contains the likes of Sachin Tendulkar, Jacques Kallis, Ricky Ponting, Kumar Sangakkara, Brian Lara, Sunil Gavaskar and Steve Waugh. He opened the innings for the Australian Test team at a time when we'd set the goal to score at four runs per over—a big ask—and he did his best to get the ball rolling every time he took strike by unleashing powerful drives or hitting balls over mid-wicket. We all treasured our baggy green cap but it had extra meaning to him because few batsmen were made to work as hard to secure their spot as Matt. He was given his first taste of Test cricket in 1994 but it wasn't until after Australia's 2001 tour of India, when he scored 549 runs in the three-Test series at an average of 109.8, that he cemented his place in the team. It's worth pointing out the secret to his success during that trip to India was that in the weeks before we left he spent plenty of time playing against spin bowlers in Brisbane on churned-up pitches—and it worked a treat when he had to face the music on the subcontinent.

He held the world record Test score, with 380 against Zimbabwe before Brian Lara hammered 400 against England. In terms of Australia's greatest one-day international players, he rates alongside Michael Bevan and Dean Jones. He is religious and would cross himself after a century. I think the man upstairs looked after him one particular night in South Africa when Haydos did a nude surf on the cable car that took the team to the top of Table Mountain—1086 metres above sea level—after Australia won the opening Test of the 2006 series against South Africa. Adam Gilchrist spilt the beans on this story and it's worth repeating. The team was taken up there late at night to sing our victory song 'Under the Southern Cross' and, as Gilchrist recalled, our opener stripped down to his birthday suit, pushed the latch to open the manhole in the roof of the car, and despite the dangerous winds that swirled around him he cable-car surfed wearing only an Australian flag draped around his shoulders. *That* was Matt Hayden, whether it was giving lip to the world's fastest bowlers to fire himself up, or stripping for the ride of his life thousands of feet above the earth; he had the ability to surprise anyone. When he retired I said it had been an honour to play alongside Matt Hayden and that it was a privilege to call him my 'mate', and I meant it. I also meant it when I said he'd be picked in any of the teams I have played for and I'm making good on that right now by naming the big Queenslander as one of my openers.

JUSTIN LANGER

Look, I'm a big fan of Australian colloquialisms. I love Australia—I've got an Australian flag outside my house— but the line 'She'll be right'? Nup. Nah. That's not how it works. Having the attitude 'She'll be right' means everything

*will just stay mediocre. I hate it. To tell you the truth 'she'
actually won't be right. Not unless you do something about it.
You're the one who can change things. They don't change
by themselves.*

—'J.L.' ON DIGGING IN

Full name: Justin Lee Langer

Nickname: J.L., Alfie

Birthdate: 21 November 1970

Birthplace: Perth

Major teams: Australia, Western Australia, Middlesex, Rajasthan Royals, Somerset

Role: Opening batsman

Batting style: Left-hand bat

Bowling style: Right-arm medium

Cricket relative: Uncle Robbie Langer (Robert Samuel Langer, WA & WSC Australia)

TESTS: 105

Test debut: v West Indies at Adelaide, 23–26 January 1993

Last Test: v England at Sydney, 2–5 January 2007

Test runs: 7696

Highest score: 250

Average: 45.27

Strike rate: 54.22

Test centuries: 23

Catches: 73

ONE-DAY INTERNATIONALS: 8

Runs: 160

Highest score:	36
Average:	32
Strike rate:	88.88
ODI centuries:	0
Catches:	2

To pick Matthew Hayden as an opener and not select Justin Langer as his partner would be like separating Charlie Brown from Snoopy, Batman from Robin or Skippy the Bush Kangaroo from Sonny. They were an outstanding partnership and after the West Indies dynamic duo of Desmond Haynes and Gordon Greenidge they formed Test cricket's most successful opening combination with 5655 runs from 113 innings. They provided Australia with a rock solid foundation and any selector who had them at their disposal would be a mug not to name them—and I'm not a mug!

J.L. is one person you'd want alongside you in a foxhole. He's a fighter, he's very loyal and I have no doubt he would be the bloke who'd throw himself on to a grenade to save everyone else. When he made his debut for Australia against the West Indies in Adelaide in 1993 he was hit on the helmet by the first ball he faced in Test cricket, from Ian Bishop. The ball crashed into his helmet so hard he told people he saw three Bishops run in to bowl the next ball at him. In that same innings he copped a Kenny Benjamin cannonball in the belly before he was caught on 20 while hooking a Benjamin fireball. If the two deliveries that left him bruised and shaken up didn't make him appreciate Test cricket was combat with a bat and pads, he was sure to realise it when he was at the other end of the wicket as a Curtly Ambrose delivery broke David Boon's arm and yet another cracked Steve Waugh on the shoulder. After his tough initiation into the big time, Langer gave some insight into his pugnacious batting style in the second innings of that match when he scored a fighting 54 that *almost* guided Australia to a historic victory and Test series triumph. Unfortunately Australia fell one painful run short of creating the upset.

Justin Langer was a player of great character. He was respectful, he had time for friend and foe, and he played cricket in the same way he conducts himself as a man, with what I consider a great decency. I have no doubt his character is as much the reason for his success as the coach of Western Australia and the Perth Scorchers back-to-back title-winning Big Bash League team as his knowledge and ability to communicate. His approach as an Australian player was to put the team first and to do anything for it. I wasn't at the 2006 Test against South Africa when he was left badly concussed by a Makhaya Ntini bouncer. But it's not hard for me at all to picture him—a few days after being advised by doctors that he'd risked death by batting again in, ironically, his 100th Test—padding up and preparing to bat when it looked as though Australia might need his skills with the bat to win the match. And with the advice from medical staff ringing in his ears there he was, running up and down in the change room trying to convince himself that he'd be okay. *That* was the attitude that made Justin Langer a mainstay in whatever team he played for.

While plenty of people are well aware he is a devotee of martial arts and does such things as spar with the former world boxing champion Danny Green for fun, something that isn't as readily known is that in 2009, while playing for the English County team Somerset, he surpassed Sir Donald Bradman as Australia's greatest scorer of first-class runs when he hit fellow Aussie Matt Mason to the boundary along his way to 107 against Worcester. He'd come a long way from the 13-year-old who 'borrowed' a bat that his father had in his study that was used by J.L.'s all-time hero, former Australian skipper Kim Hughes. Even though he had been told by his dad he wasn't allowed to use it, that was the bat he scored the first of his centuries with. 'I thought if it's good enough for Kim Hughes, it's good enough for me,' was Justin's view.

J.L. was said to have been offered the opportunity to coach England before the 2015 Ashes campaign, and while J.L. said he'd remain in Perth for the sake of his four daughters, my personal belief is he knew the kangaroo tattooed on his backside would've given him a swift kick he'd never forget!

RICKY PONTING

I always just tried to think about being a leader, no matter where I was at. If I was a young bloke in a team I thought I could be a leader just with energy, the way I train and trying to make myself a better fielder and player. Because I thought if someone else saw me doing that, they'd want to do it no matter how old they were. So when I came in the side and Mark Waugh was the best fielder, I was going to train harder every day to make sure I was better than him, and if I got better than him maybe he'd want to chase me.

—'PUNTER' ON LEADERSHIP

Full name:	Ricky Thomas Ponting
Nickname:	Punter
Birthdate:	19 December 1974
Birthplace:	Launceston, Tasmania
Major teams:	Australia, Tasmania, Hobart Hurricanes, Antigua Hawksbills, ICC World XI, Kolkata Knight Riders, Mumbai Indians, Somerset, Surrey
Role:	Top-order batsman
Batting style:	Right-hand bat
Bowling style:	Right-arm medium
Cricket relative:	Uncle Greg Campbell (Tasmania & Australia)
TESTS:	168
Test debut:	v Sri Lanka at Perth, 8–11 December 1995
Last Test:	v South Africa at Perth, 30 November – 3 December 2012
Test runs:	13,378
Highest score:	257
Average:	51.85
Strike rate:	58.72
Test centuries:	41
Catches:	196
Test wickets:	5

ONE-DAY INTERNATIONALS: 375

Runs:	13,704
Highest score:	164
Average:	42.03
Strike rate:	80.39
ODI centuries:	30
Catches:	160
ODI wickets:	3

I spent a lot of time with Ricky—although, I call him Rick these days because he's over 40—at the Australian Cricket Academy in Adelaide. Even though he was only 17 he'd been saddled with the title of 'future Australian captain' and if he thought that was a burden, it never showed. His quality as a batsman was undeniable and his understanding of all things cricket was quite incredible. He had a tremendous appreciation for the tactics and strategies, and if a school student devoted themselves to their studies like he did cricket they'd go a long way. Rick was only 17 when he was picked for Tasmania in 1992 and he was a baby-faced 21-year-old when he made his Test debut against Sri Lanka in Perth in 1995. Even though he was dismissed four runs short of his century in that match, it didn't seem to matter much that he copped a dodgy lbw decision because as his teammates we realised he'd be around for a very long time.

I remember Rick as probably the best player of the short ball I ever saw. He'd really take it on. His pull shot was magnificent and there's a school of thought that no one played it better than him. The pull is a courageous shot because when the batsman plays it, he knows the ball is heading at his chin—and at pace—and he has to commit to it because there's no backing out. Like so many of Australia's great batsmen, he wasn't tall but he possessed a beautiful sense of awareness at the crease. He was nimble and calm and fearless. I thought for quite a while that he'd be Test cricket's greatest run-scorer because he was *that* good. However, I think Sachin Tendulkar has taken that mantle from the reach of everyone.

Nevertheless, Rick was a batsman who shone on the brightest stage. While other players were suffocated by pressure, he treated it as oxygen and I point to the 2003 World Cup final against India in South Africa as an example of that. Rick blasted 140 off 121 deliveries and his knock set the tone for us to roll India, a team who was crushed by the weight of expectations from a billion fans who demanded that they beat us. In another effort that summed him up, Rick scored centuries in each innings of his 100th Test match in 2005 when Australia played South Africa. I also think it says plenty for his fortitude—and, I guess, longevity—that he batted 196 times as a No. 3 Test batsman, a position regarded by the greats as the toughest place to bat. While he played in an era where Australian batsmen such as the Waugh brothers, Matt Hayden, Adam Gilchrist, Mike Hussey, Michael Clarke and Damien Martyn dominated the world's bowling attacks, the statistics suggest he was top of the class. In his 168 Tests he hit 71 international centuries; scored the most centuries in a calendar year by an Aussie (seven in 2006); passed 1000 Test runs in a calendar year on five occasions; was the first batsman to score over 1000 runs at four different grounds; and was one of only five batsmen to have scored back-to-back double Test centuries. That effort was only enhanced by his brilliant fielding. His 196 catches—the most by an Aussie fieldsman outside of the wicketkeeper—also proves he had a safe pair of hands, and if ever there was a marksman in the field it was him. He featured in plenty of run-outs with some great throws.

Rick was also a very good captain. He was tactically astute and a good communicator; he was a skipper who could manage his players and who never expected his players to do something he wasn't prepared to do himself. He certainly led by example and I think it was fitting that his final match in Australia was a Sheffield Shield final victory. It pleases me to think of the impact he had on the team's young players, such as Jordan Silk. His ability to inspire is the reason why I have no doubt he'll be a part of the Cricket Australia system in the near future as a batting consultant, if not coach, because he has so much to offer.

There was a time when Rick and his family lived a few streets away from me at Cronulla, and I remember finding a few golf balls among the shrubs in our garden. It was a mystery at first. When I looked to see the angle from where they were hit, I realised the cheeky bugger was having a swing in his backyard! I'm not fibbing when I say my first reaction was to search for the Big Bertha in my golf bag to return serve!

MARK WAUGH

I can remember my first cricket match when I was seven, probably because I got a duck that day. My first really strong memory of watching Test cricket is the Lillee/Thomson/ Walters/Chappell era. I can recall watching Doug Walters hit Bob Willis for six at the WACA off the last ball of the day to bring up his hundred. I liked the way Walters played.

—'JUNIOR' ON CHILDHOOD MEMORIES

Full name:	Mark Edward Waugh
Nickname:	Junior
Birthdate:	2 June 1965
Birthplace:	Canterbury, New South Wales
Major teams:	Australia, New South Wales, Essex
Role:	Batsman
Batting style:	Right-hand bat
Bowling style:	Right-arm medium, right-arm off break
Cricket relatives:	Brothers Steve Waugh (NSW & Australia), Dean Waugh (NSW & SA), Daniel Waugh (NSW under-17s)
TESTS:	128
Test debut:	v England at Adelaide, 25–29 January 1991
Last Test:	v Pakistan at Sharjah, 19–22 October 2002
Test runs:	8029
Highest score:	153*
Average:	41.81
Strike rate:	52.27
Test centuries:	20

Catches:	181
Test wickets:	59
ONE-DAY INTERNATIONALS:	244
Runs:	8500
Highest score:	173
Average:	39.35
Strike rate:	76.90
ODI centuries:	18
Catches:	108
ODI wickets:	85

I rank Junior as perhaps the most naturally gifted batsman I ever saw. Through his flicks, cuts and drives he added an artistic expression to the game, and as a No. 11 who treated every run like a lottery win, I was envious of the way in which Mark Waugh did it all so easily. He was a very elegant player and one who was blessed with all of the shots, but what I've realised I admired most about Mark was he kept it all very simple—when he was out he'd fallen to either a good ball or poor shot. With Junior it was never a case of his being out of form or failing because of mental issues, he was a batsman who just played the game and you could tell he loved every moment. He was pure class and I think it says a lot about his approach to the game that when he was once asked to name the batsmen he enjoyed watching, he answered Sachin Tendulkar, Brian Lara and Adam Gilchrist—as batsmen they were brothers to different mothers.

Junior was made to wait so long for his baggy green cap he was nicknamed 'Afghan', as in the so-called 'forgotten war' in the 1980s. However, he declared his intent as a batsman during his Test debut against England at Adelaide Oval in 1991 when he was selected at 25 years of age to replace his older brother Steve (older by four minutes). He was sent to the crease with Australia lurching at 4–104 and he peeled off an elegant century, becoming the 15th Aussie player to score a century upon debut. Later on, Junior would reveal he went into the game unaware of the pressure involved in Test cricket and that was what probably allowed for him to 'breathe'. He finished at stumps on what was described as a 'glorious' 116 not out. I think Junior summed up his confidence when, after Allan Border congratulated him on a job well done when he returned to the dressing room, Junior said, 'You should have picked me years ago.'

Like all cricketers he had his tough times. He bagged two pairs in the Test series—four Test ducks in 15 balls—during the 1992 tour of Sri Lanka. While the boys nicknamed him 'Audi'—because the four zeroes looked like the motor car's logo—he remained philosophical. Rather than curse his misfortune Junior reasoned anyone can get out for a duck, saying it only takes a good ball to end an innings (and I can vouch for that!). However, his place in the Australian team was being scrutinised, and as much as he tried not to let that run of outs scar him, he admitted that he started wondering where his next run would come from and how the gaps that seemed to be in the field were no longer there. He of course overcame that.

While some of his harsher critics wanted him to be more like his twin brother and fight for every run, he maintained that he did not understand the so-called 'gritty innings'. A gritty innings is when a batsman grafts for each and every run in a day-long innings when he could go out and hit the same 60 or 70 runs in a few hours. It was Junior's basic instinct to attack. Few who saw his innings in the final Test against the West Indies in Jamaica during the 1995 series will forget how he and Steve scored over 300 runs between them, and some believe Junior's cuts helped turn the tide in our favour.

Although he loathed the limelight—he did not like the fame that went with being a high-profile cricketer—he was born for the big stage and he shone brightly in the 1996 World Cup when he overcame the heat and humidity of the subcontinent to peel off three centuries in the tournament. As a fieldsman he had safe hands, and before Ricky Ponting took it from him Junior had the record number of Test catches with 181. I don't think I've ever seen a better slips fieldsman—if Mark was artistic with the bat he was a poet on the field. He took some spectacular catches at second slip and possessed a level of anticipation that I thought bordered on ESP. He could field at silly point just as brilliantly for the spin bowlers and looked at home whenever he was required to field at short mid-wicket or mid-wicket. Mark accepted a role as a selector for the Australian team in 2014 and I was happy to hear of that appointment because he has a lot to offer. I am sure he will encourage players to back themselves and trust their natural skills.

STEVE WAUGH

*Winning leads to complacency. It's just human nature. So
you need to be constantly aware that this is going to happen.
It can be a trap. You can't rely on past success and so you
must go forward facing the truth head-on. What I mean
by this is that sometimes it's necessary to make hard or
unpopular decisions that ultimately benefit the team
(or the organisation). Even when these truths are things
that you don't want to hear, that you don't want to believe.
Like cutting a popular player from the next Test series.
Assuming nothing also means that you don't have to continue
to follow a path or direction that's no longer working.
It's never too late to review and re-focus.*

—'TUGGER' ON WHY YOU SHOULD ASSUME NOTHING

Full Name:	Stephen Rodger Waugh
Nickname:	Tugger
Birthdate:	2 June 1965
Birthplace:	Canterbury, New South Wales
Major teams:	Australia, New South Wales, Ireland, Kent, Somerset
Role:	Middle-order batsman
Batting style:	Right-hand bat
Bowling style:	Right-arm medium
Cricket relatives:	Brothers Mark Waugh (NSW & Australia), Dean Waugh (NSW & SA), Daniel Waugh (NSW under-17s)
TESTS:	168
Test debut:	v India at Melbourne, 26–30 December 1985
Last Test:	v India at Sydney, 2–6 January 2004
Test runs:	10,927

Highest score:	200
Average:	51.06
Strike rate:	48.64
Test centuries:	32
Catches:	112
Test wickets:	92
ONE-DAY INTERNATIONALS:	325
Runs:	7569
Highest score:	120*
Average:	32.90
Strike rate:	75.91
ODI centuries:	3
Catches:	111
ODI wickets:	195

Steve may have been Mark's twin but he was his opposite in so many ways. He was determined, gritty, dogmatic and described throughout his playing career as a 'street fighter' because he placed such a high price on his wicket. He was one player who was prepared to wear deliveries on his body and he did not care if he needed to play ugly to score runs. I remember him as a cricketer who was so focused, so determined he refused to give the opposition an inch. His mental strength was incredible and he loved Test cricket because he saw it as a test of character and of mettle. He described sledging as 'mental disintegration' and I think that was a far better term to use. He saw it as getting into the batsman's head by turning the screws and making the opposition ask questions of themselves. He—supposedly—did it in Trinidad to Curtly Ambrose during the 1995 Frank Worrell series when Ambrose had to be dragged away from his famous mid-pitch confrontation with Tugger by his skipper Richie Richardson. It's one of the defining sports photos from that era and some say it symbolises our team's determination to dethrone the Windies as the kings of cricket. Twenty years after that flashpoint, Ambrose, who at two metres tall towered over Steve, revealed that it threatened to escalate into a fight and that he had even threatened to knock Steve out. Apparently his pace partner Kenny Benjamin had made his blood boil when he suggested Steve had 'cursed' at him and the more he thought about it the angrier he became. Ambrose thought he'd been disrespected and when he demanded to know whether Steve swore at him the paceman was not impressed by the Australian's answer. And he lost it. When Steve took strike Australia was 3–14, and while Australia was dismissed for 128, Waugh finished unbeaten on 63 after three tough hours in which he copped plenty of short stuff. 'I was left standing there thinking, I've smashed open a hornet's nest here, what am I going to do? wrote Waugh of the stand-off. 'It's on TV, there are millions of people watching, you can't look like a coward and back away now. You've got to stand there and pretend you're tough.'

There was nothing false about Steve's toughness because I don't think he ever asked any player to do what he was not prepared to do himself. Before his back injury forced him to stop bowling, his medium-pacers took the fight to the Windies with short-pitched deliveries and, just like his exchange, it won him few friends in the Caribbean. However, he always backed himself and I don't think there is any greater example of his fighting qualities than his last ball century on the second day of the SCG Test against England in 2003. Australia had already won the Ashes but Steve's place in the team was being questioned and the selectors did not do anything to calm the situation when they said they could not guarantee him anything. It was a challenge and when Steve was sent in to bat with Australia at 3–56 in the chase for 362, he looked like a man on a mission. He made 47 when the last drinks break was taken and with the advice of the media personality Andrew Denton ringing in his ears, 'Don't be home before six', he unleashed on the English attack. Denton had won the right to carry the drinks at a charity auction and he would later say he was the last person to see Steve before he became a god. In the final over of the day Steve was up against the spin bowler Richard Dawson, and with five runs needed for his triple figures he just blocked them. He hit three off the fourth ball and Adam Gilchrist gave him his shot at a magic moment when he found a single. I wasn't surprised when Nasser Hussain took his time to set the field and chat to Dawson—it was mental disintegration or games-manship—but I couldn't help but feel annoyed as he made my mate wait. When the moment came, Waugh swung and the ball sped to the boundary. It was a special moment and for so many people it epitomised the fighting qualities of the national team's skipper.

The success Steve, and Australia, enjoyed in the latter stages of his career was a far cry from when he made his Test debut against India in 1985 when he scored 13 and 5 at the MCG as a 20-year-old. Australia had lost a number of experienced players to either retirement or those who were suspended for going on rebel tours of South Africa. It was a tough initiation, but Steve being Steve kept his eyes and ears open and the lessons he learnt from the school of hard knocks served him well. I also take heart in knowing that as a father of a son who loves playing cricket—his son Austin has played for a few representative teams—the former Test skipper, who was inducted in the Cricket Australia Hall of Fame as soon as he was eligible, passes on his observations about his 15-year-old's technique via his son's club coach because kids don't listen to their parents, even if they happen to be a former Test captain! My James is exactly the same, although I took it as a triumph that James acknowledged recently that I knew a bit about cricket. Steve Waugh is a teammate who I think can hold his head high because, as we saw that day against Ambrose, he was one guy who, come hell or high water, walked the walk.

ALLAN BORDER (CAPTAIN)

If I wasn't playing well, I hated it. I hated getting out in stupid ways, and that was when the fuse could blow. I was the same if the team wasn't playing well. Brad Pitt says in the movie Moneyball, *'I hate losing. I hate losing more than I even want to win.' I reckon I'm exactly the same.*

—'A.B.' ON DEFEAT

I played with no fear when I made my Test debut against New Zealand in 1993 after only a handful of first–class games for NSW because I believed I belonged there. (GETTY IMAGES)

Lord's was never more beautiful a place than the Second Ashes Test in 1997 when I snared 8–38. (PATRICK EAGAR/PATRICK EAGAR COLLECTION VIA GETTY IMAGES)

The Australian team always shared in each player's success and I was proud of the response my eight wickets at Lord's received from the boys.
(LAURENCE GRIFFITHS/ ALLSPORT)

Mike Atherton dancing to what the West Indies fast bowlers called 'chin music'. (DAVID MUNDEN/POPPERFOTO/GETTY IMAGES)

Brian Lara, a brilliant foe, was always a great challenge to bowl to but you never knew what kind of mood he would take strike with. (BEN RADFORD /ALLSPORT)

I know many Indian supporters still haven't forgiven me for the day Sachin Tendulkar was given out lbw for a duck when he ducked into my bouncer at Adelaide Oval in 1999. (HAMISH BLAIR/ALLSPORT)

James has asked what I know about bowling when I've offered to show him a few tricks of the trade. He was too young to remember that we celebrated my being named Man of the Match against the Windies in 2000 after I finished with match figures of 10–27.
(DARREN ENGLAND/ALLSPORT)

Dismissing Brian Lara was always a special occasion but the reason I was ecstatic when Stuart MacGill caught him at the WACA in 2000 was because he helped deliver my 300th Test wicket. (HAMISH BLAIR/ALLSPORT)

When Australia won its record-breaking 12th straight Test victory in 2000, Michael Slater, Justin Langer, Stephen Waugh, me and Mark Waugh had special reason to celebrate because we'd played in each of them. (HAMISH BLAIR/ALLSPORT)

I was far from the best player to wield the willow but I gave it my all . . . sadly it wasn't enough to keep Windies bowler Mervyn Dillon from uprooting the stumps at Adelaide Oval in December 2000. (TONY LEWIS/ ALLSPORT)

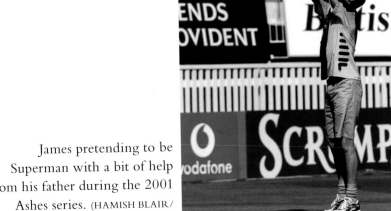

James pretending to be Superman with a bit of help from his father during the 2001 Ashes series. (HAMISH BLAIR/ ALLSPORT)

I never lost the sense of accomplishment whenever I took a wicket, hence the celebration when Mike Atherton fell lbw to me at Lord's during the 2001 Ashes campaign. (WILLIAM WEST/AFP/GETTY IMAGES)

A leap of faith, catching England's Michael Vaughan in what many considered to be a miracle catch in Adelaide in 2002. (NICK WILSON/ GETTY IMAGES)

Opening the shoulder blades on my way to 50 against the New Zealanders in 2004, it felt like I was back having a crack in the Far West competition. (HAMISH BLAIR/GETTY IMAGES)

I had dreamt of this moment for so long, raising the bat to acknowledge the applause of the Gabba crowd for reaching 50 against the New Zealanders in 2004. (JONATHAN WOOD/ GETTY IMAGES)

One day when I really was walking on air, being congratulated by the boys after smashing my first (and only) Test half-century against the Kiwis. (HAMISH BLAIR/ GETTY IMAGES)

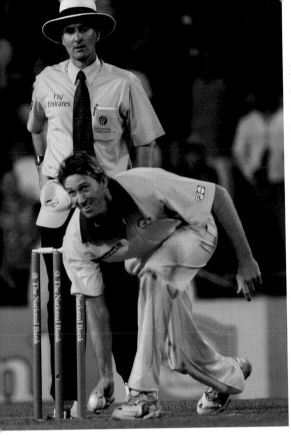

Having a bit of fun at the risk of outraging New Zealand during the 2005 Twenty20 international in Auckland by impersonating Trevor Chappell's infamous underarm bowl.
(HAMISH BLAIR/GETTY IMAGES)

Dad was happy to tell everyone my sister Donna was the best fast bowler of his children. We share a laugh after I took my 500th Test wicket during the Lord's Test of the 2005 Ashes series.
(HAMISH BLAIR/GETTY IMAGES)

Who says my wicket wasn't worth anything? England's Simon Jones shows his disappointment in not dismissing me after Geraint Jones dropped a chance at Lord's. (PATRICK EAGAR/PATRICK EAGAR COLLECTION VIA GETTY IMAGES)

Holly and James enjoy the applause of the Lord's members with me after taking my 500th Test wicket. (HAMISH BLAIR/GETTY IMAGES)

After I injured my ankle while warming up for the Birmingham Test of the 2005 Ashes series our physiotherapist Errol Alcott worked a miracle to get me back on the field for the next Test. (TOM SHAW/GETTY IMAGES)

Mike Hussey and I congratulate each other after our record last wicket stand of 107 runs against South Africa at the MCG in December 2005. I was pleased 'Huss' was prepared to trust me with the strike. (WILLIAM WEST/AFP/GETTY IMAGES)

Holly watches as I cook up a storm at a sausage sizzle for the McGrath Foundation at Sydney's Hyde Park in 2006.
(GREG WOOD/AFP/GETTY IMAGES)

The end of an era: Shane Warne, Justin Langer and I playing our farewell Test at the SCG against England in 2007. It is a great memory.
(JACK ATLEY/BLOOMBERG VIA GETTY IMAGES)

Shane Warne (R), me and Justin Langer (3rd) walk on to the pitch ahead of the Australian team on day one of the Fifth Ashes Test Match between Australia and England at the Sydney Cricket Ground on 2 January 2007 in Sydney, Australia. (HAMISH BLAIR/ GETTY IMAGES)

Sri Lanka's Russel Arnold became my final international wicket when I dismissed him during our 2007 World Cup Final triumph in Barbados. (HAMISH BLAIR/GETTY IMAGES)

La vita è bella or life is beautiful. Sara and I on our wedding day . . . the most passionate and caring person I know.

Holly, me, Sara and James on a family holiday at Table Mountain in 2011.

Sara is an adventurous person who would love for the kids to experience the colour and adventure of living in India. It was at the Gurudwara Bangla Sahib, the Sikh Temple in New Delhi, where Sara, James, Holly and I volunteered for 'Langar'.

Full name: Allan Robert Border

Nickname: A.B.

Birthdate: 27 July 1955

Birthplace: Cremorne, New South Wales

Major teams: Australia, New South Wales, Queensland, Essex, Gloucestershire

Role: Middle-order batsman

Batting style: Left-hand bat

Bowling style: Slow left-arm orthodox

TESTS: 156

Test debut: v England at Melbourne, 29 December 1978 – 3 January 1979

Last Test: v South Africa at Durban, 25–29 March 1994

Test runs: 11,174

Highest score: 205

Average: 50.56

Test centuries: 27

Catches: 156

Test wickets: 39

ONE-DAY INTERNATIONALS: 273

Runs: 6524

Highest score: 127*

Average: 30.62

Strike rate: 71.42

ODI centuries: 3

Catches: 127

ODI wickets: 73

Allan Border deserves to be regarded as one of the toughest cricketers to have ever played the game—in any team, from any era and for any country. When Australia played the West Indies at the peak of their powers in the 1980s and '90s—and they seemed to be touring Australia *every* summer back then—'A.B.' was their main target by virtue of his being the team's captain and grittiest batsman. The West Indies' pace attack operated back then with the belief that if the opposing team's head was cut off, the body would follow; and it really was the case that if you nailed Border, you nailed Australia. However, I doubt whether they ever found an opposing captain who proved to be as stubborn or as resilient as Border. And it wasn't only the West Indies, because every team had their fire-breathing dragons: Pakistan boasted Wasim Akram and Waqar Younis, England had Bob Willis, India Kapil Dev, New Zealand rolled out Richard Hadlee, and South Africa unveiled Allan Donald. Border slayed them all. No bowler could ever claim that Border was his bunny and honestly think anyone would believe him. I once read that the fiery West Indies fast bowler Curtly Ambrose refused to talk to the Australian team—at all—but he always reserved the greeting 'Morning, skipper' whenever he saw Allan. I think that says volumes about Allan.

While A.B. openly admits he wasn't a natural leader, he led by example. If the old Australian Cricket Board had based his payments on the number of bruises and chipped fingers he copped during a series, Allan would be a very wealthy man. As a kid I watched his battles on television and it was inspiring to see him standing his ground and leading by example. It made me want to get out there and help him. When I bowled at the old drum behind dad's machinery shed every afternoon, I *always* pretended it was Allan throwing me the ball and giving me the instructions to 'rip and tear'. It remains a special moment in my life when that dream was actually fulfilled, because in my first Test against the Kiwis at Perth in 1993 he did just that and I was walking on air.

In later years when he was dubbed 'Captain Grumpy' by the media—because he took no joy in being congratulated for a big score in a lost Test—I told people he deserved to be known as 'Captain Courageous' because what his critics seemed to forget was he'd carried the hopes of the nation for so many years. He had the burden of building Australia—a team he captained to seven series losses straight after being made captain when Kim Hughes resigned and subsequently went on a rebel tour of South Africa—into one of the best teams in the world, and he did. Under his guidance the Aussies won our first World Cup in 1987, and there was a ticker-tape parade throughout the national capitals when Border's men won the Ashes in 1989. Border has admitted in the early years of his captaincy there were concerns for his mental state as he found himself in some dark places. There was one occasion when he was asked at a press conference how he felt and Allan responded with, 'How the f— do you think I feel?' I can only imagine that having to do what he did for such a sustained period of time can get to you. He gave his blood and sweat for Australia, and even in the brief time I played under his captaincy I appreciated he expected nothing but the best from his men, and I had no problem with that.

I have named Allan as my team's captain because, well, he deserves it. He was the constant in the Australian team, captaining Australia in 93 consecutive games in a decade. In that period, I understand England had eight captains, New Zealand seven, India and Pakistan six, the West Indies five, Sri Lanka four and South Africa, who were eventually readmitted, had two. He suffered more losses than he enjoyed victories, but the team and the culture he handed to his successor, Mark Taylor, was one that led Australia to a golden era. Allan's place in Australian cricket is acknowledged by the Allan Border Medal, which is presented to that nation's best cricketer every year. The Australian Cricket Academy is based at the Allan Border Field in Brisbane and since 1996–97, India and Australia have contested the Border-Gavaskar Trophy, the prize for some of the most intense matches in the modern era. I'm pretty certain both men—Sunil Gavaskar was India's warrior—wouldn't want it any other way.

ADAM GILCHRIST

[My father] always used to encourage me, particularly at the end of [practice] sessions to just hit the ball. I would do some technique work but he always threw an extra 20 at the end and he'd say 'just slog it now, just go for it'. And that's what it's about. The most fun part of batting is seeing a ball, lining it up, trying to hit it in the middle and for one split second you and only you in the whole world know that you've got it. That's a really enjoyable feeling.

—'GILLY' ON THE JOY OF SIX

Full name:	Adam Craig Gilchrist
Nickname:	Gilly or Churchy
Birthdate:	14 November 1971
Birthplace:	Bellingen, New South Wales
Major teams:	Australia, New South Wales, Western Australia, Deccan Chargers, ICC World XI, Kings XI Punjab, Middlesex
Role:	Wicketkeeper-batsman
Batting style:	Left-hand bat
TESTS:	96
Test debut:	v Pakistan at Brisbane, 5–9 November 1999
Last Test:	v India at Adelaide, 24–28 January 2008
Test runs:	5570
Highest score:	204*
Average:	47.60
Strike rate:	81.95
Test centuries:	17
Catches:	379
Stumpings:	37
ONE-DAY INTERNATIONALS:	287
Runs:	9619
Highest score:	172
Average:	35.89
Strike rate:	96.94
ODI centuries:	16
Catches:	417
Stumpings:	55

As wicketkeeper, Adam was the most important bloke on the field for me and the other members of the fast-bowling attack when he joined the Australian team in 1999. He was crouched behind the stumps for most of my career and our rapport was built quickly upon a deep sense of trust. On those days when it felt like I was bowling on quicksand and the ball was coming out of my hand like a sponge, I'd seek his counsel because 'Gilly' saw my action day in, day out and could tell what I was doing wrong. His observations made him an invaluable ally. Some might say he didn't have the acrobatics of a Rod Marsh or the finesse of Ian Healy, but he was a tremendous wicketkeeper—it's important to remember most of his career was spent keeping to Shane Warne. That was a job that would have challenged any keeper because each and every ball Shane bowled was a hand grenade with the pin pulled out. While he took some incredible catches, I have no doubt Adam will be remembered by historians—and those who saw him play—as the game's greatest wicketkeeper-batsman of all time. He provided Australia with a luxury no other international team had (although some might say Sri Lanka's Kumar Sangakkara came close), in being a destructive force—a wrecking ball— at the crease. Whether it was in the Test whites or coloured clothing of the one-day arena, he scored his runs quickly and brutally. I think it says plenty that the fact he scored 81 per 100 balls in Tests and 96 in one-day internationals puts the likes of the great West Indian Viv Richards in the shade. His career is summed up in some savage innings, including his 149 off 104 balls in the 2006 World Cup final in Barbados. In that match he slammed 13 fours and 8 sixes after taking a tip from his batting coach Bob Meuleman to wear a squash ball in his glove to allow him to hit straighter. Unfortunately, that final was also my last game so I never had the chance to apply that technique to my own batting. He didn't reserve his big hitting efforts to the 50-over game— his 57-ball Ashes century at Perth meant he missed equalling Viv Richards' world record by one ball. However, he does hold the record for the most sixes in Test cricket—he blasted 100 of them in his 96-match career—and they weren't slog shots, they were masterful strokes and he hit them so sweetly it was always a pleasure to watch him at full cry.

Adam was given his chance to play Test cricket a few days shy of his 29th birthday and he didn't need much time to establish himself as having a cool head in a crisis. In only his second Test he was sent out to bat when Australia was in serious trouble against Pakistan at 5–126; the team was 243 runs short of victory. The Pakistanis boasted pace aces Wasim Akram, Waqar Younis and Shoaib Akhtar but they were all but hit out of the game by Gilchrist who, as the man picked to replace a crowd favourite in Healy, needed to win over the public. He and Justin Langer peeled off 238 runs in 59 overs and while Langer was dismissed just before Australia reached the target, the savagery of Adam's 149 runs from 163 deliveries sent out a powerful message. The feeling we in the Australian team developed about Gilly after that was that if we were in trouble and he could stay out in the middle for an hour, he'd steady the ship. If Australia was travelling well we knew he'd twist the knife in the opposition's belly by playing his shots and keeping the scoreboard ticking over, each run taking the game further away from our opponents.

Apart from his statistics, Adam also left a great legacy for the game through his respect for cricket. He gained universal applause for deciding to walk in the semi-final of the 2003 World Cup after being given not out when he tried to sweep Aravinda de Silva's second ball. Australia was 0–34 after five overs and everyone looked stunned when, after the umpire Rudi Koertzen turned down the appeal by saying the ball had hit Gilchrist's pads, he walked back to the pavilion. It was sportsmanship at its best. His decision had no impact on the result, even though Ricky Ponting was dismissed in the next over and Matt Hayden not long after that; we won the match and ultimately the final against India. However, Adam won the respect of the cricket world for what's rightly remembered as a magnanimous decision when it was within his rights to continue batting. It summed up the behaviour of someone I consider a good bloke.

SHANE WARNE

Playing cricket, I was always about strategy, tactics, reading people, all that sort of stuff. When you sit at a poker table and you don't know anyone, you've got to work out ten people straightaway. You've got to work out who's the pro, who's there just for the fun, doesn't really care if they lose, who's been saving up for a year to play in the tournament. You can

*pick on them a little bit. And I think with poker, there
are two different things. I know basic mathematics and
probability . . . but then there's instinct. I'm a bit of both.
I know the basic probability: position, pot odds, that sort of
thing. But I'm instinctive, too.*

—'WARNEY' ON LIFE AS A POKER STAR

Full name:	Shane Keith Warne
Nickname:	Warney
Birthdate:	13 September 1969
Birthplace:	Upper Ferntree Gully, Victoria
Major teams:	Australia, Victoria, Melbourne Stars, Hampshire, ICC World XI, Rajasthan Royals, Rest of the World XI
Role:	Bowler
Batting style:	Right-hand bat
Bowling style:	Leg-spin
TESTS:	145
Test debut:	v India at Sydney, 2–6 January 1992
Last Test:	v England at Sydney, 2–5 January 2007
Test wickets:	708
Best bowling in an innings:	8/71
Best bowling in a match:	12/128
Five wickets in an innings:	37
10 wickets in a match:	10
Average:	25.41

Strike rate:	57.4
Economy rate:	2.65
Catches:	125
Test runs:	3154
ONE-DAY INTERNATIONALS:	194
Wickets:	293
Best bowling:	5/33
Five wickets in an innings:	1
Average:	25.73
Strike rate:	36.3
Economy rate:	4.25
Catches:	80
ODI runs:	1018

I don't know what more I can add to the millions of words that have already been written about Warney, but here's my offering: Shane Warne was, without a doubt, a cut above every cricketer I can think of. I believe he has had as big an impact on the game as Don Bradman, although off the field he may have felt more comfortable with The Don's peer—and playboy—Keith Miller, who legend suggests may even have been able to teach Shane a few things. In saying that, I have little interest in what people might think of what Warney has or hasn't done off the field. I stand by him as a highly regarded friend. As far as bowling is concerned his skill level was incredible. He had a vast array of deliveries and while they confounded the best batsmen in the world, what really amazed me about Shane's bowling was his unerring accuracy. His ability to hit the same spot ball after ball after ball was testimony to his mental strength and competitive nature. Those two traits combined make him cricket's answer to Halley's Comet that's visible to the naked eye every 75 or so years—a phenomenon. Most leg-spinners bowl knowing they have to buy their wickets, but Shane was never dominated and he was also deep into the mind craft side of the game, and by that I mean he could think a batsman out. He plays the professional poker tour these days, and if he can 'read' his opponents in the casino just as he did the batsmen's body language when he held court with the six-stitcher he'll be a card shark. He tormented the best in the business and I guess that came from Shane's firm belief that if he had the ball in his hand he was in control of proceedings. I'm well aware some may call that attitude wishful thinking, but the statistics and scorecards note it definitely worked.

Nine years after we retired I have no doubt that Shane and I were lucky to have been thrust together by destiny or chance or the stars aligning as members of the Australian bowling attack because we were at opposite ends of the spectrum as far as bowlers go (and individuals for that matter). We were mates and everything clicked—and it helped that we also had control over the ball because that made the batsmen we bowled to sweat bullets. It pleases me to think that while people always consider blistering pace bowlers as the most formidable pairings—Jeff Thomson and Dennis Lillee always come to mind—a bloke with skinny legs and a basic haircut and a guy with bleached hair and bling played 104 Test matches together and took a combined total of 1001 wickets (Warney took 513 and I bagged 488) and of those matches Australia suffered only 18 defeats. It pleases me to have been a part of something so special. I don't know if I would have taken the same number of wickets had Shane not been in the team and I guess it's debatable whether we would have won so many matches if Shane had successfully pursued an AFL career with St Kilda. Steve Waugh once suggested that in Shane and me he had 'four men', meaning we could tie up an end or take wickets. It made us, in his words, 'attacking and containing' bowlers, which is a rare commodity. One thing I know we did was build pressure, some called it water torture, but we prided ourselves on giving the batsmen no respite from either end, and something we quickly learned in the early days was that any batsman could crack under pressure—and by the end of our Test careers there were 1001 occasions when that rang true.

I believe Shane was Australian captain material. He had a tremendous grasp on the game's tactics and offered what I thought were good strategies. You only need to realise what he did for the English country team, Hampshire, a team that flourished under his leadership, to understand why I believe that. I think he gained the next best honour, albeit an honour with no title, when he was named the Australian bowling attack's leader. He was the person we all went to for advice, to use as a sounding-board, the bloke who we saw as the man with all the answers. He also knew how to lift his bowlers, because whenever Australia was screaming for something to happen, Shane would summon a miracle with a flick of his wrist and a brilliantly bowled delivery that would leave batsmen questioning all that they had believed was true. The only thing I would advise to those who might find themselves pitted against Shane on the poker tour is this: just remember, as the world's greatest bowler he always had an ace up his sleeve.

BRETT LEE

The longevity, that's my proudest achievement. It's not taking [over] 300 [Test] wickets or 380 one-day wickets for your country . . . it's putting your body through so much stress and so much strain and knowing you can come out the other side. I had ten operations, six ankle ops. For some people, one ankle operation is game over. So I endured the comeback time and time and time and time and time again and putting my body through hell—but I've enjoyed it.

—'BING' ON BEING A WARRIOR

Full name:	Brett Lee
Nickname:	Bing
Birthdate:	8 November 1976
Birthplace:	Wollongong, New South Wales
Major teams:	Australia, New South Wales, Sydney Sixers, Kings XI Punjab, Kolkata Knight Riders, Otago, Wellington
Role:	Bowler

Batting style: Right-hand bat

Bowling style: Right-arm fast

Cricket relative: Brother, Shane Lee (NSW & Australia)

TESTS: 76

Test debut: v India at Melbourne, 26–30 December 1999

Last Test: v South Africa at Melbourne, 26–30 December 2008

Test wickets: 310

Best bowling in an innings: 5–30

Best bowling in a match: 9–171

Five wickets in an innings: 10

Average: 30.81

Strike rate: 53.3

Economy rate: 3.46

Catches: 23

Test runs: 1451

ONE-DAY INTERNATIONALS: 221

Wickets: 380

Best bowling: 5–22

Five wickets in an innings: 9

Average: 23.36

Strike-rate: 29. 4

Economy rate: 4.76

Catches: 54

ODI runs: 1176

Not long after the 2014–15 Big Bash League kicked off I was asked whether Brett Lee, who was 38 at the time and determined to hit the 150 km/h mark for the 21st consecutive season, deserved to be acknowledged as the benchmark for pace bowling. I didn't need much time to reply that he did. Most express pace bowlers have, at best, a career lifespan of ten years. As Bing pointed out, cricket has plenty of stories of fast bowlers who could generate incredible pace, but none of them lasted at the top level for two decades like Brett. He learned to bowl fast and mean at Oak Flats just outside of Wollongong. Bing proved to those of his ilk—the express pace aces—that they could extend their expiry date if they were prepared to work as hard as he did on their fitness and treat the injuries that are unfortunately part and parcel of their vocation. In the pursuit of his explosive pace, Brett subjected his body to incredible stresses and painful injuries. His career almost ended before it even started because he suffered stress fractures when he was a teenager, which meant he needed his trunk covered in a plaster cast, and he also needed a series of ankle surgeries. For some bowlers one ankle injury means the end of their career, but Brett endured six and kept bouncing back. He was someone who had the fortitude to fight on when it would've been so easy for him to simply pack it all in and take up surfing—or, in his case, modelling. While he captured 310 Test wickets and 380 one-day international scalps, Brett admitted he considered his longevity his greatest triumph because it demonstrated his mental toughness. I think it also proved that he had the need to bowl fast and furious because, at his peak, Brett was blessed with the ability to bowl at 160 km/h—that's 100 mph in the old language—and he was exceptional. He had a raw, pure pace and it was that firepower that made him unique in world cricket and he loved it: his celebrations showed this when he took a wicket—the high leap and click of the heels or the 'chainsaw'.

'Lethal' Lee terrified plenty of batsmen over two decades but as he grew older he developed his game and became a smart bowler; he was able to apply his experience to various situations—including his incredible farewell appearance for the Sydney Sixers in the 2014–15 Big Bash League final against the Perth Scorchers. With the Scorchers needing eight runs off the last over to win the title, the English Test batsman Michael Carberry hit his first delivery for four, his second for two and the third for a single. Nathan Coulter-Nile was bowled for one, Sam Whiteman went the very next ball and with the score level on 147, the Pakistani international Yasir Arafat managed to get some bat on it and he scampered through for the winning run. I thought those final balls were a brilliant—a near perfect—display of a paceman keeping his head and controlling the controllables.

Brett was more than an express pace bowler who liked to rattle the batsmen with short-pitched stuff. After Shane Warne and I retired he stepped up for Ricky Ponting and knew when to hit the turbo button and when to slow down the pace a few notches and contain the batsmen. In the nine Tests that followed my retirement he took 58 wickets at 21.55, and that's a phenomenal record. His value to the Australian team was acknowledged with the 2008 Allan Border Medal and it was thoroughly deserved. He was a good athlete, and could handle the bat as well. Some of the biggest sixes I ever saw were struck by Bing. He had a full swing at it and would nail it. He wasn't a slog merchant, his Test batting average was 20.15 and with five half centuries I don't think he was all that far off from being an all-rounder. One of the nice guys off the field, he said his aggression came from the battle with himself and his body; for him it was getting out there and making his body push through barriers. Away from the cricket field Brett has thrown himself into his other love—music. His song 'You're the One for Me', which he wrote during the 2006 ICC Champions Trophy in India, was recorded as a duet with Bing and Bollywood star Asha Bhosle. I think the fact he jumped at the chance to play the leading male role in the romantic comedy *UnIndian* says a lot about his spirit of adventure and not wanting to have any regrets. I think it's a good message.

CRAIG MCDERMOTT

All our fast bowlers have to have some aggression in them, it's just how they use that sometimes. You can be too aggressive and actually forget about what you're trying to achieve at the other end. I was guilty of that in my time as well on the odd occasion. It's a fine line you walk. I had a number of ups and downs in my career until I got it right in about 1990.

—'BILLY' ON BECOMING CRICKET AUSTRALIA'S BOWLING COACH IN 2011

Full name:	Craig John McDermott
Nickname:	Billy
Birthdate:	14 April 1965
Birthplace:	Ipswich, Queensland
Major teams:	Australia, Queensland
Role:	Bowler
Batting style:	Right-hand bat
Bowling style:	Right-arm fast
Cricket relatives:	Sons Alister McDermott (Queensland), Benjamin McDermott (Brisbane Heat)
TESTS:	71
Test debut:	v West Indies at Melbourne, 22–27 December 1984
Last Test:	v Sri Lanka at Adelaide, 25–29 January 1996
Test wickets:	291
Best bowling in an innings:	8–97
Best bowling in a match:	11–157
Five wickets in an innings:	14
10 wickets in a match:	2
Average:	28.63

Strike rate: 56.9

Economy rate: 3.01

Catches: 19

Test runs: 940

ONE-DAY INTERNATIONALS: 138

Wickets: 203

Best bowling: 5–44

Five wickets in
an innings: 1

Average: 24.71

Strike rate: 36.7

Economy rate: 4.03

Catches: 27

ODI runs: 432

At 19 years of age Craig McDermott was thrown into the deep end of the pool when he was named in an Australian bowling attack that contained Geoff Lawson, Rodney Hogg, Murray Bennett and Greg Matthews, as Australia's third-pace option against the West Indies in the Melbourne Test of the 1984–85 season—and he swam like a fish! He finished his baptism of fire with six wickets and he followed that up with four scalps on the spin-friendly SCG pitch. Those two efforts set the bar for the big red-headed Queenslander's next 69 Test appearances because 'Billy the Kid' was an exceptional bowler. After making his debut for Queensland at 18 he was introduced to international cricket during the era when Allan Border was rebuilding the Australian team.

From the outset Craig proved he was a quality bowler who possessed what was needed to lead the attack. At 20 he took 30 wickets during the 1985 Ashes series and then he bent his back and worked hard in Eden Gardens in Chennai to play his role in Australia's first World Cup triumph (over England) in 1987. While he was strong and trained hard off the field, he was sidelined by a series of injuries. As well as suffering the strains and stresses that go with the job Craig was cursed with an unlucky dose of bad health: he suffered what turned out to be a life-threatening twisted bowel during the 1993 Ashes series; he needed a hernia operation; in 1994 he was sent home early from South Africa with a knee injury; he suffered a leg injury in New Zealand; and, most significantly of all for me, he injured ankle ligaments when he jumped off a sea wall while on a run during the 1995 tour of the West Indies. I say 'significantly for me' because that injury provided me with my big chance to prove myself as a member of the Australian attack and I might add, just for the record, that no, I did not push him! Craig had more than his fair share of setbacks but he fought back time and time again to resume his mantle as the nation's strike bowler.

For all of his trials and tribulations he still took 291 wickets at 28.63; he captured 203 one-day international wickets and 303 for Queensland at a shade over 25. I learnt a lot from watching Billy. He was a hard trainer, he maintained his quality and I liked that he bowled outswing. On his day he had the ability to blitz through any team's batting line-up like Epsom salts. He was involved in many lion-hearted efforts for Australia but perhaps the one he is best known for is the 8–97 he bagged against England at Perth in 1990–91, an innings in which England was cruising at 2–191 to be all out for 244. He was a quality player, a great bowler, but I think for all that he's achieved—and what he offered Australian cricket—he's terribly underrated. I'm glad that he's back in the national team's fold as the bowling coach because when I was a raw fast bowler he helped me and I see that he has plenty to offer. Before he joined the team in 2014, he suggested that young fast bowlers ought to follow the gymnastics programs that young gymnasts training for the Olympics use in order to be as 'strong as an ox'. When the Australian team's bowlers were falling like flies to injuries, McDermott maintained the best preparation for a fast bowler was to put the joggers on and get some kilometres in their legs; he reasoned fast bowlers will run 20 kilometres a day. In his first stint as the Australian team's bowling coach he had the likes of Peter Siddle and James Pattinson run three sessions of five kilometres a week. The great thing about Craig McDermott, apart from his status as one of Australia's top fast bowlers, is that he has lived the dream . . . and the nightmare. His experience and his ability to explain aspects of the art of fast bowling will be beneficial for the new breed coming through, such as NSW pace ace Pat Cummins who, despite being named Man of the Match after his Test debut in South Africa when he was only 18, has had his own hurdles to overcome.

JASON GILLESPIE

*This is ridiculous. I was just lucky that the shots came off
and I had a bit of a laugh all the way. It's unbelievable.
It's a fairytale really. Hansel and Gretel and Dizzy's double
hundred, it's one and the same. Absolute fairytale. He
[Matthew Hayden] reckoned he's going to do a nude run of
the oval if I got 200. I said if I got 200, I'd do a nude lap too.*

—'DIZZY' ON SCORING 201* IN A TEST AGAINST
BANGLADESH

Full name:	Jason Neil Gillespie
Nickname:	Dizzy
Birthdate:	19 April 1975
Birthplace:	Darlinghurst, New South Wales
Major teams:	Australia, South Australia, Ahmedabad Rockets, Glamorgan, Yorkshire
Role:	Bowler
Batting style:	Right-hand bat
Bowling style:	Right-arm fast
TESTS:	71
Test debut:	v West Indies at Sydney, 29 November – 3 December 1996
Last Test:	v Bangladesh at Chittagong, 16–20 April 2006
Test wickets:	259
Best bowling in an innings:	7–37
Best bowling in a match:	9–80

Five wickets in
an innings: 8

Average: 26.13

Strike rate: 54.9

Economy rate: 2.85

Catches: 27

Test runs: 1218

ONE-DAY INTERNATIONALS: 97

Wickets: 142

Best bowling: 5–22

Five wickets in
an innings 3

Average: 25.42

Strike rate: 36.2

Economy rate: 4.21

Catches: 10

ODI runs: 289

It's a bit harsh naming Dizzy Gillespie at No. 11, after all he did score a Test double hundred against Bangladesh. Something I envied about Jason as a batsman was he had a solid defence and he made the opposition bowlers earn his wicket. I wasn't in Chittagong in 2006 when Dizzy scored 201 not out in his final Test after being sent out as night watchman. He racked up his first-ever hundred with a cover drive and it was the team's masseuse Lucy Frostick who mentioned the possibility of him scoring a double ton as she worked on his muscles after stumps. Dizzy said he realised that the pitch had a few runs in it and—with the urging of Michael Hussey—he didn't throw his wicket away, and created a great piece of history when he struck a boundary. Jason, who retired as the nation's sixth highest Test wicket-taker with 259 wickets from his 71 Tests, deserves to be acknowledged as an outstanding Australian bowler. He said perhaps the most surreal moment of a double ton, however—apart from scoring the runs—came after the match when he was quizzed by journalists about his batting. I would have loved to witness it—the party the boys would have had on the roof of their hotel to celebrate Dizzy's milestone would have been one for the ages!

Depending on which side of the ledger you sat, Jason was either my brother in arms or my partner in crime because between us we have the most wickets for an opening combination for Australia. When you think of the Lillee–Thomson and Lindwall–Miller combos, it's quite a decent record to share. Dizzy was a quality bowler, he bowled from a good height, he got bounce and seam movement, and he could get the ball through at a good pace. If anything he should have taken more wickets than his final tally, and I am the first to acknowledge that the way he bowled helped me get my many wickets. Jason bowled similar to me but he was quicker, and when the ball did something off the wicket the batsman couldn't adjust so he had a lot of play and misses rather than nicks. In my case, since I wasn't as quick, if the ball seamed off the wicket the batsman had enough time to adjust, allowing for the ball to find the edge. He was made to work hard as a member of the national team because he was given the job of running uphill, or bowling into the wind. Steve Waugh had plenty of confidence in his ability and it was justified. I remember him as a great bowler who, while he was named Wisden Cricketer of the Year in 2002, was the unsung hero of the Australian team. His effort to take 7–37 against England at Headingley during the 1997 Ashes series was described by some as a genuinely 'terrifying' display of fast bowling during his 13.4 overs. It was something special and England, who'd been chugging along at 2–103, were bundled out for 172.

He suffered a terrible broken leg when he and Steve Waugh collided trying to take a catch off Colin Miller's bowling during the First Test against Sri Lanka in Kandy in 1999. It was ugly and poor old Dizzy didn't realise how bad the damage was until he tried to stand up. Steve had a badly busted nose and they were both taken away in a panel van to the local hospital before a helicopter, which was generously arranged by Sanath Jayasuriya, spared them a bumpy five-hour drive to Colombo. Dizzy had his leg in a cast that went from his foot to his upper thigh and while I felt gutted for him I never had any doubts whatsoever about him returning strong and savage. Since his life after cricket Jason has made a mighty impression as a coach by guiding the tradition-steeped English County team, Yorkshire, to its first County Championship victory in 13 years. When the English team's head coach, Peter Moores, and the England and Wales Cricket Board parted ways after they failed to qualify for the quarterfinals of the 2015 World Cup, Dizzy was mentioned in despatches as a possible replacement. As the unofficial chairman of the old Australian Fast Bowlers Cartel, I thought, Good luck, I hope you get it—he definitely wasn't going to be stripped of his membership. I believe Jason has the traits needed to be a successful coach: he's a good and honest bloke, he's very good with people and is obviously a good manager, and that's important because at international level the job isn't about teaching people how to play cricket, it's about extracting the best out of them. That's something Jason has been doing since he was a 17-year-old who was razzed by his mates in the Adelaide Cricket Club's C-grade when they heard him say he would represent South Australia by the time he was 19, and Australia when he was 21. He was called by his mates the 'Lion of Adelaide' and he responded by marking out a long run-up at training and raining fire and brimstone upon them. The club coach noticed and because he liked what he saw, Dizzy was named to make his A-grade debut. Jason said that 'Lion' sledge made him hit the 'go' button and he devoted himself to making the cut. As a bloke who benefited enormously from his presence I'm glad that he did.

ANDY BICHEL

I thought, well, I'm going all right at cricket why don't I give it a try and go to Brisbane and have a crack at it. It was the best thing I ever did. I played three grade games then played for Queensland so I was very, very lucky. If you have got

*some ability, instead of sitting back and wondering whether
I should or shouldn't have tried, you can always go and have
a go for two or three years in grade cricket and then you can
come back. Your club will still be there and you can join back
in and maybe pick up that job you left behind and carry on.
I think I was given those opportunities and you only have to
ask and you might receive, so you just never know.*

—'BIC''S ADVICE TO COUNTRY CRICKETERS, 2013

Full name:	Andrew John Bichel
Nickname:	Bic
Birthdate:	27 August 1970
Birthplace:	Laidley, Queensland
Major teams:	Australia, Queensland, Essex, Hampshire, Worcestershire
Role:	Bowler
Batting style:	Right-hand bat
Bowling style:	Right-arm, fast-medium
Cricket relatives:	Uncle, Donald Bichel (Queensland)
	Cousin, Chris Sabburg (Queensland)
TESTS:	19
Test debut:	Australia v West Indies at Adelaide, 25–28 January 1997
Last Test:	Australia v India at Adelaide, 12–16 December 2003
Test wickets:	58
Best bowling in an innings:	5–60
Best bowling in a match:	6–125

Five wickets in an innings:	1
Average:	32.24
Strike rate:	57.5
Economy rate:	3.36
Catches:	16
Test runs:	355
ONE-DAY INTERNATIONALS:	67
Wickets:	78
Best bowling:	7–20
Five wickets in an innings:	2
Average:	31.57
Strike rate:	41.7
Economy rate:	4.53
Catches:	19
ODI runs:	471

A few days after Andy Bichel's Test career ended in 2003, our skipper Steve Waugh wrote him a letter that outlined how much he had inspired people. Tugger said something along the lines that he would have loved to have had ten players with Bic's character and commitment, and while it was the ultimate compliment, it was also warranted. I remember Andy Bichel as being the type of player who, if he knew he risked getting injured trying to stop a four or take a catch, he wouldn't baulk—he was all heart and it's why I loved playing with him. He was one of the most unselfish cricketers I met, and while he wasn't a natural—he wasn't born with the raw pace of Bing or the height of Dizzy—he worked hard. He was physically strong and each of his 58 Test wickets were the result of determination at it's very best and of someone who left nothing in the tank.

Bic represented Australia in 19 Tests and was named the 12th man in just as many. I have no doubt it must have hurt him to be named to carry the drinks so often—there was one match when Steve forgot to tell him and he'd marked out his run-up because he expected to be bowling—he never allowed for it to show and he never allowed for it to stop him from smiling. And yet, his career had plenty of highlights. He dismissed Brian Lara on *seven* occasions during the 2003 tour of the West Indies; he took 60 wickets in a season for Queensland on two occasions; he was the Sheffield Shield Player of the Year in 1996–97; in 2005–06, at the grand old age of 36, he was named the Pura Cup Player of the Year after scoring 452 runs and taking 50 wickets; he hammered 125 against Sri Lanka in a tour match; and, make no bones about it, Andy Bichel was one of the reasons why we won the 2003 World Cup, because apart from his 16 wickets at 12.3 (and that included 7–20 against England), the gritty Queenslander featured in two match-winning stands with Michael Bevan, one of which was a 73-run ninth wicket stand. Bic or Michael Kasprowicz would be picked in the Australian 12 at the expense of the other, but it was not a problem because they weren't only great mates, they lived in the same street in Brisbane! The story goes that when Bic was left out of an Aussie squad, he demanded to know who had replaced him. Upon hearing it was Kaspa (Kasprowicz), his response was said to have been, 'Well, that's all right then.' Since his retirement, Bic has coached Papua New Guinea's national team and had a stint on Cricket Australia's selection panel. From all reports he did both jobs with his trademark enthusiasm and wholeheartedness. I remember Bic as someone who looked you in the eye when he had something to say, and his handshake was vice-like.

MICHAEL KASPROWICZ

I always found [a lot came down to belief]. You have to enter every match with a total belief that your preparation is right—not only your own preparation and skills, but all your mates around you. Generally during my time in the side you really noticed it. There was that total belief in the dressing room and it got you through those moments.

—'KASPER' ON SELF-BELIEF

Full name:	Michael Scott Kasprowicz
Nickname:	Kasper
Birthdate:	10 February 1972
Birthplace:	South Brisbane, Queensland
Major teams:	Australia, Queensland, Essex, Glamorgan, ICL World XI, Leicestershire, Mumbai Champs
Role:	Bowler
Batting style:	Right-hand bat
Bowling style:	Right-arm fast-medium

TESTS: 38

Test debut: Australia v West Indies at Brisbane, 22–26 November 1996

Last Test: South Africa v Australia at Johannesburg, 31 March – 4 April 2006

Test wickets: 113

Best bowling in an innings: 7–36

Best bowling in a match: 8–92

Five wickets in an innings: 4

Average: 32.88

Strike rate: 63.1

Economy rate: 3.12

Catches: 16

Test runs: 445

ONE-DAY INTERNATIONALS: 43

Wickets: 67

Best bowling: 5–45

Five wickets in an innings: 2

Average: 24.98

Strike rate: 33.2

Economy rate: 4.51

Catches: 13

ODI runs: 74

Michael Kasprowicz never left anything on the field, including the time in 1998 when, due to injuries, he was forced to carry the brunt of the Australian pace attack's workload during the tour of India. He lost eight kilos—one for each wicket he took—as a result of battling fatigue, heat exhaustion and, of course, the home team's quality batsmen. He remembered the job of having to go out day after day and bowl in 40–50 degree heat, on grounds that were like deserts, as the most challenging thing he ever did as a cricketer. I wasn't on that tour but I knew he bowled throughout that series with his trademark purpose and commitment, and that rather than look for shade to sit and cool his heels he was always up for one more over. He became known as a subcontinent expert because the conditions favoured his reverse swing, but Kasper described himself as the 'fashionable bowler for the unfashionable tours'. That was his call; I saw him as a quality bowler with enormous stamina, a quality I think he gained from the training he undertook to make the Australian Schoolboys rugby union team. He repeated his lion-hearted effort of 1998 during the 2004 tour of Sri Lanka, when I wasn't available, and finished with 12 hard-earned wickets at an average of 25.16.

Kasprowicz made his first-class debut for Queensland against Western Australia when he was just 17 years of age. While he should have been preparing for another school year he was locking horns with the likes of Graeme Wood, Tom Moody, Mike Veletta, Tim Zoehrer and Tom Hogan— and what an education! It was the first step of an incredible journey because over the following 19 seasons he broke plenty of domestic records—he retired the second-highest taker of first-class wickets in Queensland with 501 scalps—while each of his 38 appearances in the baggy green cap allowed young bowlers to appreciate that the currency of their art is blood, sweat and tears. One of Kasper's most memorable efforts was his 59-run partnership with Brett Lee during the 2005 Ashes series at Edgbaston. He was dismissed three runs short of victory, after scoring what I thought was an impressive 20 runs under intense pressure, when he gloved a contentious catch to their wicketkeeper Geraint Jones off Steve Harmison.

Like his good mate Bic, Kasper was an unselfish player; he was all for his team and his teammates and that approach made him valuable. However, I have to admit I hated it when I had to glove to the big Queenslander during fielding drills. Kasper pegged the ball back at you so hard I always thought one of his missiles would put a hole in my hand. In terms of his unselfishness, I thought it said a lot about his character that when he called stumps at the ripe old age of 36—and after battling a string of injuries—he hung up his maroon cap because he thought it was time to give a younger bloke his chance.

15

SPORT INSPIRES

Champions aren't made in gyms. Champions are made from something they have deep inside them— a desire, a dream and a vision.

—Muhammad Ali

Long before Nelson Mandela became South Africa's first black president, I understand he was an amateur boxer who ran two hours' roadwork every day and then trained like hell by throwing leather in the gym. During his 27-year imprisonment, he followed a strict training regimen. I think it says a lot about the power of sport—and athletes— that when Mandela became a politician upon gaining his freedom in 1990, he viewed sport as a unifying force at a time when his nation was finding its feet and apartheid was being dismantled. Mandela realised sport would have a more positive impact on his people than protests, petitions and peace talks. One year after Mandela became president, his nation hosted the 1995 Rugby World Cup. When the Springboks—whose green jersey was perceived back then by black South Africans as a symbol of apartheid—played New Zealand in the final, he convinced the nation to pull together by making a point of wearing a Springboks jumper. South Africa won the World Cup 15–12 and as he watched people of mixed race celebrate as one, President Mandela revealed the reasons why he believed sport could be a catalyst for good. He said: 'Sport has the power to change the world. It has the power to inspire. It has the power to unite people in a way that little else does. It speaks to youth in a language they understand. Sport can create hope where once there was only despair. It is more powerful than government in breaking down racial barriers.'

I believe there are some athletes who inspire others by striving to be better people. The world heavyweight champion Muhammad Ali is definitely inspiring in this way. Ali was a showman, he was charismatic, he was a humanitarian, an activist and, from what I've gathered from reading a little bit about him, he is a man of principle. I like the story about him attending a graduation ceremony at Harvard University in the 1970s and someone in the crowd yelled 'Give us a poem', and Ali responded by saying 'Me, we'. Apart from being described as the shortest poem in the English language, many people have interpreted it as a great summary of the collective human condition—that we are all in 'it' together.

There has been a host of other great athletes who have inspired the world, including the German long-jumper Carl 'Luz' Long, who is remembered for his actions during the qualification round for his event at the 1936 Berlin Olympics. Long defied Hitler's ideology of the supremacy of the Aryan race by helping Jesse Owens when it appeared as though this descendent of slaves from Alabama was in danger of disqualification after several fouls. As Owens sat on the track in obvious despair, Long advised him to jump a few centimetres before the take-off board to have a better chance of making the final. His advice proved to be so good it actually relegated him to the silver medal, because Owens won the gold. However, in full view of Hitler, Long overcame any disappointment he may have felt to congratulate Owens. In later years when he reflected on that victory, the man regarded as one of the world's greatest athletes said of that moment: 'You can melt down all the medals and cups I have and they wouldn't be a plating on the 24-carat friendship I felt for Luz Long at that moment.'

Long and Owens remained friendly after the Games and when the German fought in World War II he sent his friend in America a letter with a request should he die in battle: 'When the war is over, please go to Germany, find my son and tell him about his father. Tell him about the times when war did not separate us and tell him that things can be different between men in this world. Your brother, Luz.' The Olympian died of his wounds during the battle of Sicily and Owens sought out his son after the war and spoke of a friendship that was forged in the most incredible of circumstances.

It's great to see someone compete at the top of their game, because they prove there are no boundaries to what can be achieved and I think they inspire other people to better themselves. I was in England playing County cricket when Cathy Freeman won her gold medal for the 400-metre event at the Sydney Olympics. I consider her effort to rise above the immense pressure she was under to win as one of the best. I also couldn't help but be impressed by the will to win that the swimmers Ian Thorpe and Michael Phelps displayed every time they dived into the pool. And I'll never forget the thrill I felt when my skipper Steve Waugh, at a time when he was under massive pressure to hold his place in the Australian Test team, hit Richard Dawson's last ball of the day for four to rack up his record-equalling Test hundred at the SCG in the 2002–03 Ashes series. I remember Pat Rafter showing that winning isn't everything when he displayed great grace after losing a Wimbledon final, and I was in awe of Anna Meares coming back from having suffered a broken neck in 2008 to win gold at the London Olympics, because she must have overcome so many dark thoughts to get back on the velodrome.

Despite the amazing achievements of these athletes, there are three (outside of cricket) who have made a lasting impression on me in the way they have performed. They are Roger Federer, Steve Redgrave and Usain Bolt. Each is different in so many ways but they are blessed with the right stuff to be acknowledged as champions. I would love to have been able to apply aspects of the greatness I see in them to my own game, because, in my opinion, they are inspirations. I've detailed below what excites me about them.

ROGER FEDERER, TENNIS

I enjoyed the position I was in as a tennis player. I was to blame when I lost. I was to blame when I won. And I really like that, because I played soccer a lot too, and I couldn't stand it when I had to blame it on the goalkeeper.

—ROGER FEDERER

Born:	8 August 1981, Basel, Switzerland
Titles:	17 Grand Slam titles
	One Olympic gold medal—doubles (2008)
	One Olympic silver medal—singles (2012)
	Swiss Davis Cup team (2014 champions)

I view Roger Federer as sport's consummate professional athlete. He is a quality player whose reputation is enhanced by playing the game with what I've long considered to be a sense of nobility. He refuses to allow anything to faze him while he is on the court, whether it is a poor call by the umpire, a bad shot, an opponent who may have tried to put him off his own game by throwing a tantrum, or even the disappointment of perhaps not living up to his own expectations. That was what I strove for, I wanted to perform day in, day out. I like the idea that Federer proves it's possible to be in control for the entire game—I tried to live by that creed throughout my career, but there were times when I failed to do so. I just wanted to go about my business, and while I did to a degree, I wasn't perfect and I couldn't quite achieve that level of control Federer has attained. It amazes me that he makes the mental side of tennis, a game where it's not uncommon for some players to have brain explosions and meltdowns, look so easy. I doubt whether anyone could be critical of the 'Fed Express', because of the way he has conducted himself over the years. I've long believed that particular trait is what sets him apart from all other athletes—he's second to none for calmness.

I can relate to the fact that Federer's success didn't come easily. I've read about him going through some tough times before breaking through for his first final, the Marseille Open in 2000, a match he lost. I can only imagine before that moment his defeats and disappointments must have challenged his belief that he had a future in the cutthroat world of the Association of Tennis Professionals. I went through my own trials and tribulations as a young cricketer, and I appreciate that rather than feeling sorry for himself he trained harder, he practised smarter and enjoyed small victories along the way, such as qualifying for that first final in 2000, even though he lost to fellow countryman Marc Rosset. From 2002–12—the year he celebrated his 300th week as the world's No. 1—he was the world's most dominant tennis player. I appreciated that while other players seemed crippled by nerves on the big stage, he thrived when the spotlight was on him.

I met Federer when we took a break during the 2005 Ashes campaign to attend the Wimbledon final. He was coached by fellow Australian Tony Roche, and just before his win over Andy Roddick, Adam Gilchrist and I were invited to visit him in the dressing room. We found ourselves in the surreal situation of talking to him for 20 or so minutes before he went out to contest one of the most famous events in world sport. His mother is South African and he knew a bit about cricket. We talked about a few things as he loosened up and prepared, and his calmness made a huge impact on me. He was relaxed, happy and friendly and keen to engage in a conversation. We wished him well and as we returned to our seats he walked out to centre court to wipe Roddick all over the lawn. That brief brush with Roger Federer gave me a tremendous insight into how he could switch on when it mattered most. I played a bit on the NSW country tennis circuit when I was young and I have a distant relative named Vivian McGrath who was considered the original wonder boy of Australian tennis. He was famous for his two-handed backhand, which was a revolutionary stroke back in the day, but I've also read that he could have been considered a great had he trained harder. I'd like to say Roger listened to my advice and took my tips, but I think he always had it in control. While I'm no expert, I have noticed how Federer's head remains statue-still after he hits the ball. That interests me because when I watched a batsman who was in full cry, I always considered that poise, that stillness, as a sign of the calmness inside his mind; it exerted what I saw as a graceful control of the body and soul.

The statistics note that Roger Federer has held the world No. 1 ranking for 302 weeks; in an all-time record, he has reached each Grand Slam final on at least five occasions; he's qualified for the Wimbledon final on ten occasions and won seven. Federer's name sits alongside Fred Perry (Great Britain 1933–35); Don Budge (United States 1937–38); Rod Laver (Australia 1960–62); Roy Emerson (Australia 1961–64); Andre Agassi (United States 1992–99) and Rafael Nadal (Spain 2005–10) as one of only seven men to have won a career Grand Slam. His full list of achievements could fill the next 20 pages but I think his mastering the mind game day in, day out is a far greater feat than all the trophies he's won. There's been a lot said and written about Federer over the years and one of the comments I believe resonates most was offered by the American player James Blake when, after being asked to nominate the world's top tennis player, he said: 'If you poll the top 500 tennis guys in the world, about 499 are going to say Roger. The only one who won't is Roger himself because he's too nice about it.'

I believe that view says a lot about the spirit of the athlete.

STEVE REDGRAVE, ROWING

Self-belief is probably the most crucial factor in sporting success. The bodies are roughly equal, the training is similar, the techniques can be copied, what separates the achievers is nothing as tangible as split times or kilograms. It is the iron in the mind, not in supplements, that wins medals.

—STEVE REDGRAVE

Born:	23 March 1962, Buckinghamshire, United Kingdom
Titles:	Five Olympic gold medals (1984–2000)
	One Olympic bronze medal (1988)
	Nine World Championship gold medals (1986–1999)
	Two World Championship silver medals
	One World Championship bronze medal
	Three Commonwealth Games gold medals (1986)

Steve Redgrave addressed the Australian cricket team during our 2007 World Cup campaign in the Caribbean, and we hung off his every word. Apart from being one of the greatest Olympians of all time, based on his feat of winning *five* gold medals in *five* consecutive Olympics, he expresses the language of the pursuit of excellence—grunt and strain— eloquently. There are plenty of sports that lay claim to being the toughest of them all; rugby league, ice hockey and boxing all put dibs on that tag, but my personal view is that not many match the demands and rigours of rowing. While my insight is restricted to some training on the rowing machine, I am certain it's a brutal sport that must force the competitors to ask a lot of questions of themselves. For Redgrave to dominate the rowing world for close to 30 years is extraordinary, and while he was a supreme athlete my impression from listening to him address the Australian team is he was also extremely gracious. A lot of what he said came back to inner courage.

After Redgrave won his gold medal at Atlanta in 1996, the strain was getting too much. He was famously quoted as saying that if anyone ever saw him near a boat again they had his permission to shoot him. However, he was persuaded to return for the Sydney Games and, while no one shot him, his career appeared to have reached an unfortunate end when he was diagnosed with diabetes in 1997. He proved a setback is only what you make of it because he slogged on to win an historic gold in Sydney. I drew inspiration from his response to a reporter's question directly after the win, asking him when he knew he'd won the race. When Redgrave said it was after 250 metres, the journalist thought he'd meant to say with 250 metres to go. But Redgrave reiterated that such was his self-belief, and understanding of his ability, he felt as though the race was won after he'd completed the first eighth of the course. I interpreted that as an example of the supreme sense of self-belief an individual needs to achieve their goals in sport—and life. The foundation to Redgrave's confidence was hard work and iron-willed discipline. I found it inspiring to discover that during his preparation for an Olympics, he only ever allowed himself one day away from training every three weeks, for 49 weeks of the year. If nothing else, his record proves that old-fashioned toil is rewarded. Although he was also unique because he was technically adaptable—from what I understand he's one of the few oarsmen in Olympic history to have won a gold medal rowing both strokeside and bowside.

In retirement Sir Steven Redgrave (he was knighted in 2001) has devoted his energies to raising money for a variety of charities. I consider him an athlete who exemplifies the idea that many of sport's battles are won in the mind, not just in the stadium.

As a postscript to his willingness to provide his nation's old foe, Australia, some insights into the business of winning in what was the lead-up to our triumphant World Cup campaign, it made me smile to learn that after England's skipper Michael Vaughan learned he had spoken to us, he put in an urgent request for Redgrave to go visit his team, too, and share a few pearls of wisdom.

USAIN BOLT, ATHLETICS

I've learned over the years that if you start thinking about the race, it stresses you out a little bit. I just try to relax and think about video games, what I'm gonna do after the race, what I'm gonna do just to chill. Stuff like that to relax a little before the race.

—USAIN BOLT

Born: 21 August 1986, Trelawny, Jamaica
Titles: Six Olympic gold medals (2008–12)
11 World Championship gold medals (2009–13)
Two World Championship silver medals (2007)
One Commonwealth Games gold medal (2014)

Jamaican juggernaut Usain Bolt is tall, powerful and charismatic, and in 2009 he became the fastest human to have ever stepped foot on the planet when he scrambled over 100 metres in a lightning fast 9.58 seconds. I view him as a genuine showman and the fact he can talk the talk *and* walk the walk means Bolt shapes up as the ultimate sportsman. I know he likes to showboat before a race, but I have always seen that as a sign that he's enjoying himself and encouraging the crowd, and the *billions* of people watching him on television, to share in the moment. In 2015 when he was asked about his preparation ahead of the World Championships, he said: 'I never doubt myself, I look forward to competition . . . If I can execute right . . . then I know I'll run fast.' I think that most athletes would agree that view simply highlights the faith that comes with great preparation. Bolt is someone who I think not only inspires people by the way he always comes through, but I think the *way* in which he competes is something athletes should want to emulate. When he takes his place on the starting line the whole world watches because he's proven that whenever his spikes strike the track, magic can happen. And the unexpected often happens even before he gets to the starting blocks; like the time he competed at the 2015 London Anniversary Games, when he videobombed a television journalist by dancing behind him as he gave his spiel.

I like that Bolt proves there are no limits. I remember reading, after the one-time fast bowler broke the 100 metre world record during the 2009 World Championships in

Berlin, that some physicists claimed they'd worked out the formula for his amazing feat. The discovery was published in the *European Journal of Physics* and the team said their model had pinpointed the power and energy he needed to expend to defy the drag caused by air resistance, something they said was made even stronger by his imposing 196 centimetre (6 foot 5) frame. The mathematical model that was proposed suggested the following:

- His 9.58 seconds was achieved by reaching a speed of 12.2 metres per second, which was the equivalent of about 43.5 km/h.
- His maximum power occurred when he was less than one second into the 100 metre sprint and he was only at 50 per cent of his maximum speed.
- This demonstrated what was called the 'near immediate effect of drag', when air resistance slows moving objects.

He is yet another example of an athlete who started with nothing. I've read that he was raised in a village a three-and-a-half hour drive from Jamaica's capital of Kingston. From all reports it's a place with no streetlights, limited running water and where old men still ride donkeys. It was the place where he played cricket with an orange for a ball and he was raised on yam and dumplings. By achieving such greatness, Bolt proves that natural ability and championship qualities can be found anywhere. While it's important that those traits are harnessed properly, Bolt has also proven that pure enjoyment is as vital as tough training, harsh dieting and regimented goal-setting.

16

THE WORLD'S BOWLING SCENE

*Aww, mate, I just shuffle up
and go wang.*

**—Jeff Thomson on one of cricket's most fearsome
bowling actions**

To be the No. 1 team in the world you need a quality bowling attack. No team can be loaded with the best batsmen and cursed with poor bowlers and expect to make much ground in the ICC's rankings. If you have a strong bowling unit, especially a pack of fast bowlers who are hungry and mean, it has a positive effect because they have the spirit and ability to lift their team. That's the reason I believe South Africa has been up around the mark as the world's best—as has Australia in more recent times—because of their attack.

After I retired I didn't watch too much cricket. After turning on the television and seeing a few overs bowled, my inclination was to think how happy I was to not be doing that anymore, to switch it off and do something else. However, in more recent times, due to my roles as coach of the MRF Pace Foundation and as a commentator, I've closely monitored the current breed of pace bowlers. I have noted my observations below. There is a great battalion of pacemen in world cricket and these are the ones who I really enjoy watching. In one or two cases, they are players I'd like to see more of, and for a variety of different reasons.

THE AUSTRALIANS

Australia's tradition of pace bowlers goes back to Fred 'The Demon Bowler' Spofforth, who terrorised the English in the 18 Tests he played against them in the nineteenth century. His prowess is emphasised by the fact he took 94 wickets at an average of 18.41. He was followed by the likes of Albert 'Tibby' Cotter, Ray Lindwall, Jeff Thomson and Brett Lee. Australia is now in a position where it has some tremendous bowlers ready to make their mark after the early stages of their careers were frustrated by injuries that led to long stints of rehabilitation.

They have come through and I have no doubt the likes of Pat Cummins, Mitchell Starc and Josh Hazlewood have it in them to spearhead an exciting new era of pace for their skipper Steve Smith.

Mitchell Johnson (Test strike rate: 50.8)

Dennis Lillee identified Mitch as a 'once in a generation bowler' when he was just a kid from Townsville. While I know Dennis later regretted casting that spotlight upon him because of the expectations that accompanied his comment, at his very best Mitch really is a special gem. He bowls around the 150 km/h mark and when he gets it right he swings the ball well. He was outstanding in the 2013–14 Ashes series when he terrorised England, taking 37 wickets at an incredible 13.97. While critics are a part of every fast bowler's life—and Mitch has had more than his fair share over the years—I think he silenced them that summer.

I've stressed that a fast bowler needs to know himself and his game, and I think there was a time a couple of years ago when a few little things weren't quite 'there' in Mitch's game. By working hard with people such as Troy Cooley at the Cricket Academy and Dennis Lillee, he sorted out his run-up and a few other technical issues. I also think he benefited from the 'trifecta', and I'm certain those three factors combined to help him be the force he was in the 2013–14 Ashes. They were: his life off the field was going well for him, he was fit and he was strong.

Throughout that series we saw a Mitchell Johnson who had great control, and when he combined that with his pace he became what the media calls a 'lethal bowler'. He was our best. When you have a spearhead exuding the confidence he did that summer, and you see that look of fear in the opposition batsmen's eyes when they faced him, the impact on the rest of the team is extraordinary.

People have asked me why he was so successful during that series. The reasons were straightforward: he's a left-armer; he bowled express pace; he swung the ball well; and he bowled with great control and aggression. It was a formidable combination and there wouldn't have been too many batsmen in the English squad—or even many around the world, for that matter—who had come up against such a volatile mix.

I don't like the theory that suggests pace bowlers need to slow down to attain accuracy and control. I prefer Mitch's approach, which was to preserve (and persevere with) his pace, even though he was sorting his game out, because he appreciated his speed was what made him unique. If a bowler can remain fast as he gains greater control—just as Mitch did—they can become 'very special'.

At the time of writing this book I am at Lord's where, in the Second Test of the 2015 Ashes series, Mitch seems to have tapped back into his true self, even after some people had all but written him off. As Mitch seems to be proving, that is always a silly thing to do to a champion bowler. In the opening Test in Cardiff he finished with 0–111 and 2–69, and was taunted by my old mates in the Barmy Army singing in the terraces: 'He bowls to the left, he bowls to the right. That Mitchell Johnson, his bowling is shite!' A week or so later, I said to whoever wanted to listen that I didn't think his match figures reflected his bowling—he had bowled much better than his figures suggested. I felt that he was consistently swinging the ball *and* getting it through at a reasonable pace. My prediction at Cardiff was that if he continued on that path it would only be a matter of time before he took a good haul—and it didn't take long. Another important indicator that he was on song for a big series was that he hit 77 in the second dig of the First Test. I've noticed over the years that when he scores a few runs, the wickets follow; maybe it just builds his confidence. As history now notes, Mitch bounced back in the Second Test, where he not only took 3–53 and 3–27, but that old look of terror also reappeared in the English batsmen's eyes.

Mitchell Starc (S/R: 55.7)

He's a quality bowler who definitely knows his one-day game inside out. In the one-dayers he targets areas with the new ball, he swings it, he attacks the stumps, and he generates speed up around the 150 km/h mark. I love that he also has a very good yorker, which he bowls at will. This is something I regret very few bowlers even attempt these days.

I have no doubt that the way he goes about his business is why he's regarded as the world's No.1 limited-overs bowler. We saw what he did to be named the Player of the Tournament in the 2015 World Cup and it was sensational. I think Mitchell has come to realise that Test cricket is a different beast. It's a fact you can't bowl the same lines in that format as you do with the white ball; you can't attack the stumps the same way, nor can you bowl yorkers all the time.

It really pleases me to see Mitchell is working out the nuances of Test cricket, because he has decent control and I really want to see him emulate at Test level the amazing feats he's already achieved at just 25 years of age in the one-day arena. It only stands to reason that the more opportunities he gets with the red ball, the more chance he'll have to get to know his Test game.

I think it's important that when people hear commentators talk about fast bowlers being aggressive, they realise it doesn't mean we go out in the middle and yell abuse, curse and carry on . . . although some do. Instead, what they're referring to is body language: keeping your head up and soldiering on when things aren't going so well. They're the little insights a bowler picks up along the way; they come with experience. It was well reported that Shane Warne was critical of that aspect of Mitchell's performance during the First Test of the 2014–15 Test series against India in Brisbane. I think if you can ignore the headlines and the outcry that accompanies the fallout from that type of situation, a fast bowler can use it to his advantage. It can either fire you up to prove your critics wrong or you can let it have a negative impact on your game.

I haven't spent all that much time with Mitch, but from what I have so far seen he has an enormous, and exciting, future ahead of him. He's also reaching the age where a male's bones 'harden', and that ought to mean there's less likelihood of him suffering the injuries that frustrated his career in the early years. He looks the goods, and I hope for Australia's sake he can convert his mastery of the one-day game to Test cricket. If he can, it will go a long way to ensuring Australia is the No. 1 cricketing nation for many summers.

Ryan Harris (S/R: 50.7)

Unfortunately, Ryan was forced to retire when two different scans of his right knee during the tour match against Essex indicated he would be unable to get through the 2015 Ashes series. While he took it stoically—as you'd expect from a man like him, based on the performances he put in for Australia—I really felt for him, because whenever I watched Ryan bowl I couldn't help but think he was a bowler you'd want in your attack. Throughout his career I'd heard people refer to Ryan Harris as the workhorse of Australia's attack. I always believed he deserved to be regarded much more highly than that. He was a fighter, as tough as an old army boot, and he was born with that wonderfully 'mad' mentality that meant he was prepared to not only bowl all day for his team, but he'd slog through it at a good pace and with quality.

I have no doubt that Ryan worked hard during the 2014–15 Aussie summer when he was 'cotton-wooled' by the powers that be and told to prepare for the upcoming Ashes campaign. As it turned out, his knee had been through one too many campaigns. I think one thing all young fast bowlers should take from Ryan Harris's career is that the role of the fast bowler is *not* (despite what you'll hear some people say) about keeping it tight and this 'n' that. The job of the fast bowler is to take wickets and he gets them by bowling to a game plan and building pressure. When the fast bowler's role is stripped back to its most raw definition, the fast bowler must take wickets if he wants to stay in the team. That's what Ryan's value to Australia was in his 27 appearances—the big-hearted bloke collected 113 wickets and he slogged his guts out for each and every one of them.

Josh Hazlewood (S/R: 44.1)

My old teammate Mark 'Junior' Waugh, who serves as a national selector these days, tipped Josh after his starring role on the 2015 tour of the West Indies to eventually surpass my record for the most Test wickets taken by a fast bowler. If that's the case, I'll be the first to congratulate him. I agree that he has started his Test career brilliantly. However, if Junior's prediction is to be fulfilled, Josh will need to look after himself to ensure he achieves one of the hardest goals a fast bowler can hope to attain because of the brutal nature of his job—and that's longevity.

I realised early in my Test career that I needed to do things differently in order to be able to perform at that intense level over a long period. That was why I sought the toughest and wisest strength and fitness conditioner I could find—Kev Chevell. It's up to Josh if he wants to follow a similar path, but I will say I'm a massive supporter of his. He seems to be a good young bloke from the country and from what I have observed he appears to have a very good work ethic and a desire to succeed. I really do hope that he's around for a long time because I can see great potential in the way he bowls.

A lot of people compared Josh to me when he was picked as a 17-year-old to play for New South Wales against New Zealand, but the truth is that the media seem to do that to every tall kid who comes along nowadays and bowls a good line and length. I don't know if Josh has taken the comparison as a sledge or a compliment, but I don't mind admitting that I feel proud some people see something in him that reminds them of me.

He was given a taste of international cricket as a member of the Australian one-day team at 19 but unfortunately he was sidelined, suffering from stress fractures and other strains. From what I understand he's come through all of that with an approach that *nothing* is going to stop him from getting to where he wants to be, and I applaud that. While his early progress was frustrated by those injuries, I'm sure that (like the smart blokes) Josh would fully appreciate that it took a lot of hard work for him to make the Australian team and now he has his baggy green cap in his kit bag, it's going to take a lot of hard work to stay there. I believe he has a lot of things in his favour. He has a simple action, he's tall (196 centimetres), he can get the ball through well, and he swings the ball; and the reason I'm happy with what I see is there doesn't seem too much that can go wrong.

I also view Hazlewood as a bowler who'll always hit good areas, and if he can build up pressure with whoever it is he's bowling in tandem with, at the other end, he'll take plenty of wickets. He started his Test career with a boom—he took 34 wickets in seven Tests at an average 19.94—and I'd say as long as he stays focused and works hard, he'll be just fine.

Something else I like about the boy from Bendemeer in the New England region of New South Wales is that I can see he has a quiet belief in himself, and he seems to have worked his game out. It's obvious he has a simple approach. By now it should not be a shock to anyone that I'm a huge fan of a fast bowler keeping his game as simple as possible because that means he won't have to undergo too much change or a complete revamp to unravel any problems.

THE SOUTH AFRICANS

Fanie de Villiers was aggressive, but I can't really think of too many openly aggressive fast bowlers from South Africa who you'd say were from the same mould as Brett Lee. A typical South African cricketer is seen by many of his opponents as stoic, disciplined and competitive—they play hard and enjoy the contest—but I believe that Australia's cricketers differ to their South African counterparts in that they're prepared to back themselves. The Aussies don't have what you'd call that fear of losing, and I'm afraid that's what has held the Proteas back over the years. However, they do boast great bowlers and the three I've picked are all ranked in the ICC's top 20 pace bowlers. They are also the reason why in recent years South Africa has had the world's most dominant attack.

Dale Steyn (S/R: 41.5)

He's ranked No. 1 in the world and has held that mantle for quite some time. He's a quality bowler. At the time of writing this book, he'd played in 78 Tests and taken 396 wickets, and his strike rate of 41.5 is right up there with the best of all time. I think that says a lot about Steyn as a bowler and competitor.

I really appreciate that he exudes that never-give-up attitude you want in a spearhead; he runs in hard all day long; he'll bowl all day if need be; and he can swing the ball. He goes about his business in a quieter manner than most—he doesn't 'chat' all that much to the batsmen—and he gives the impression that for him cricket is simply a matter of getting on with the job. That seems to have been the Steyn way for quite a long time. Mitchell Johnson challenged him for the No. 1 crown previously and he might again, although I have a feeling Mitchell Starc could be the next cab off that rank.

Steyn is not as tall as most other pace bowlers, but he's definitely found ways of taking wickets by utilising his pace, by swinging the ball and bowling to good areas. Indeed, he became the fastest South African—and the 15th fastest in world cricket—to reach 100 Test wickets, and the way he's built on that reinforces my belief that he's worked out his role in the Proteas system. The 32-year-old realised you need to take wickets but even more importantly understood that a fast bowler needs to find ways and means to achieve that. A fast bowler has the most physical part in the game—he leads from the front—but Steyn isn't your typical aggressive, in-your-face type of bowler. I view him as being in the mould of the great West Indian Michael Holding, who would refuse to bowl at all rather than dig a short one in at a tail-ender. There'll be those people who'll suggest that, just as Holding did 30 years ago, Steyn is doing his bit to prove to younger cricketers that cursing and over-the-top aggressiveness isn't a prerequisite to being effective. However, he definitely doesn't lack fire. He made everyone sit up and take notice when he took 10 wickets in the opening Test at Johannesburg against the Kiwis in 2007–08, and I think batsmen realised he was to be respected when one of his short deliveries unfortunately sent the New Zealand batsman Craig Cumming to intensive care.

He's still ranked highly in the one-day game, but from what I've observed Steyn seems to have the same game plan for both formats, and I'm not so sure if that's the best path to follow in one-day cricket. He doesn't bowl all that many yorkers or too many slower balls, either, so that suggests he has one speed—literally—of going about things. As I've already said, Dale Steyn's strike rate of 41.6 is incredible. That's over five wickets a Test, so regardless of my observations on his approach to the limited-overs game, it's still very hard to fault him. He definitely deserves the title of a champion bowler.

Vernon Philander (S/R: 47.9)

He needed only *seven* matches to take 50 wickets, making him the second-fastest player in Test history to reach that milestone. There're a number of reasons why I praise Philander for doing as well as he has in his career so far.

Firstly, he's kept it quite simple: he doesn't bowl express pace; he swings the ball just enough; he seems to get a bit of seam movement; he attacks the stumps relentlessly; but above all he strikes me as an intelligent bowler who bowls to the areas he knows a batsman doesn't like, and he has the ability to nip the ball around.

Philander has found a way to take (at the time of writing this book) 121 wickets in 29 Tests—and at a strike rate of 47.9. I like that he's replicated the success he's so far enjoyed at Test level in the one-day arena, and I attribute a lot of his success to the simplicity he utilises to bowl good areas and to extract just enough movement to trouble the batsmen.

The Australian team that toured South Africa in 2011 were the first to get a taste of what the now 30-year-old had to offer. He won the Man of the Match in his Test debut after taking 8–78, and then took a second innings haul of 5–15 to spearhead the home team to a stunning victory in Cape Town. He followed up that performance with another five-for in the Second Test to secure him a well-deserved Man of the Series medal.

Morné Morkle (S/R: 56.2)

Morkle was identified by Allan Donald as something special a decade ago—Allan, nicknamed 'White Lightning', was impressed by the bounce and pace Morkle could extract as a result of his height (he's 196 centimetres tall). Though he's been living in the slipstream of Steyn and Philander for a long time, that hasn't stopped him from being effective. Indeed, I think there's an argument that his bounce complements what that pair brings to the table, and it rounds out what's been the world's most formidable attack for a few years.

I like to see that Morkle works very hard to bowl at good areas. That effort was rewarded during the 2015 World Cup jointly hosted by Australia and New Zealand, when he assumed the lead role of the attack and his 17 wickets allowed him to finish as the tournament's fourth-highest wicket-taker behind Starc, Trent Boult and Umesh Yadav. He also took six more wickets—at a better average and strike rate—than Steyn. Perhaps that World Cup might be his springboard to even better things for the Proteas from here on in.

I'd like to see more yorkers from Morkle in the limited-overs format because he can execute them well when he wants to. If he needs proof of their impact he only needs to see what they've done for Starc's wicket-taking ability in the white-ball game: they've propelled him to the head of the pack.

Morkle has his idiosyncrasies, especially at the top of his run-up. While most fast bowlers will stop and settle themselves before they commence their run-up, he prefers to do a little turn and then charges straight in to bowl. While it's different, I'm not going to say he should do this or he should do that, because he has obviously worked out what's good for him. I think his style only serves to highlight that cricket is about routine and what works for the individual.

THE NEW ZEALANDERS

The Kiwis have always had willing fast men but injuries seem to plunder their reserves of talent and it's obviously been the cause of great frustration for them over the years. I can remember watching Sir Richard Hadlee, the man regarded as New Zealand's greatest cricketer, on the television and, apart from being a great competitor who carried the hopes of his nation on his shoulders, in my eyes he seemed to be the complete fast bowler. Over the years we've seen the likes of Dion Nash, Simon Doull, Ewen Chatfield, Chris Martin, Shane Bond and Danny Morrison compete hard and well for their country. However, I think the partnership we saw between Tim Southee and Trent Boult during their charge to the 2015 World Cup final was one of the most exciting in recent times for our cousins across the Tasman Sea. I'll be watching their progress keenly because I think they could spearhead the Black Caps to greater heights.

Tim Southee (S/R: 62.1) and Trent Boult (S/R: 56.8)

I think it is safe to say both these players have come of age and I was impressed by some of the spells I saw this pair bowl during the 2015 World Cup. Southee has played 41 Tests and taken 144 wickets, and with more Test matches under his belt he will only continue to improve. As a bowler who can swing the ball, Southee steps up to another level on any deck that offers swing. And one of the most exciting things he has going for him is his age—he's only 25.

I heard a lot of people pay tribute to Brendon McCullum during the World Cup. It was certainly well deserved because he backed up his captaincy with some great knocks, but make no mistake about the contribution Southee and Boult made to their team getting to the final. It was sensational. New Zealand has unearthed two quality fast bowlers who should help make a difference in the years to come. They're going to grow together and they've already formed a great partnership, with Southee the right-armer and Boult the left-armer and both enjoying good control. As is the case with the top performers, they bowl to good areas and both get the ball through quite well.

Boult, who has taken 123 wickets from his 32 Tests, has the ability to swing the ball and we saw how effective he was—the second most successful bowler behind Starc at the World Cup. Both Southee and Boult have a lot of cricket in them, and something they'll benefit from is the Kiwi approach to the game: they enjoy themselves and they back themselves. A fast bowler needs that attitude, but he also needs to foster it in the rest of his teammates because these qualities are the things that can make the difference. I view these two as quality bowlers. There is nothing flamboyant about either of them. They work very well together and, just as importantly, I love that they have a go!

THE INDIANS

The subcontinent is perhaps the toughest place on earth for anyone with an aspiration to be a fast bowler. The wickets are dead and are much better suited to the spinners. It's hot and it's bone dry, and most days it feels as though your feet are pounding into a concrete slab. However, I am finding in my role at the MRF that there are hundreds upon hundreds of local boys with the courage to put their hands up, because they have the dream to be the X-factor for their national team, just as the great Kapil Dev was. I don't use the word 'courage' lightly—those young men are volunteering to commit themselves to a tough life in unforgiving conditions, and I admire the enthusiasm in which they want to embrace the role. I have worked with quite a few high-calibre fast bowlers coming through the Indian system, and if we can get it right, it will make the Indians an even more formidable outfit.

Umesh Yadav (S/R: 53.6) and Varun Aaron (S/R: 66.8)

Neither had played a lot of Test cricket at the time of writing this book, but they both have the ability to bowl at 150 km/h. Yadav has taken 43 wickets in his 13 Tests, and that suggests he definitely has a lot of potential. I certainly wouldn't like to see that raw pace he possesses stifled in any way, because if he can continue to generate that pace he'll be a wicket-taker. As I said, the wickets in India aren't conducive for fast bowling: the harder you hit the deck, the slower it comes off. To be successful on the subcontinent you need to be a quality player, just like Kapil Dev was (although he was more a fast-medium-paced bowler who could swing the ball beautifully). The two young guys have the firepower to become genuine forces, so I'm hopeful they'll be used in the right way, because both of them provide India with a strong base to build on.

It's important to find ways to take wickets in India. I tried to take them with each *new* ball, because when it gets older you work on it for reverse swing, and that's a trait you need to have on the subcontinent. Like Yadav, Aaron has good control. This pair is improving; they have a great attitude and I have no doubt at all that they have it in them to go a long way.

Ishant Sharma (S/R: 65.2)

He's been around since 2007 and started out of the blocks at a million miles an hour. However, Sharma went through what I imagine was a frustrating patch where he didn't play as well as he probably would've liked. Whether that was because he excelled overseas but found returning to India's conditions a tough ask, I really don't know. He's still there though: he's played 62 Tests and taken 187 wickets. I think he's done very well for India. As I have said a few times now, to run in on those flat wickets and defy the heat and the humidity isn't easy: you need to be a lot fitter and stronger to do that in India than in other countries. Sharma is only 26, so he has plenty of time and should have many more opportunities to add to his wicket tally. Something I have noticed about him is that if the selectors put him under scrutiny—particularly if there's the risk he might lose his place in the team—he invariably responds by taking wickets.

THE PAKISTANIS

While India has struggled to find a pool of pacemen, across the border in Pakistan they're coming out of the woodwork and on their day, they're lethal. If you cast your mind back, Imran Khan, Sarfraz Nawaz, Wasim Akram and Waqar Younis were all quality bowlers who provided Pakistan with clout. And the many others who have followed—such as Umar Gul, the explosive Shoaib Akhtar and Mohammad Asif—have always made it seem that no matter what the state of play might be in Pakistan—involving controversies, revolts or scandals—it is a nation that has the ability to produce quality pacemen. In my role with the MRF Pace Foundation, I would love to find the key to unlock that in India. I've heard someone say that perhaps the first step will be to instil the attitude the young Pakistani pacemen have into their Indian counterparts—the love of knocking the stumps out of the ground with a fireball.

Wahab Riaz (S/R: 56.9)

He's only played 12 Tests and taken 35 wickets, but I was impressed by both the potential and the fire this player showed against Australia in Adelaide during the World Cup where he played with great aggression and good pace. I liked that he had the batsmen jumping around and dancing to his tune. He had skipper Michael Clarke caught off a short ball. He should also have had Shane Watson caught off a short ball but the fieldsman fluffed a straightforward opportunity. It was a really tough period for the batsmen, and while I think Riaz showed a bit of inexperience, he'll definitely be better for that hit out. It's important that Riaz keeps learning. What I thought was encouraging was the fact that he got aggressive and he bowled short. But what let him down was that he didn't really adjust when Australia got on top. I was also disappointed that he was fined by the ICC after that match for his well-publicised run-in with Watson. Their duel was compelling viewing and highlighted both the intensity of the match and the fact that it mattered. I thought it was ridiculous to punish passion.

Mohammad Irfan (S/R: 71.2)

I haven't seen Mohammad bowl 'live' but he is 216 centimetres tall, and while he's only played in four Tests I think it's safe for me to suggest that if anyone is going to get pace and bounce out of the wicket, he should be the man! He might not be as coordinated as other fast bowlers, but if he can stay fit and well, his height alone should ensure he'll enjoy some success. I don't know how many injuries he's suffered during the course of his career—he's 33 and has been used more regularly by the Pakistan selectors in one-day internationals than he has Tests—but I'd imagine his pace and swing will be unique, and I am sure he has plenty of people in his ear advising him to use his height to his advantage.

THE WEST INDIANS

The West Indians were once the most feared pace bowlers on the planet, and over the years names such as Wes Hall, Michael Holding, Joel Garner, Colin Croft, Courtney Walsh, Malcolm

Marshall, Andy Roberts and Curtly Ambrose were enough to strike fear into the hearts of even the bravest of batsmen. No one understands where it went wrong, but there are plenty of theories in the Caribbean for the great demise: the rise in popularity of American sports such as basketball; the lack of amenities to encourage and foster talent; internal politics that have taken a terrible toll; and the fact that they haven't been winning too many matches, let alone series, over the last 20 years, resulting in kids losing interest in cricket. There're a few bright lights on the Windies pace scene. I think Jason Holder, at 201 centimetres, might be the lightning rod the Windies crave to encourage more kids to bowl fast, while Kemar Roach is also dangerous on his day. However, at the moment, the West Indians are living off past glories from 30–40 years ago. The champion batsman Brian Lara put me in the picture when he was in Australia working as a commentator during the World Cup. He pointed out that we were at an advantage by having a cricket academy because they don't have one in the West Indies. I don't understand how that has been tolerated by the authorities. I want to see them receive assistance from the ICC and other nations to improve. I believe the West Indians can rise to be a great cricketing empire again but it will take a concerted effort by the ICC to achieve that. It'll take a lot of commitment, hard work and cash, but it would be worth the investment and would definitely be to the game's advantage. Because when the Windies were at their peak in the 1970s and '80s, cricket fans around the world would flock to watch them—there was an insatiable appetite for Calypso cricket.

Jerome Taylor (S/R: 59.2)

He's the guy flying the flag, and I thought he performed very well against the Australians in the two-Test series in 2015. He was well rewarded for his efforts with a first-innings haul of 6–47 in the Second Test. However, Taylor didn't have any back-up, which I can only imagine must've been frustrating for him. Jamaican-born Taylor isn't as tall as the West Indies bowlers from the past, but he gets the ball through well, he swings it and has that aggressive streak I talk about. He is the man leading the attack and I hope for his sake, and for the greater good of West Indies cricket, that he can get some support—and soon.

Taylor enjoyed a dream run when he was called up to play for the West Indies in the final match of the one-day series against Sri Lanka in 2003, because he'd played in only one game for Jamaica. He was selected for the 2006 Champions Trophy and became known to the Australian team when he took a hat-trick against us in the opening group game. It was a great effort. I think it says a lot for his depth of desire and is testament to old-fashioned determination that nine years down the track he's maintained the rage.

THE ENGLISH

The wickets in England are a bit slower and the ball tends to nip around a little bit, but the old enemy has a long and proud history of producing quality fast bowlers. Off the top of my head I can nominate the likes of Harold Larwood of

Bodyline fame (or as he preferred to call it 'fast leg theory bowling'), while others who come straight to mind include Freddie Trueman, Frank Tyson, Brian Statham, Bob Willis, John Snow, Ian 'Beefy' Botham (although he was considered an all-rounder), Darren Gough and Andy Caddick. I enjoyed bowling in England. I averaged over six wickets a Test, and I really enjoyed the County season in 2000 when I played for Worcester. Something I quickly realised when I first played in England was the need to bowl at a fuller length than we do in Australia, to really hit the wicket; and if you can swing the ball and make it nip around, it can help make life exciting. I really loved bowling with a Dukes cricket ball. People ask how that ball would go in Australia, and my belief is that it might be a little bit too good. I think you'd get a bit more bounce on our decks and there'd be more seam movement; and since it bounces well, it would turn the tables in the bowler's favour.

Jimmy Anderson (S/R: 57.6)

He's played in more than 100 Tests and taken over 403 wickets, but he's someone who I think is very hard to gauge. Some days Anderson looks like a world-beater; he swings the ball and can appear unplayable—like he did in the opening Test of the 2015 Ashes series at Cardiff. But on other days he appears to be pedestrian, and by that I mean when the ball isn't doing anything (as was the case at Lord's in the next Test) he seems to be nullified. England is in a position where they need Anderson and Stuart Broad to fire and do well, and when they don't it definitely has a negative impact on their chance of winning. I think Anderson has the talent and the potential to be the world's No. 1 bowler, but he won't reach that mark until he learns to rely less on swing for his wickets.

Stuart Broad (S/R: 56.8)

He's tall, he runs in hard, hits good areas, gets bounce, gets some seam movement and moves the ball a little bit—so he has all the attributes that are required to be a really good bowler. And I think he's improved as a result of getting more opportunities to bowl. He was the pick of England's bowlers in the first two Tests of the 2015 Ashes series and he crowned those performances with his 8–15 in the fourth Test at Trent Bridge. It was a phenomenal effort, where the Aussies were skittled for 60 in the first innings. He isn't afraid to say his piece, and while that has been criticised as 'carrying on', I think a fast bowler needs to be prepared to back himself and to have a bit of fun with the media and the crowd. He's developing a real toughness with age and that's helping turn him into a very good bowler. While I've said Anderson relies heavily on swing to enjoy success, Broad is one bloke who I think has it in him to do well in any conditions. I was at a function where Broad was interviewed on stage and he said that I was his hero when he was in short pants and dreaming of bringing the Aussies down; I was flattered, it was a huge compliment. I'd like to have a chat to him one day to learn a bit more about his philosophies. He and Anderson bowl well in partnership, especially if the ball is swinging well for Anderson and Broad is hitting the deck with a bit of seam and bounce.

17

THE LITTLE
MASTER

Before we left, I remember [Bradman] said to Sachin
that he loved the way he batted and of all modern
players he reminded him the most of himself.
You can't get a greater accolade than that...

—Shane Warne on the meeting between him,
Bradman and Tendulkar

When umpire Daryl Harper gave Sachin Tendulkar out lbw for a duck off my bowling during the Adelaide Test in 1999 many of the Little Master's fans were outraged and the Cricket Australia headquarters received an unwelcome insight into just how fanatical some of Sachin's supporters are, because a few death threats were directed at me via their office. As you would expect, the authorities treated the matter very seriously but I really didn't think there was too much to worry about. It was only some angry—and I don't mind saying, *misguided*—fans letting off some steam. The reason I say misguided is because Umpire Harper made the correct decision when he raised his finger to give Sachin out. I have said it before that Indian supporters have never forgiven me for dismissing their idol that day, and 16 years after the event I've noticed that the emotions still run strong; there are posts on the internet that describe me as a 'cheat'— and worse—because my appeal for Sachin to be given out when he ducked into a ball as it was heading straight to the stumps was rewarded.

I'd like to think that after all the tough battles we fought over the years, Sachin and I share a mutual respect. Although, in saying that, I hasten to note that he has been quoted in a book as saying I was the only opponent he ever sledged throughout his long and illustrious career. I rate him as one of the greatest batsmen to have ever drawn breath, but I feel as though we're going to debate that lbw decision at Adelaide until we're old men. He wrote in his autobiography that Harper's was a poor decision, but I'll maintain until I'm blue in the face he was definitely out.

The drama unfurled when I bowled a bouncer that didn't bounce. However, when Sachin ducked to avoid the short ball he'd anticipated, it hit him plum on the shoulder and that prevented the six-stitcher from hitting the stumps. Sachin is only a short guy and he ducked that low I could actually see the bails; I believed there was no doubt he was out and I appealed. Harper, who had umpired 95 Tests, had no alternative but to give Sachin out because he was in front of the stumps and he did not play a shot. It created a maelstrom of outrage throughout the subcontinent and within Australia's Indian community. Like me, Harper—who I found to be a very fair match official—has copped it on the internet. I've heard second-hand that it is the one decision from his 13-year career as an international umpire that he would like to forget because it comes up so often from Sachin's supporters and the Indian media. However, he has never wavered in his belief that Sachin was out and I understand he made an interesting point in light of Sachin's well-publicised disappointment 15 years after the event in an interview with *Cricinfo*. Harper has been quoted as saying there was no mention of Sachin feeling aggrieved by the decision in the report that he filed as India's captain after the match finished.

Throughout his 24 years in top-flight cricket, Sachin Tendulkar defined calmness and composure whenever he was at the crease. While those traits (allied with his talent, obviously) underpinned his success, it says a lot that he was able to block out the weight of expectation he carried—from over a billion fans who considered him a god—whenever he took strike. Sachin was earmarked for greatness long before he made his Test debut against Pakistan as a 16-year-old wunderkind in 1989, and in that match he gave an insight into his mental toughness when he batted on in a blood-stained shirt after being whacked in the mouth by a Waqar Younis delivery. I've read the stories about how Sachin spent hours in the nets as a kid, and how after he either retired or was dismissed in one match he'd be ferried to another ground to bat in another game. In 1988, he and Vinod Kambli scored a 664-run partnership (both finished with unbeaten triple centuries) in India's most prestigious schoolboy competition, the Harris Shield (in 2013 schoolboy Prithvi Shaw scored 546). At 17 he scored the first of his 51 Test centuries, against England at Old Trafford. He was one who liked to be in control. While you never knew what you'd get from Brian Lara when he took strike, Sachin was always the same. It was impossible to use Sachin's ego against him, and he was prepared to tough it out and wait for a bad ball from which to score runs. Everything he did appeared to be so measured; he was technically correct, mentally strong and very disciplined. His longevity—24 years at the top after making his Test debut, apparently four short years after he started playing with a hard cricket ball—puts him in a league of his own. I also can't think of too many other cricketers who matched his insatiable appetite for scoring runs and I doubt whether anyone will surpass the incredible 15,921 runs he scored in 200 Tests at an average of 53.78. Sachin has an inner-confidence and he appeared to almost loathe being the centre of attention. I also observed Sachin to be self-assured and confident in who he is—there were no insecurities. If that's having an aura then, yes, he had an aura.

He also proved patience is a virtue and one of the most astounding examples of his willpower occurred while I was sidelined after an ankle operation during the 2003–04 season. He was caught in slips a few times trying to drive the ball through cover. Those dismissals compounded his form slump and after he posted scores of 0, 1, 37, 0 and 44 leading into the fourth and final Test of the Border–Gavaskar Trophy— with the series locked at one all—he decided to eradicate the cover drive from his game for that match. Just like that! I don't think any other batsman could have emulated the monk-like devotion to a cause that he showed during that innings, especially when the Aussie attack tried to constantly tempt him to unleash one of his prized off-side drives off either front or back foot by bowling at his off stump. He refused to take the bait, and in the 613 minutes he was at the crease for his unconquered 241—and in which he'd faced 436 deliveries—he didn't even look remotely interested in playing the cover drive. His decision to refuse to play at any of the many balls the Aussie attack pitched outside his off stump was like the spider who lures the fly into his web. The bowlers changed tack and did what he wanted; they bowled at him, and in one of the game's great master classes, he used the pace off the ball to score runs.

The first time we crossed swords was in a one-day international tournament at Sharjah in the mid-1990s when he was 20. I remember in the build-up to the series, all of the talk centred around this young bloke and how he would be cricket's next great batsman. I was keen to see how he performed. When I ran in to bowl he was on six runs and he attempted to play the pull shot, but because I managed to get extra bounce from the ball, he hit it straight to Mark Taylor at short mid-wicket. The next time we opposed one another was in Test cricket in a one-off Test in Delhi and I dismissed him for a duck when the ball found his inside edge and uprooted his leg stump. While our meeting had a great start—for me, at least—it only got harder. In nine Tests I dismissed him on six occasions, and every time I got him was a great cause for celebration. The reason for this was obvious—he was so skilled and, on his day, quite brutal.

That brutality was rammed home in the 1996 World Cup when we played against India in Mumbai. He scored 90 off 84 deliveries before being stumped by Ian Healy off Mark Waugh's bowling. I enjoyed a good start in that match until Sachin pulled one of my deliveries for four and that appeared to be the catalyst for him to hit the 'go' button. Regardless of whether it was a poor delivery or a peach of a ball, he had no problem despatching them around the ground. During the post-mortem I realised we had made a mistake in that innings—he got away with what I think could have been called a lucky shot when he hit that four but we changed our approach to bowling at him. Rather than continuing to bowl just short of a good length, we pitched the ball up and tried to get him with a yorker. It was *never* going to trouble him, especially on his home ground (on a typical subcontinent pitch that favours the batsman) and in front of a home crowd who treated every shot as though it was a gift from heaven.

Bowling just short of a good length worked better for me in Australia and other countries that favoured bounce, because I could (and did) use it to my advantage when we faced off for World Cup matches in England and South Africa. When we played India in the Super Six stage of the 1999 World Cup, the stakes were high because a loss would have ended our campaign; we naturally earmarked Sachin as a dangerous man but I had him caught behind for a duck by Adam Gilchrist. Then, in the 2003 World Cup final played at Wanderers in South Africa, India was trying to run down our 360 and when Sachin blasted my second ball of the innings to the boundary we took that as his signal of intent. I bowled my third ball to him at a similar length but it was a tad shorter and because it bounced a little more, he hit it straight up in the air and I caught it to dismiss him for four—the groans from the Indian-dominated crowd were deafening.

While I mention two success stories, there were plenty of times when he was mentally switched on and I gripped that ball knowing he had it in him to really destroy any bowler. He rarely spoke while he batted, but Sachin certainly let me know he was out there when we played in the quarterfinal of the 2000 ICC Champions Trophy in Kenya because he decided to *sledge* me! I was shocked because it went against his character, but he made it clear from the outset that day he wanted to be in charge. Sachin recalled this encounter in a book called *SACH* and revealed he'd concocted a plan to try and upset my rhythm because it was an overcast day and there had been some light rain—conditions he thought were tailor-made for me to be dangerous. He said he wanted to put me off my game and his account of the sledge was that

he said a genteel: 'Today I will hit you out of the ground'.
I remember the language being a little more colourful but
after all this time that's splitting hairs. He was quoted as
saying that he believed the jibe got under my skin and that
I sprayed the ball around because he made me as angry as a
bear with a migraine, but I wasn't upset by his 'gamesmanship'. While I was surprised he had a go at me, I accepted
that as being a part of cricket. I'd learnt not to be put off
by any batsman long before we crossed paths that day in
Nairobi. Something I can clearly remember in the lead-up to
his sledge was that he attempted to pull one of my deliveries
in my opening over, and I watched as it went straight up
into the air. I thought to myself, Beauty, that's out. There
was a stiff breeze behind my back, however, and I watched
as the ball kept going . . . and going . . . and going. Ever the
optimist, I believed Sachin would be caught, but the breeze
carried the ball over the boundary for six. It was incredibly
frustrating to watch it just plonk over the rope and I guess
he thought the universe was on his side that day. It provided
Sachin with the confidence he needed to chirp. Fifteen years
on and I'm still not sure whether I ought to feel honoured
or offended, because Sachin has maintained I was the only
opponent he ever gave a spray. It certainly set the tone for
him in that match because he went for it and set the Nairobi
Gymkhana Club Ground alight. He was in a mood and teed
off at *every* ball, and his 39 runs from 38 deliveries included
three sixes and the same number of fours. It provided the
Indians with a flying start.

After all those years there have been many Indians who've been quite keen to remind me of the time I was given a tongue-lashing by their hero and all I can do is smile and say, 'It's just a part of the game.' What I also tell them is I have fond memories of opposing Sachin Tendulkar, who was a great batsman and a worthy opponent. The greatest compliment I can offer him is to say that he was someone who never failed to force me to dig deep and draw out my competitive best.

18

DR JEKYLL AND PRINCE LARA

Where is Brian Lara?

**—Former South African president Nelson Mandela
upon his arrival in Trinidad**

Brian Lara is regarded as one of the finest stroke players from any era since Don Bradman. If you use big centuries as a gauge for greatness, critics say he deserves to sit at the right hand of 'The Don' having scored massive hundreds with the same consistency. I'm a former opponent who readily recalls his quality, his flamboyance, his poise and courage against pace bowling. He was someone who wanted to play all of the shots in the book, and as is the case with all of the game's genuine free spirits, he never wanted to be tied down. I think the fact that Sachin Tendulkar once said it was a 'joy' to watch him bat says volumes about Brian's ranking among cricket's elite.

I remember Brian and Sachin as the best I ever bowled to. When he was on song, I'm not sure if there was ever a better batsman in the world than 'The Prince'. What made him a formidable opponent was he had the skills to match his sense of daring. While he'll be forever remembered as the batsman who scored an unconquered 400 during the 2004 Test series against England, and for hitting an unbeaten 501 for Warwickshire against Durham in an English County match in 1994, I found it interesting to learn that he nominated the 213 he scored against us at Jamaica's Sabina Park in the Second Test of the 1999 series as his best effort.

That series started with Brian under pressure as the captain of a team the Caribbean people would not accept. After decades of watching the West Indies rule international cricket with intimidation, fire and brimstone, the country found itself suddenly represented by a team ranked by many critics as 'second tier'. That burned them but their frustration turned to outright fury by the end of the First Test when we rolled them for 51 (it would be their lowest ever total before England routed them for 47 in 2004). I think what would have added to Brian's intimidation was that the confirmation of the Windies' fall from grace occurred in front of his home crowd. He copped it—and how!

If I had any thought the pressure that may have been weighing on his shoulders would play into our hands, I was given a rude shock as he put on a masterclass. He and Jimmy Adams batted and batted . . . and batted for the entire second day of the match against an attack that contained

Shane Warne, Jason Gillespie, Stuart MacGill and myself. Both of them were in the zone and we finished the day footsore, bone-weary and wicketless. Brian was destructive. He not only scored his first Test century in two years but he and Adams put on a record fifth-wicket partnership of 322, and it gave their team a foundation for a famous 10-wicket victory. Brian would say 16 years after his gutsy effort that the reason he prized that innings so highly was because of the context in which those runs were scored. 'The criticism I got even before the Test match was so great, it was not looking promising at all,' he said. 'Through the immense pressure, physically and psychologically that I was going through at the time, I really had to muster a lot of courage and commitment. I went and produced what I thought was the best I've ever batted under that situation.'

It really was an incredible effort, especially under the circumstances. And as someone who saw too much of him that day, I agree the innings was built on courage and commitment. It is one of quite a few examples that I call upon when I explain to people why I always rated his wicket so highly. However, while he'll always be remembered by me as a champion batsman, I found Brian had a touch of Jekyll and Hyde about him. Something I realised early in our contests was that you really never knew what to expect when it was his turn to bat.

There were times when he would come to the crease and appear so focused that the air literally crackled with anticipation, but there were those other occasions when mentally he seemed to be all over the place and from my perspective he appeared a mess. I've heard people say there is a fine line between genius and insanity, and there were days when his antics out in the middle made me wonder whether he walked that fine line. For instance, I vividly remember a Test we played in Antigua because Matthew Hayden chirped him, and it wasn't really anything that could be considered too bad or over the top, but for reasons best known to Brian he just lost it—and in a big way. He stood in his crease and yelled at the top of his voice: 'SHUT UP! SHUT UP! SHUT UP!' I remember thinking to myself, This will be interesting, because Steve Waugh obviously smelt blood, and a few seconds after Brian's final demand for us to 'shut up', he moved to field at short cover and promptly engaged in what was described during Steve's era as our Test Captain as a spot of 'mental disintegration'—he turned the screws.

Throughout my career I never once felt as though I was the underdog, even when the likes of Brian Lara, Sachin Tendulkar, Jimmy Adams, Mohammad Yousuf, Kumar Sangakkara, Rahul Dravid, Graeme Smith or Jacques Kallis were on song, because I knew the plan I was bowling to and I knew what I wanted to achieve. That mentality meant I didn't ever say to myself 'I don't want to bowl at this bloke', nor did I ever despair and ask myself 'How do I get this guy out?', even when they were scoring freely. I was always armed with a plan and I trusted the plan. When Brian came in to bat, I sometimes felt as though I lifted by at least ten per cent. My game plan early in his innings was to bowl around the wicket and bowl full outside off stump with a packed slips, gully and point region. My intention was to tempt him to slash at the ball because he was a batsman who wanted to play his shots and craved the chance to showcase his flair and flamboyance. However, I stacked the field so if he got it slightly wrong I had six or seven blokes ready to take the catch, and I know the field I set played on his mind. Sometimes I thought Brian may have felt as though the Aussies were suffocating him.

Of course it wasn't always one-way traffic because there were those times when he'd drop anchor and the sight of him hitting the ball seemed as natural as watching a bird fly or a fish swim. Brian scored some big double hundreds against Australia—and it is worth noting he scored nine centuries in total against us—and on those occasions he was ferocious. He was always a batsman who, regardless of the situation, would play the shot he wanted, and when he was in that frame of mind it didn't really matter what you bowled. I bagged Brian Lara's wicket on 15 occasions in Test cricket. The second most successful bowler to dismiss him was André Nel of South Africa who got him eight times. We had some great duels and the honours were evenly shared, but my approach was to allow Brian to be his own undoing; it was simply following the old edict of giving someone enough rope to hang themselves. You see, I realised if I bowled enough balls in the right area it would only be a matter of time before he got himself out, and as sure as night follows day, that's what happened. There was a stage when people joked that it looked as though I could get him out at will because he allowed me to frustrate him. Brian wouldn't have realised this, but he actually helped me formulate the way I bowled to him the first time we spoke, during the 1995 series we played in the Caribbean.

Over the years Brian spent a lot of time in our dressing room after a match and he was always warmly welcomed. He was seen as a nice guy—and he is—he's charismatic and likeable, and I formed the opinion that he was someone who liked to be liked. It was obvious he was happy to enjoy himself and we shared some good times over the years. Something I remember about that series was that it was the only one I ever played in that had a rest day (we didn't need it in Bridgetown because we won that Test in three days), and I found myself on a replica pirate ship called the *Jolly Roger*, which was a popular party cruiser, and there I was in Brian's company. I was still buzzing from my first five-for at Test level and Man of the Match award. Brian had become one of my wickets in the second innings when he nicked one of my deliveries to our wicketkeeper Ian Healy for nine runs. Despite the 10-wicket defeat he was in good spirits and he started the conversation by saying, 'Well played.' I thought that was nice, but before I had a chance to reply he continued with, 'That ball wouldn't have got anyone else in world cricket. I'm in such good form I was good enough to nick it . . . I'm telling you, no one else would have got near it.' From that first sentence he spoke to me he struck me as a very confident guy and I realised you'd need that brand of self-belief to bat like him and to be so good. At that stage in my life I was still a shy young fellow from the bush, and I didn't say too much. I was happy just to think that I was contributing something to the Australian team and I didn't take any offence to Brian's comment about his talent being the reason I dismissed him . . . there was a compliment in what he said, but I sometimes thought it was directed at himself! In any case, after the function I thought long and hard about what he'd said—'*That ball wouldn't have got anyone else in world cricket*'—and I constantly replayed in my mind the delivery that brought him undone. I realised that my approach to bowling at the left-hander was for the ball to hit the wicket and go away off the wicket, and if I picked that length up it moved ever so slightly, forcing the batsman to play at it in an area where the chances of nicking the ball increased significantly. In opposing Brian you needed to throw in a couple of factors—that he liked to be flamboyant *and* he wanted to dominate the attack—and I realised that could be used against him.

Thanks to Brian's input on the *Jolly Roger* I found a formula and it served me well over the years that followed. It sometimes pays to listen. The scorecards from our old battles noted that it wasn't a one-sided battle because on the days he dug in, Brian gave nothing away. One of those knocks was in Adelaide during the 2005–06 series when he scored 226 against us, and 24 boundaries were included in that score. It was yet another Lara masterclass and in the process Brian became Test cricket's highest run-scorer when he overhauled my old skipper Allan Border's 11,174 runs by hitting a single to fine leg off my bowling early on the second day's play. He was in total control for each of the 402 minutes he was at the crease, until I set him up by making it appear as though I planned to send down a bouncer but instead bowled it full at the stumps. It was the only ball of the 298 he faced during that knock that he misread, because he was bowled when he gave himself room to try and hit me over third man. While he scored a double century, I was still happy as a bowler that I'd set a trap and it had worked.

I wonder how Adam Dale, who was a right-arm fast bowler from Victoria, must have felt about his fate as a bowler when his first match in the baggy green cap saw him pitted against Tendulkar in Bangalore in 1998, and a year later he was thrown in against Lara in Antigua! Some might have considered it a curse but Adam collected Tendulkar's scalp when he bowled him for 177. And while it would have been seen by some as a David versus Goliath type of battle, I reckon Adam was like me in that he would have enjoyed the challenge fate had picked for him—two of the toughest batsmen on the planet to match wits and pit skills against.

I think Australia's current opener, David Warner, has that same destructiveness, but unlike Brian his confidence is in your face. Brian didn't need to do that because while he wasn't quite as intimidating as Viv Richards—I thought from watching him on television that Viv had the aura of a prize-fighter—he was born with the strut and swagger that characterises the great West Indians.

He also had a good sense of humour, as Adam Gilchrist can attest. Adam tells a great story about Brian when he was keeping to Brad Hogg during a game in Grenada—it might've been a one-dayer in 2003. In between deliveries, Brian would chat to Gilly and not only tell him the shot he was going to play to the next ball but where he was going to hit it—and he did! As you can imagine, it blew Gilly's mind . . . it was amazing and gives an insight into what made Brian one of the sport's great entertainers.

I spent time with Brian during the 2015 World Cup when we did some commentary together and what I learned gave me a better insight into what enabled him to dominate in so many of his 131 Tests; to score a century against every Test nation; to hit Test cricket's highest score of 400 not out; to hammer 501 not out in English County cricket; to score 11,953 Test runs; to record 34 Test centuries; and to notch 48 Test half-centuries. And while he finished with an average of 52, it's incredible to think he scored 18.8 per cent of the West Indies team's runs over his career. He was the tenth of 11 children, and with money scarce his first bat was carved from the branch of a coconut tree by one of his older brothers. They'd pick the hardest orange they could find and play cricket in the street. Brian said the fact that he had six older brothers bowling at him gave him an advantage over other kids his age because he said there was nothing quite like matching his skills against the 'tough guys' who gave him no quarter. He said, 'If you wanted an innings out on the street you had to work for it.'

At a time when West Indies cricket is on the ropes, I was interested to learn of his frustration with the system in the Caribbean because, as he complained, there is no infrastructure, no sponsorship, no money and no cricket academy—things we Australian players all take for granted. He is extremely passionate about West Indies cricket and I think the powers that be over there need to utilise him better than they do, because as a kid who graduated from batting against the older kids with his coconut-branch bat on the streets of Trinidad to conquering the world proves, there are no boundaries for greatness. I don't know if we'll see another Brian Lara but, for the sake of West Indies *and* world cricket, I certainly hope we do . . . the game needs its entertainers.

19

TAKING STRIKE

And Glenn McGrath dismissed for two,
just 98 runs short of his century.

**—Richie Benaud, on yet another innings of rich promise that was cut
down too early**

There's no number 11 in history who hasn't done
his best, whether he's got 0 or 106 not out.

—Mike Whitney, proud Australian No. 11 (1981–92) and scorer of 106

Statistically, my 35 ducks and three pairs ranks me alongside the likes of Englishmen Monty Panesar, Devon
Malcolm and Phil Tufnell, India's Bhagwath Chandrasekhar,
the West Indian Courtney Walsh and New Zealand's Chris
Martin as the so-called 'most wonderfully inept' batsmen to
have ever played Test cricket. Steve Waugh joked early in
my career that I should approach batting companies to pay

me *not* to use their bats; but the truth is that the incredible amount of scrutiny I was placed under whenever I was on strike actually made me an attractive proposition to sponsors because their brand received maximum exposure, well at least for the few balls or minutes I hung around.

I never had any trouble picking up the ball when it left the bowler's hand; the root of my problems, especially in the early days, was that I lacked the technique needed to get myself set, and I also didn't ever allow myself enough time to play shots. While I know there were jokes made about my batting—such as the old line that suggested a stocking had more runs in it than my chunk of willow—I took my role as a batsman extremely seriously. Something I read in a cricket book when I was a kid rang true: a batting line-up consists of 11 players and it doesn't matter if you're an opener, No. 5, No. 8 or 11, your job is to go out and show a commitment to score runs or at the very least hold up your end. I took it seriously, so much so that my teammates said I'd often return to the dressing room fuming about being on the wrong end of a dodgy decision. I know *they've* claimed that I'd rant and rave and carry on that 'there's no justice in this game', throwing my bat to the ground and hurling my gloves into the locker—by the way they give their accounts, I'd still be paying off my fines if the ICC match referee heard what I had to say about another dodgy delivery. On the flipside, my bowling mate Jason Gillespie said he was ecstatic when I was dismissed cheaply—and even more so if he heard me carrying on about the umpire—because he thought that signalled an 'easy' day for him and the other bowlers, knowing I'd be fired up to bowl well. Since my retirement I've also heard that other blokes used to hide their faces and laugh at my carry-on after being dismissed, which is something I'm pleased I never saw because I was so serious about trying to contribute to the team as a batsman, I think seeing that would've *really* sent me over the edge. Batting—it was a source of so much anguish and frustration, but ultimately it provided me with one of my most treasured moments in cricket.

My batting was something that, for whatever reason, people became fascinated by, but they weren't watching me to marvel at lusty cover drives or hook shots, they wanted to see me sweat and poke and prod for singles that were worth their weight in gold. I heard the jokes from the outer, that some bloke's near-sighted 90-year-old grandmother was a better bat than me (and I would've liked to have seen it). But perhaps the cruellest jibe of all was the time Steve Waugh— who I nursed to his historic double century in Jamaica—said I'd wake up one day and realise I was actually left-handed. It wasn't an easy road and I am often asked about my trials and tribulations at the crease. What I thought I would do here is detail the development of my batting career from starry-eyed slogger to a so-called rabbit who bettered his average by a multiple of ten in one innings. I thought I'd roughly chart my battle with the bat from my days as a Narromine bush-basher to being a specialist No. 11, who turned down the opportunity to bat at No. 3 in an SCG Test.

It wasn't always pretty, but one thing I always did as a batsman was this: I gave my best.

IN THE BEGINNING

My dad has a dry sense of humour. When I made the Australian team and my batting was put under a spotlight and I was exposed as being, well, technically flawed, he didn't do my reputation any favours or instil much confidence in the public that I might hold up the tail against the likes of Wasim Akram. He said with a straight face and deadpan delivery that, in his opinion and judging from our family's backyard Test matches, my sister Donna was the best batter—and possibly even best bowler—of all his kids. I'd like to think my efforts out in the middle, and not Dad's joke, defined how the public viewed me as a batsman!

I know I've said on many occasions that my bowling benefited from the fact that no one at the Backwater club saw anything special in me when I was a kid trying his hardest to get a bowl, because it meant no one ruined my action. The general consensus was that it would be a waste of time and effort showing me how to bowl because I didn't have any talent and I was destined to utilise my height and play in the bush basketball league anyway. However, the flipside to that is I didn't receive a skerrick of batting coaching for the same reasons, and in the years that followed I paid heavily for not being given a solid foundation—or better still, sound defence—in the town's cricket nets. I was left to my own devices, and as a kid left to his own devices, I adopted the philosophy of 'when in doubt hit out'. That helped me score a few runs in the bush, especially when I was a teenager. It was also around this time that I bought a 'piece' of Viv Richards from Greg Chappell's cricket store in Brisbane . . .

There's a great saying in cricket and sport in general that suggests even if you're not a good cricketer, you ought to look the part. So when I changed clubs from the Backwater XI to join the Rugby Union XI, I figured if I wanted to give myself a fighting chance of scoring some runs, I ought to invest in a decent bat. I ordered a Stuart Surridge Jumbo, the humped-back bat made famous by Viv Richards—the man who was undoubtedly cricket's most damaging batsman in my childhood years. Apart from the appeal of it being the Master Blaster's preferred weapon of choice, what lured me to pay the princely sum of $100 for it was the blurb in the catalogue describing it as perfect for the cricketer who liked to hit the ball long and far, and that was definitely me . . . if only in my dreams.

Some blokes boast they have the prettiest girlfriend or the fastest car, but after all these years I reckon I had claims on owning the best chunk of lumber in the NSW Far West. After I joined the Rugby Union XI to get a better go at bowling, the captain gave me the chance to bat higher up in the order and I was pleased to discover that *when* I connected with the ball, the bat lived up to the manufacturer's promise of sending the ball long and far—and I *loved* both the feeling and sound of the ball hitting the meat of the blade and soaring towards the boundary. I scored quite a few 50s and 60s that season and the first scoring shot was often a six straight down the ground. The reality is, there was never any science to my batting, it was simply a matter of winding up and waiting for the ball to bounce on the synthetic pitch and getting lucky *when* I connected with the ball on the rise, because I whacked the bejeezus out of it.

GOING THE BLUFF

When I joined the Sutherland Cricket Club in the Sydney grade competition, I had this crazy thought that I could perhaps start afresh as a batsman if I could convince the officials there that I was a dab hand with the willow. Now that I think about it that was a gutsy (maybe silly) call, because two of the officials I was trying to sell myself to as a 'gun' were the former opener John Dyson and wicketkeeper Steve Rixon, who'd played a combined total of 43 Tests between them and knew a bit about who could bat and who couldn't. However, I didn't allow the fear of being caught out to hold me back. When they asked where I batted, I replied 'I open', and I could almost hear them thinking what a stroke of luck it was that they had a kid on their books who could open both the batting *and* the bowling—but, I'll give them this much, they were smart. They realised the standard in Narromine couldn't have been too crash hot, so they decided rather than open I'd start in the Second XI at No. 7 and they'd watch to see how I went. Well, I did well to contain my smile to think I'd bluffed them, but the problem with cricket is you get found out sooner or later. I pushed on, oblivious to common sense pleading for me not to set myself up for a mighty fall.

In the first innings I took strike at No. 7—and I smile when I think of how the guys at Backwater and in the Rugby Union XI must have reacted when they heard on the bush wire that I was batting at No. 7 on the finely manicured turf wickets in Sydney—and I was bowled first ball. Surprisingly, after I trudged back to the boys, I was patted on the back and told 'bad luck, could've happened to anyone' and I nodded quietly in agreement that, yes, it was a good ball. In my second knock I was bowled for another first-ball duck, but I noticed on that occasion there weren't as many of my teammates commiserating about the misfortune of being brought undone by a ball that would've dismissed even the best of the team's best. I'll give the selectors at Sutherland this much—they were patient with me. I was given a *third* chance at No. 7, but when I was bowled for my third consecutive golden duck, I realised my goose was cooked when the captain walked over and said that in all future matches I'd bat at No. 11 until I proved I was worthy of anything higher. Sadly, I couldn't argue, I'd been found out and I didn't have a leg to stand on.

WRATH OF THE WINDIES

I knew if I was ever going to cop any unwelcome punishment when I batted, it was going to be during the 1995 Test series against the West Indies, which was played in their backyard. I'd decided—at the urging of Steve Waugh and my skipper Mark Taylor—it was time to give the West Indian pacemen a taste of their own fare when they came in to bat. While I never bowled with the intention to hurt them, there were plenty of people who thought it was sheer madness for someone who couldn't even hold a bat to go out of his way to aggravate them—it was, they thought, the equivalent of a miniature poodle baiting a Doberman. I had no problem in bowling what the Windies refer to as 'chin music' to their pace brigade of Courtney Walsh, Curtly Ambrose and the Benjamin brothers Winston and Kenny, because I thought they needed to be unsettled. Also, my mission to take the fight to them was meant to be. After all, when I was a kid, that was what I'd committed myself to doing for Australia if my dream to have a crack at the Windies was ever realised— and 1995 was my chance. It only took a few deliveries when I was on strike for me to realise that none of them liked to dance to the short and sharp stuff I'd served back to them in the opening Test in Barbados. I can vividly recall Walsh, someone I regard as one of the truly great bowlers, trying hard to give the impression it didn't bother him because he'd laugh, shrug his shoulders and try to look cool and collected after having yet another bouncer whistle past his chin. However, his eyes betrayed him. I could see he didn't much enjoy being on the receiving end of what he'd subjected batsmen to regardless of their competence, and that inspired me to keep going.

Mark Taylor welcomed my aggression. He figured it sent the message to the West Indies that on this particular occasion Australia would be competing in front of the eight ball for a change, and I like to think the team lifted with that. Obviously I knew there'd be retribution—*of course I realised that*—but I also knew from watching the Windies pace attack on the television during my childhood that it didn't matter how anyone bowled to them, you could've underarmed a ball to them back in the day and they'd still want to stick it to you. I was committed to rattling them, however there were plenty of people who feared for my safety and I was to learn upon my return to Narromine that my poor grandma, Vera, was petrified the Windies were going to leave me battered and bruised as part of their square up. I never dwelled on that, because I realised if I allowed the thought of what I might receive preoccupy my mind it would have been terrifying! However, I vowed to myself that come what may, when I was called upon to bat I'd keep my nerve. Rodney Hogg, the former Australian bowler who is now an accomplished after-dinner speaker, tells a great story of when he played against the West Indies in the eighties. Thinking he was about to be hit by a Michael Holding beamer, Hogg half-turned his back, but it was actually a slower delivery, which hit his pads and he heard the ball brush off them and rattle his stumps. After he was dismissed, the first thing 'Hoggy' said he did when he reached the safety of the dressing room was phone his wife and ask her to erase the videotape of the game because he didn't want his son to grow up thinking his father was a coward. I was prepared to wear a few bruises to save myself from such an indignity. I'd heard stories, too, of how Merv Hughes, who scored 72 in a Test against the West Indies in 1989, would go missing when he thought Allan Border may have been considering him to bat as a nightwatchman. That was never me (although, I guess that was never going to happen). However, I know some of my teammates, Steve Waugh was among them, thought there was a lot of bravado in the way I walked to the crease, but hand on heart I can honestly say my only fear whenever I took strike during that series—and every series that followed—was of being embarrassed by my struggles with the bat. During the early days of that tour I quite foolishly tried to prove to the West Indies that I wasn't scared of them by not wearing extra armour, such as an armguard or a chest pad. Upon reflection that was a silly, ego-driven reaction. I think it may have been Tubby Taylor or perhaps our coach, Bobby Simpson, who pointed out that I'd be of no value to the team if I was sidelined with busted ribs or a broken arm. It was a valid point, so from that moment on I strapped on as much gear as I possibly could when it was my turn to bat.

Nevertheless, I gained an enormous amount of inspiration from watching blokes such as Steve refuse to back down from the pace and intimidation Ambrose and Walsh rained down upon him. I tried to emulate his . . . well, if not his actions with the bat, then at least his defiant body language, when it was my turn to face the music. When I was sent out to bat in the Fourth Test of that series—and I was yet again welcomed with calls from the members of their pace attack urging whoever had the ball in hand to 'kill him'—Steve was on 197, and his body showed just how much he'd suffered for each of those runs. His wrist was bruised, the elbow of his right arm was red and throbbing like an ambulance siren after he was struck there, a couple of his fingers were smashed by a short-pitched delivery, and other parts of his body were tenderised after being peppered by the Windies' brothers-in-harm, who I think were hell-bent on proving that particular day why they were called a pace *battery*.

I had only one intention as I marched from the pavilion towards the crease, and that was that I wouldn't let my mate down when he was so close to a double century. I would not get out to a soft dismissal; I would not throw my wicket away; I would instead dig in, stand my ground and not back away from the ball. It was all rip-roaring stuff and while I was summoning as much courage and determination as I possibly could from deep within me, I was to learn later that the ever-pragmatic Steve was already consoling himself, as he stood up the other end of the pitch, that 197 not out in Jamaica wasn't a bad knock!

I can vividly recall one of the many things I realised that day—based on the speed in which the ball dangerously zipped past my nose in a blur of red—was that I hadn't made myself too popular with our hosts. But I'm proud to say that despite the bombardment, I stuck to my guns and helped to 'nurse' Steve along the way to becoming only the fourth Australian, behind Neil Harvey, Bob Simpson and Bill Lawry, to score 200 in the Caribbean. When he was dismissed for his 200, caught Lara bowled Kenny Benjamin, he left me stranded on three. By the end of the tour my scores when tabled together could've been confused for the postcode in a suburb of Mumbai because they read 4, 0, 0, 0*, 3*. However, we became the first Australian team since 1973 to win the trophy in the West Indies' backyard, and I worked just as hard to make each of those seven runs (at an average of 2.33) as I did for each of the 17 wickets I took during the series.

COACH WAUGH

As I said, Steve 'Tugger' Waugh is a logical bloke— pragmatic was the word I used—and I guess it was because he realised there could be more occasions when we'd be forced to face the music together, caused by such things as a batting collapse, that he decided to appoint himself as my batting coach. He said my biggest problem was I looked like a batsman until I had to play a shot. He was adamant it was simply a matter of getting the basics right—I was told the same about dancing—and the first thing we attacked was my defensive technique. To help get my arms working in unison, he'd use the phrase 'rock the baby' to illustrate how to play a straight bat. Every time I dropped my left arm he'd yell 'You dropped the baby'. Steve stuck with me for a lot longer than most other coaches would have, but eventually even he'd had enough and found more important things to do, such as sorting out his sock drawer. His parting words of advice were to go to the bat manufacturers and hit them up for money in return for promising I wouldn't use their bats, but I think such an approach could have been interpreted in court as blackmail.

However, I'd like to think that Tugger would admit after all of these years that his efforts weren't in vain, because I did improve over the years. My crowning moment towards the end of my career was when I mastered the slog sweep and hung in long enough on quite a few occasions to help a few of my teammates—Steve included—get to their hundreds. And, I'm pleased to say his exercise aimed at getting my arms moving in unison certainly paid off when James and Holly were born because, mate, I never dropped the baby . . .

HEARTBREAK AT THE SCG

One of the most disappointing efforts of my career remains the Second Test against South Africa at the SCG during the 1994–95 summer, when all that stood between a gritty Australian victory and devastating defeat was their bowler Fanie de Villiers, a few lousy runs and . . . yours truly. When I was sent out I planned to dig in, but when the moment came the best I offered was flimsy opposition with a little defensive push straight back to de Villiers. What cut deeply as I made the long walk back to the dressing room was that while I could always accept being dismissed by a good ball, I had fallen to a regulation delivery on that particular occasion; caught and bowled for one run after Australia was set what seemed an easy enough target of 117 to win.

We collapsed, and while my teammates tried to console me in the aftermath of it by saying such things as 'It shouldn't have been left up to you', I vividly recall the way I felt as I walked past the Members. It was sickening. I felt as though I'd let Australia down. I thought it was a disaster at the time, but as I've grown older and witnessed genuine tragedy, I realise that the disappointment I felt that afternoon was far from the end of the world.

STRUCK BY THE BUZZARD

I returned from the 1996 World Cup unscathed but I was rocked by a delivery I copped in grade cricket for Sutherland upon our return.

I'm asked if I ever feared for my safety and the answer is no, never. I've told the tale before that the only time I was given a chance to bat higher in the order for the Backwater XI was because none of the others were overly keen to face a pace demon from the Trangie Cricket Club. I got out cheaply, dismissed by a good ball, but the point is that I wasn't worried about facing up to a fast bowler. I always trusted my reflexes to keep me out of harm's way. I watched the ball and, while I copped a few on the gloves and one or two on the body, I think the reason I never got too badly hurt was because I didn't play hook or pull shots all that often (if ever). I took heed of the screen character Dirty Harry's advice that 'A man's got to know his limitations'—and I knew them. I found that on the occasions when I was struck by the ball it didn't hurt straight away. I figured the adrenaline of the moment masked the pain, but I *always* felt it later on.

The worst hit I took was a ball that got me square on the helmet, delivered by my old NSW teammate Brad 'Buzzard' McNamara during a Sydney grade cricket semi-final at Bankstown Oval in the 1995–96 season, and it rattled me. I was sent in a bit higher up the order for Sutherland—I always maintained batting at No. 11 for Australia meant I should bat at No. 6 in grade, but that never washed with my skipper—and I was cruising on five or six runs when I watched our No. 11, Stuart Clark, who in the years to follow would open the bowling for Australia, make the long march out to the centre. Stuart told me we only needed five runs to win and secure our place in the grand final, and with that I managed to hit the next ball over the top. However, any hope of it racing to the boundary was ruined by the long grass in the outfield and when we realised it wasn't going to make it, we stretched out and ran a quick three. As a result I found myself on strike for the first ball of the next over and I watched as Buzzard steamed in, his legs pumping like pistons. He attempted to bowl a yorker but it went terribly wrong and ended up a beam ball, hurtling at pace towards my head. The only defensive action I could take at that last split second was to turn my head—it was instinctive and went against everything the textbook advises you to do—and when the ball crashed into my helmet the thud was dreadful and I was certain that in one way or another I'd been harmed by it. I ripped my helmet off, expecting to find I'd been injured but rather than a ringing in my ears I heard instead wild cheering from my teammates, because a no-ball was worth two runs in grade cricket and Brad was penalised for bowling a dangerous delivery above the waist on the full. It was enough to give us the victory and allowed Sutherland to push on and win the title.

24 OF THE BEST

I was becoming the pin-up boy for the Primary Club of Australia, a club that's been about since 1974 and raises money for charity when Members who are dismissed for a golden duck make a donation. The club's purpose is to allow anyone with a disability the chance to experience what they call the joy and exhilaration that comes from taking part in any form of physical activity, so it's a worthy cause. However, I did manage to enjoy what I'd describe as my first real taste of batting success at Test level at the SCG Test during the 1996–97 series against my old sparring buddies, the Windies. I was motivated by one of my teammates—it was probably 'coach' Tugger—who cut out a newspaper article about my batting and pinned it to the spot where I prepared for the game, and let's just say I wasn't overly impressed. When the time came for me to bat, I was determined to do something.

At lunch I was unconquered on 20 and it felt funny, but good at the same time, to receive a standing ovation by the Members as I walked back towards the dressing room. Judging by their carry-on you'd have sworn I just made a ton. I lasted 57 minutes at the crease that innings and, as you would imagine, I savoured each minute.

HELPING HUSSEY

Australia was in dire straits when I joined Mike Hussey out in the middle during the MCG Boxing Day Test against South Africa in 2005. We were 9–248 and we needed to stay at the crease for as long as we could and to score as many runs as possible to set the visitors a 'chase'. 'Huss' had devised a plan where he'd stay on strike for as long as he could, and it worked. I was up the other end when what had started for Mike as a shaky knock became an innings of flowing elegance after he reached 50. When he was on 97, 'Huss' did something I don't think many batsmen would've done because they'd have been hell-bent on getting their hundred—he took the single. I well remember that, when he took the run, the South African keeper Mark Boucher yelled something like 'What have you done?', but I backed his faith, digging out one of the 56 balls I'd face during my two hours in the firing line. Huss batted for over four hours to score a gutsy 122, and we both entered the Australian record books for our 107-run 10-wicket stand. I scored 11 not out and I remember that while I felt exhausted out there,

I also felt a sense of satisfaction in knowing the longer I was at the crease the more the South Africans would be frustrated.

THE MILESTONE

Mark Waugh had a long-running bet with Shane Warne that I would never score a first-class half-century, and when I hit 55 in English County cricket he found a reason not to honour it (although he ended up donating the sum to the McGrath Foundation). Rather than pin up in my cubicle articles about my batting to fire me up—like someone had done that day against the West Indies at the SCG in 1997— the boys had started to use the sight of me going out to bat as their sign to put their whites on; just as they did that November day in 2004 when I faced New Zealand at the Gabba . . .

The day had started strangely; I was in the swimming pool doing my usual preparation for the day, laps, when Jason Gillespie, Michael Clarke and Adam Gilchrist joined me, because the three of them wanted to stretch. That was unusual because I was normally in the pool on my own. While we were in the water, two ducks flew over the wall and landed in the pool with us—and yes, this is all true— and that was a bit unnerving because no cricketer wants to get too close to ducks on the day of a Test. They're a bad omen. When Matthew Hayden opened for Australia and Queensland, he wouldn't even allow his kids to have rubber duckies in the bath; but here we were, on the day of a Test, splashing water and trying to shoo the ducks off but they wouldn't budge. They just looked at us as if we were madmen. The four of us were worried that the birds were a sign that we wouldn't score a run between us, and we went back to our rooms to collect our gear, cursing the two unwelcome guests who had darkened our doorstep.

The game was deep into the middle session of day three when Shane Warne was dismissed for ten. His was the eighth wicket to fall and that eighth wicket was my signal to get ready. I put my creams on, I kitted up in my protective gear, and when the ninth wicket fell I put my helmet on, only to see Adam Gilchrist dressed in his creams and in the throes of taping up his fingers; he was already getting ready to field! As I walked out to do my best for the team I grumbled, 'Thanks for the vote of confidence, *mate*!' Then, after I'd made it to the middle, I looked towards the players' viewing area at the Gabba—it's hard to miss because it's in the middle of the stand—and there wasn't a teammate to be seen . . . I realised they were all getting ready to field by now. With no support I took centre, walked down the pitch and tapped my bat on certain spots, because that was what I had seen batsmen do. I proceeded to hit a few balls in the middle and it felt good. When I reached 11—as 11 was my playing number it was also my lucky number—I enjoyed some good fortune (for a change as a batsman) when Brendon McCullum dropped me and Mark Richardson spilled the very next ball. I made the most of my chance by hitting a few boundaries and I noticed with each run I scored, more of my teammates sat in the viewing area to watch. As I neared the half-century mark their cheers became louder and wilder.

I scored 61 that day and there were some people who called it a fluke; they said I was lucky, but what those people didn't realise was in the two months that led up to that match, I was sidelined by some spurs on my ankle from overbowling. They grew so large along my tendons that I needed surgery. The doctor removed one but decided to leave the other two, and when I returned to training the extra movement I had in my ankle caused one of the spurs to snap off, which meant a lengthy time away from playing. While I recovered I faced the bowling machine at the SCG nets and that meant, instead of facing a couple of hundred deliveries in an entire year as a member of the team, I faced 500 a week! It was amazing and, as you'd expect, I improved as a result of the extra work. My career high score of 61 against the Kiwis that day was the first innings after all of my hard work, and I was pumped. When I returned to the rooms I pointed out to Ricky that my Test batting average was six, and for me to go out and score 61 was akin to him, a great batsman who boasted an average of 50, hitting 500! He just shook his head.

While I was far from a great batsman, some of my time at the crease—like that knock against the Kiwis—provided me with some of my career's proudest moments. Oh, and there's an interesting twist to the story about those two ducks that spooked Michael Clarke, Adam Gilchrist, Jason Gillespie and me when they decided to have a swim with us. They turned out to be more of a blessing than a curse because in that Test I hit the half-century that forced Mark Waugh to part with his cash; Pup finished with 141, Gilly 126 and 'Dizzy' Gillespie was so excited to hit a half-century he stole a scene from the Adam Sandler movie *Happy Gilmore* and rode his bat up and down the pitch like he was on a horse. It was apparently a celebration Dizzy had promised his mates in Adelaide he'd do if he ever scored a Test 50 and it was memorable! I had big raps on Pakistan's Wasim Akram as a bowler-batsman but I always had a high opinion of Dizzy's ability as a tail-ender. While Dizzy lacked the array of shots needed to be considered an all-rounder—although he scored 201 not out a few years later against Bangladesh when he was sent in as a nightwatchman—he had a tremendous defence and it allowed him to score runs.

Whenever the team returned to that hotel for future matches, I always hoped when I went down to the swimming pool to do my laps that my feathered friends would join me for a dip. Sadly, just like the excitement that came from my half-century, that's turned out to be a once-in-a-lifetime visit.

THE END

By the time my final Test came, my batting kit was a rag-tag mess. I had one-and-a-half pairs of gloves—I lost one somewhere along my trails and didn't bother to replace it—my pads were well worn and my one bat—some guys have half a dozen—looked as though it would be more useful as firewood. I'd scored 641 runs from 138 innings. I remained not out on 51 occasions, I averaged 7.36 and my strike rate was 40.82. And those stats ran through my mind in my fare-well Test, when Ricky Ponting asked if I wanted to bat at No. 3. I thought better of it and said that unless I opened, I'd remain at No. 11.

20

TEN MAGIC
MOMENTS

The starting point of all achievement is desire.

—Napoleon Hill, US author

Before writing this book, I had never tried to pinpoint my ten best moments but I figure it is worthwhile to document them because they help reinforce my message that if you have self-belief and confidence, if you're willing to make sacrifices and stay true to your goal, then there is a good chance your hard work and determination will be rewarded.

I was blessed because I enjoyed more than my fair share of magic moments in cricket and to whittle them down to ten was a tough process. I needed to be brutal towards some fond memories to brush them aside in some instances. The starting point of these achievements was when I was a kid watching the Aussies get pummelled summer after summer by the West Indies, because I had the audacity to think that perhaps I could be the bloke who helped Australia turn the tide to become the world's best team.

Other people devoted their energies to becoming doctors or scientists or farmers, but for whatever reason, the thought of me opening the bowling for my country was what stuck in my head. As I've pointed out, that dream was challenged on quite a few occasions and there was also a lot of hurt along the way that came from being overlooked for teams. I'm sure that, unlike me, the great Dennis Lillee didn't spend his first few years as a cricketer fielding in the deep among the cockatoos and galahs, waiting . . . praying . . . for the ball to be tossed to him.

I used to roll my arms over and over again, but I think rather than pick up on my signal that I wanted to bowl, my old Backwater XI skipper must've thought I was pretending to be an out-of-control windmill, because I never got the ball. At the end of the day's play I returned home and, dressed in my whites, I found myself back behind the machinery shed setting my imaginary fields. Now that I think of it, the idea that it was me against the world back then wasn't all that far off the mark.

You also need to help yourself. I joined the Rugby Union XI, and I remember having a chat with Brian Gainsford who was a highly respected country cricketer and whose daughter Melinda represented Australia at the Olympics and

Commonwealth Games as a sprinter. I was 17 when we sat down and had a yarn one day after a game. It was at a time people were telling me I should play basketball—I'd played in a few representative basketball and tennis teams—but cricket was the game I was most devoted to.

Brian put everything into perspective. He said the camaraderie cricket produced was worthwhile, but he added that while I had all the requirements needed to become a fast bowler, at that stage of my life my bowling was a bit erratic. He told me all I really needed was time and patience. That conversation was very important and it renewed my push to prove myself as a bowler. Brian selected me to play for Dubbo in the Country Cup match that included Doug Walters, Mark Taylor, Greg Matthews and Mark Waugh, and by doing so put me on my path towards playing for Australia.

While these ten moments are my personal highlights, it's important to note that without the commitment, and in some cases the courage, of the blokes who I played alongside during those 14 years, much of what appears below would never have happened. I thank them. However, I hope while you read my moments, you can recognise that each of these highlights stems back to the time I was a kid on a sheep and wheat farm 500 kilometres away from Sydney, realising that if I was going to dream, it wouldn't cost anyone any extra for me to dream big . . .

1. TEST DEBUT VS NEW ZEALAND AT THE WACA (1993)

*I think he deserved his selection. He has a fantastic line,
he's fit, he's angry and his selection was fairly predictable
from where we stood. He's got a bit of Sir Richard Hadlee
about him . . .*

—NEW ZEALAND CAPTAIN, MARTIN CROWE

It seems a lifetime ago but this match was my dream
come true. I was given my spurs much quicker than I could
ever have imagined when, after playing in only six first-
class matches, I was picked because Merv Hughes, Jo
Angel and Bruce Reid were injured. The other bowlers the
selectors had in mind also didn't perform as well as they
wanted them to in the Sheffield Shield matches leading into
the Test.

I remember how my Sutherland and NSW coach Steve
'Stumper' Rixon treated the push for me to be named in the
Test with some caution. Stumper described the call from the
media as premature and he let them know it. I remember
how he suggested I should be left to play another three or
four games for New South Wales before being thrown into
the deep end of the pool that is Test cricket. I was fortunate
because in the lead-up to the First Test in Perth, I was given
two shots at the Kiwis. I was given a crack at them for the
Australian Institute of Sport XI and took 1–21 from my eight
overs. When I played for New South Wales in Newcastle
I took 2–30 from 15 overs, and one of my wickets was

the mainstay of the New Zealand line-up, Martin Crowe. I bagged his wicket thanks to Michael Slater, who caught Crowe when he was on 15. The journalists at that game noted that I had good control over the ball; one reporter wrote I could land it on a five-cent piece, which I treated as a vote of confidence.

There were a few people saying I would get the nod, because the most likely candidates were injured. However, I refused to get caught up in the hype because I thought if I dared to believe what was being written and said, it would only lead to a terrible disappointment if I missed out, so I treated it as a case of 'whatever happens, happens'.

I was sharing a unit with Phil Alley when the first of the phone calls came through to congratulate me, and our place must've looked like a nightclub when the Channel Nine news crew arrived to do an interview. The footage that appeared on television that night showed me having a celebratory sip of beer while the Queen song 'Another One Bites the Dust' was booming in the background—that was clearly Phil's music choice.

I was quietly confident I could do the job for Australia because I'd already played against the Kiwis and had held my own. My attitude allowed me to really enjoy the experience.

Mark Greatbatch became my first Test wicket when I bowled a delivery that was a little bit short of a length, and when it went ever so slightly away from him he edged it through to Ian Healy. I remember thinking as he left the field that no matter what happened from that moment on, no one could take my first Test wicket away from me.

By the end of the (drawn) Test my match figures were 3–142, and more importantly I realised playing international cricket wasn't beyond me.

2. 500TH TEST WICKET AT LORD'S (2005)

I'm a failure. I tried to make a farmer out of my son and he became a great cricketer.

—KEVIN McGRATH AFTER HIS ELDEST SON TOOK HIS
500TH WICKET

Halfway through my career, I sat down and set myself a goal. I decided the *minimum* number of wickets I wanted to finish Test cricket with was 500, but the circumstances in which I fulfilled that goal—at Lord's of all places and during the opening Test of an Ashes tour—is what I still consider the closest thing possible to a cricketer's fairytale. It was enhanced by having Jane and the kids, my mother, father and manager and good mate Warren Craig there to celebrate the day I became the first fast bowler in Test-cricket history to take 500 wickets.

I finished the previous Test series against the Kiwis at Eden Park on 499 wickets and despite what some people suggested at the time, I wasn't keeping the 'big one' for Lord's because of the perceived prestige and memorabilia opportunities. I worked hard to try and get one of the last three

New Zealand batsmen out in that Test in Auckland, because you don't know what will happen in life and there was no guarantee I'd go on the tour to Lord's. I could've injured myself or some other circumstance could've prevented me from playing, so I was keen to reach the milestone as soon as I could, but as hard as I tried, I was forced to wait a few months.

The London bookies established English opener Marcus Trescothick as the red-hot favourite to become my 500th wicket, and they were paying $3.30 when he nicked the ball and I watched on excitedly as the delivery flew to Justin Langer at fourth slip. I held the ball aloft, like a batsman does his bat when he reaches a century, to acknowledge the generous applause from the English crowd. It was pleasing to have my family there, because the greatest sacrifice I made throughout my career wasn't the training or even those times when I played with an injury. It was the amount of time I lost not being with them.

A lot of people have asked if I dread the day when someone will take the record from me, but I don't. It's there to be taken, and I'd like to think I'll congratulate the bowler who takes it from me with the same good grace as Courtney Walsh when I overtook him. Fast bowlers know what it takes to do the job and it can involve a lot of pain, a lot of frustration and hurt. I am in possession of the record but I'm not possessive of it . . .

3. FINAL TEST AT THE SCG (2007)

What a fairytale finish!

—PRIME MINISTER JOHN HOWARD CELEBRATING
MY LAST WICKET

Shane Warne, Justin Langer and I had announced we would be retiring after the final Test of the 2006–07 Ashes series and I felt very fortunate that fate allowed me to bow out at my home ground in front of my family and friends so they could share in what I'll always remember as five emotion-charged days.

Ricky Ponting allowed me to lead the team onto the ground and that was a huge honour—I don't think I ever felt prouder as a cricketer. I saw what it meant to Shane Warne when he did it in Melbourne for the Boxing Day Test and it was quite moving. I'm grateful Rick granted me the honour. The crowd was incredible—including some of my old sparring partners in the Barmy Army—and their reaction helped to turn it into a treasured event for all of us, including our coach John Buchanan, who was also stepping away from his role with the team.

Something I liked about the way we approached that Test as a team was that it was business as usual. Coach Buchanan attacked England's most dangerous batsman, Kevin Pietersen, by saying he was a 'selfish player', and a few of us saw that as his way to keep us switched on to the job. My approach to the game was always to leave nothing on the field and despite the emotion of that farewell Test, there was no danger I was going to change tack.

On a personal level, I still can't believe I took Jimmy Anderson's wicket with my last ball in Test cricket . . . that's what I call a cricket blessing, and the result of a generous skipper, because Rick told Warnie and me to bowl in tandem when England lost its ninth wicket. After a few close calls I decided to bowl around the wicket to Anderson. I used the final ball of my over to bowl a slower delivery, which he scooped to the safe hands of Mike Hussey. It ignited an explosion of emotion, and for all I know I was walking on air as I trooped around the SCG hand in hand with Holly and James to savour the moment.

I was happy on quite a few fronts that afternoon—we'd won the match and the Ashes back; I took that last wicket; I'd been a part of a great era of Australian cricket; but I was especially pleased that James and Holly were old enough to realise what was happening, because it's become a memory for them.

4. 8–38 VS ENGLAND AT LORD'S (1997)

I still think you couldn't bowl back then!

—FAX SENT BY MY FIRST CAPTAIN, SHANE HORSBOROUGH, WHO DIDN'T GIVE ME A BOWL FOR THE BACKWATER XI

Playing cricket at Lord's is a unique experience, there's no place like it anywhere else in the world because it's steeped in tradition and that inspires you to think of the Ashes greats who've played there: W.G. Grace, Monty Noble, Fred

Spofforth, Jack Hobbs, Harold Larwood. It's very special and while I felt the same reverence as you do walking into a church, I think that feeling extends to the spectators in the outer ground. At every other venue in world cricket there's a cacophony of noise when a bowler runs in for the first delivery, but at Lord's the silence is deafening, and it shocked me. I recall how the hairs stood up on the back of my neck and they tingled as I took a big breath before launching into my run-up. I actually went to Lord's the day before I played my first game there, because I didn't want to get overwhelmed by the atmosphere or the history of the place while I was playing. I took my time, looked at the ground, sat down and got lost in the experience of it all, and I have no doubt that doing this helped calm my nerves when I was eventually tossed the ball.

When I saw the honour boards in the visitor's dressing room during that first visit, I wanted my name to join the first Aussie—a spin bowler named George Eugene Palmer who took 6–111 in the inaugural Test in 1884—on the bowler's board. Like me, Palmer was the team's pest who drove his teammates crazy with his practical jokes, so there was a bond and maybe old George looked favourably upon me in that match because I couldn't do a thing wrong. I started my first Test spell at Lord's with three wickets for two runs—Mark Butcher, Mike Atherton and Alec Stewart all fell cheaply from my opening 13 balls—and I remember thinking if ever there was a bowler's paradise, Lord's fitted the bill that particular day.

I made it a point to stay in control of my emotions, because I realised there was no need to do anything except plug away, and I was benefiting from the English batsmen. It was incredible. I remember poor old Alec Stewart letting the ball go but it came back at him from up the slope and he was clean-bowled. The stars had seemingly aligned for me over London that day and I made the most of it. At the end of their innings, when I dismissed Andy Caddick lbw and England was routed for 77, our coach Geoff Marsh wrote my name and 8–38 on a piece of masking tape and stuck it to the board. I savoured the moment as I walked back towards the dressing room. I waved to Mum and Jane and I was surprised when I saw the then prime minister John Howard give me the thumbs up . . . it wasn't a bad day at the office!

As you'd expect, the statisticians noted England's total was the lowest recorded by an English team in the 20th century; it was their second-lowest since the end of World War II and the 13th lowest Test score since 1877. My 8–38 was the best by an Australian bowler, eclipsing the 8–84 Bob Massie took in 1972, and it was the third-best innings haul by an Aussie against the old enemy since Arthur Mailey took 9–121 in 1920–21 and Frank Laver's 8–31 at The Oval in 1909.

Lord's was always kind to me because in the three Tests I played there, I was named Man of the Match on each occasion. However, when I think about that first match, when nothing could go wrong, I still can't help but shake my head and ask myself whether it really happened.

I remember reading once that the Australian political figure Doc Evatt, who was the only Australian president of the General Assembly of the United Nations, wrote that Australians would be prepared to go to war to defend that 22 yards at Lord's, and while I wouldn't quite endorse that sentiment, I certainly loved the place.

5. FIRST FIVE-WICKET HAUL, BARBADOS (1995)

The greatest dynasty world cricket has known is on the verge of collapse thanks to a bold young Australian who dared to put the wind up the Windies.

—ROBERT CRADDOCK, *THE DAILY TELEGRAPH-MIRROR*

Australia started the tour of the West Indies on the back foot when our attack's spearheads, Craig McDermott and Damien Fleming, were sent home with injuries. While I'd played in a few Tests, I was suddenly presented with an opportunity to prove myself and I lapped it up because I wanted to earn my stripes. It's worth noting that injuries had provided me with all my opportunities. When I joined Sutherland I was earmarked for third grade but was picked for the second-grade team that went on a tour of the South Coast; I received my baggy green cap to play against the Kiwis because the 'go to' bowlers were all injured; and in the Caribbean, unfortunate circumstances—McDermott injured himself jumping off a wall and Fleming hurt his shoulder—meant they had to return to Australia.

I was used as the second-change bowler in the opening Test of the series in Barbados. I targeted the Windies pacemen with the short stuff they liked to serve and they made it clear it wasn't appreciated. Mark Taylor and Steve Waugh devised the plan to hook into their bowlers when they had to bat and I respected the fact that it had Waugh's fingerprints over it, because before his back gave way and stopped him from bowling his medium-pacers, I don't think any bowler in international cricket bowled as many bouncers as he did at the West Indies. I viewed what he did as gutsy and I didn't need much prompting to agree to do what I could to not only unsettle them, but take their wickets.

That style of bowling didn't win me too many fans among the Windies line-up, but I did finish the second innings with 5–68 and Australia won the Test. I felt as though I'd broken through as a fast bowler and had genuinely contributed to the team. I grew in confidence after that and I never looked back. The Windies made a point of letting me know they didn't think too much of me, because they'd yell 'Kill him, man' when I took strike, but that wasn't enough to faze me. I took strength from the scenes in Jamaica from the Aussie supporters in the crowd chanting *'Ooh aah, Glenn McGrath'*— it was the first time I'd received that kind of attention. It really surprised me and I remember thinking it'd be special to help win the Frank Worrell Trophy for those people in the outer who were waving their Australian flags and supporting us. It was a wonderful experience, my coming of age as a Test bowler, and by the end of the series we became the first

Aussie team to bring the trophy home from the Caribbean since Ian Chappell's team in 1973.

While that tour signalled the demise of the West Indies as cricket's greatest superpower of the time, it was the beginning of Australia's ascent to the top of the mountain.

6. 61 VS NEW ZEALAND AT THE GABBA (2004)

It gave us a lot of momentum and a lot of energy to go out and play well for the rest of the game.

—AUSTRALIAN SKIPPER RICKY PONTING ON THE PARTNERSHIP BETWEEN ME AND JASON GILLESPIE

I always dreamt of scoring a Test 50—and a century, for that matter—but there were times when I wondered whether I could even get close because in order of strengths my bowling came first, my fielding was second and batting, well, batting came a distant third. That's not to say I didn't try, because I fought hard to keep my wicket. I never backed away from the ball regardless of who bowled it, and I also dug in to help a lot of great batsmen, such as Steve Waugh and Mike Hussey, to their hundreds. However, the day I joined Jason Gillespie at the crease in Brisbane proved that every dog has its day, because before the match I copped a bit of stick from the boys for taking almost as many Test wickets (454) as I'd scored Test runs (477). I wasn't too impressed. He gave me a purpose, if not a point to prove. A highlight of my knock was tonking the great Kiwi spin bowler

Daniel Vettori for six because apart from being the only one I ever struck in Test cricket, it also brought up my 500th Test run.

Something I loved about the knock was the fact I could see how much my team were enjoying it! They were cheering and hollering—laughing—at what was happening. However, in the context of the Test, Rick would later say the last wicket partnership between Dizzy and me was important because he said it 'was the straw that broke the camel's back'.

People have asked me since that knock whether I valued that 50 more than a five-wicket haul, and sometimes I come close to saying 'yes' because I saw it as a great reward for hard work. As you could probably imagine, I didn't mind letting three great blokes—Ricky Ponting (51), Justin Langer (34) and current national coach Darren Lehmann (8)— know that I'd scored more runs than them that day, but I guess history—and the stats sheet—notes all three had the last laugh!

7. THE CATCH VS ENGLAND AT ADELAIDE OVAL (2002)

It was a miracle, we weren't expecting him to catch it.

—AUSTRALIAN SKIPPER STEVE WAUGH

I loved Channel Nine's classic catch segment when I was growing up, because it left you wondering how on earth a fieldsman was able to take what should've been an impossible catch. The best one I remember was John Dyson's screamer in 1982 against the Windies when he ran backwards in the deep at the SCG and took it like a soccer goalkeeper.

I used to dive for classic catches when I was a kid on holidays; I'd get someone to throw me the tennis ball as I dived into the swimming pool and it was always a lot of good fun. Almost as much fun for me as that day in Adelaide when Michael Vaughan slogged Shane Warne out in the deep and I found myself running as fast as I possibly could.

I doubt whether too many people watching the chase gave me any chance of taking it, and even though the ball seemed to hang in the air for quite a while I realised I'd need to dive to have any hope of adding another wicket to Warnie's tally. It turned out to be a leap of faith because when I dived, the ball not only deflected off my left hand and into my right but I was amazed the ball actually stuck when I crashed onto the ground.

The catch was only a small part of what ended up as a great victory for us. It meant we'd won 10 of our past 11 Tests and it allowed Steve to be just one win off matching Allan Border's record 32 victories as the nation's Test captain. I've been asked if I had any concern about injuring myself, but that's really the last thing that comes into your mind. Most times you don't need to dive for a catch, but on that particular day it was the only hope I had. However, to be able to pick yourself up off the ground, throw the ball in the air and celebrate with your arms raised in triumph is a dream come true that I reckon any kid who watched the old classic catches or dived for a tennis ball while jumping into the pool would relate to.

8. 8–24 VS PAKISTAN AT THE WACA (2004)

The conditions are suited to fast bowlers, but McGrath was great . . . a match-winner.

—AUSTRALIAN SKIPPER RICKY PONTING IN THE POST-MATCH PRESS CONFERENCE

My goal was to always bowl the perfect match and I think I achieved it in this match; a game where the famous Fremantle Doctor—the cooling afternoon wind that blows through Perth from off the ocean—came in from a slightly different direction, which helped because when I ran in at a slightly wider angle it swung the ball a little bit.

I seemed to have total control and the funny thing is, before play started I had a premonition that *something* special was going to happen. It happened when I was asked by the director of the Save the Rhino foundation if they could have the ball from the Test to auction at a fundraising dinner. I've been a long-time supporter of the foundation because they fight for a cause I truly believe in. I became captivated by the rhino when I toured South Africa with the Cricket Academy squad in 1992. They struck me as being noble animals, and when I heard the aim of the foundation was to preserve them, I threw my support behind it because the guys who run it don't get any handouts from the government. They fight for every dollar, so throughout my career I didn't mind giving them some of my memorabilia and gear to auction off.

At first I said it wouldn't be a problem to donate the match ball from this Test, but as I started to walk away something told me I'd probably want to keep it because, for some reason, I felt that ball would mean a lot to me. The only other time I had that feeling was when I took 8–38 against England at Lord's six years earlier . . . and while it would've been nice to have woken with that feeling a few more times during my career, I certainly made hay when the sun shone! I bowled 16 overs as Pakistan was skittled for 72 and it was gobsmacking how easily the wickets fell—at one stage it appeared as though I might take all 10 wickets, but Michael Kasprowicz denied me that when he bundled out their No. 8, Mohammad Sami, in his opening over.

What added to the achievement was that the WACA was a ground where I usually struggled for success, despite it having a reputation as a fast-bowler's nirvana. On that particular day, with the Fremantle Doctor working its magic, there wasn't anywhere else I would have wanted to be.

9. 1995 TOUR OF WEST INDIES & 2004 TOUR OF INDIA

*If the question has been asked once it's been asked a
thousand times. Just who will take over from McDermott?
On the evidence tendered in the Caribbean in recent weeks
this is no longer an issue. McGrath has come of age.*

—MIKE COWARD, *THE AUSTRALIAN*

I rank both series extremely highly because they were watershed moments for Australian cricket. In 1995, under Mark Taylor's captaincy, we became the first Australian team in 22 years to win a series in the Caribbean, and in 2004, under Ricky Ponting (and Adam Gilchrist, who filled in when Rick was injured), we became the first Australian team in 35 years to win a series in India. Due to the magnitude of those moments it should be no surprise that I'm proud to say I was involved in both campaigns.

The West Indies triumph was the beginning of a dominant era for Australian cricket and it was also an eye-opener for me because I realised if I wanted longevity as an international player I needed to do things differently. I weighed 77 kilograms and I realised I needed to put on 15–17 kilograms of muscle and train tough to become unbreakable. It also taught the Australian team a few things because after that tour we understood how to win, and we went from strength to strength and dominated world cricket for a long time.

To win in India was a highlight because the subcontinent was the last frontier for the boys. We almost did it in 2001, but unfortunately stumbled at the last hurdle. The victory in India proved we'd learnt to master all conditions and was a tribute to the team's practices.

10. WORLD CUP TOURNAMENT VICTORIES IN 1999, 2003 AND 2007

In the ensuing minutes, no-one could tell me that one-day cricket wasn't as important as Test cricket.
—STEVE WAUGH ON THE 1999 WORLD CUP VICTORY.

When I saw the Michael Clarke captained Australian team celebrate the nation's fifth World Cup victory in 2015, it amazed me to think that I'd also held that trophy aloft on three different occasions.

In 1999, after a slow start, we found ourselves in the position of needing to win *every* game to qualify for the final. Australia responded to this incredible pressure, and by the time we played Pakistan at Lord's we believed nothing was beyond us. In 2003 we handled the pressure to perform much better than our opponents, India, to take it out in South Africa. And in my final campaign for Australia in 2007, we never looked in danger of even losing a game in the lead–up to playing Sri Lanka in the final, when the Cup was staged in the West Indies.

We almost had a fourth Cup triumph during my time but we were defeated by a Sri Lankan team that played better than us and mastered the subcontinent's conditions. However, I think it was that loss that gave us the hunger to succeed at those subsequent World Cups.

I was proud of every World Cup campaign I played in, but the last one, when I was named Man of the Tournament, was ridiculous! That was a great honour and rather than making me feel as though I might want to play on, that acknowledgement made it easier for me to retire fulfilled. I'd done everything I could.

21

MY MENTORS

A student was given a mentoring opportunity, in the hope that when you had somebody to lean on you, you would begin to stand a little steadier yourself, and get manliness and thoughtfulness.

—Thomas Hughes, *Tom Brown's Schooldays*

I have read that mentoring is a trusted relationship and a meaningful commitment. As someone who has benefited from having many mentors throughout my life—people who have been generous in sharing their insights and knowledge—I believe that is a fair description of the special bond that can create the difference between a person making the grade or missing the cut. If you consult the textbooks, there are descriptions for the different types of mentors; they range from *the wise leader* who has reached the top of whatever their calling is; *the life coach* who is a professional mentor; *the teacher* who fosters learning and growth by sharing their knowledge; and *the confidante* who is a trusted sounding-board.

Over the years I have benefited from each of these types of mentors, sharing their hard-earned life experiences and invaluable insights. I've found there is a truth in the saying that suggests if you want to know how to get somewhere then go ask someone who has been there. As a cricketer I've been in a very fortunate position to be able to call upon a host of wise and proven performers such as Dennis Lillee, Rodney Marsh and Steve Rixon. If they didn't know the answers to my questions they found a way to answer them with a clear-headed logic. I was also very lucky as a child because I didn't need to look too far for heartfelt guidance and advice. My extended family lived close to one another and I gained a lot from Mum and Dad, my uncle Malc and my grandparents, and something that strikes me as being important all those years ago was that the adults in our family not only asked how things were going for me, but they also took the time to listen carefully to my answer. As the years have flown by it's dawned on me to appreciate how special that commitment was, and I try to show the same commitment to James and Holly.

Something I have also realised as I've grown older is that sometimes being a mentor means knowing when it's best to stay silent, and when to speak. It's easy to offer your thoughts and observations about every little thing, but sometimes the best way to allow a person to learn is by their own trial and error. In those cases I don't think it hurts a person to hit the ground—they learn from that—but it's the mentor's role in that situation to pick them up and help dust them off.

I have benefited from the involvement of so many wonderful and decent people and I figured a fitting way to finish this book would be to acknowledge the people who have had a big impact on my life. I wanted to also share the traits I have developed and admired, and strengths I have drawn from those relationships. We're all in a journey in life and I hope what I share might help make it a more enjoyable road for some people.

MUM AND DAD

My parents, Kevin and Bev, were hardworking people who brought me up to treat people how I would like to be treated, and to live with humility and respect. If you judge the success of your parents by how you remember your childhood then mine were world-beaters because I have only good memories of growing up on the farm. I loved everything about my upbringing, from always having fresh milk in the fridge from our cows, to our annual Christmas vacation at a caravan park at North Haven, near Port Macquarie, where the days at the beach seemed to go on forever. However, it wasn't an easy life, as I have mentioned. Anyone who knows anything about farming will tell you that it is one hard slog, with early morning starts that run well into the night. But it was from watching how hard Mum and Dad toiled that their three kids, Donna, Dale and I, had our work ethic instilled in us. In terms of life's lessons, with Mum and Dad it was definitely a case of 'following their lead'. I had no problem living their values because they were good and they were solid. However, I'm sure I can speak on behalf of Donna and Dale when I say their actions were what made us appreciate the importance of 'Do as I do', because they'd get up early for a long day's work to run the household. However, regardless of drought, frost, flood or even financial stress, they always found time for us, whether it was Mum driving me for miles to play cricket, tennis and basketball, or Dad talking about the day's events at the dinner table. And while I said we lived their values, they never forced them upon us; I think we three kids simply appreciated the way they lived—and accepted—life.

I'm a big believer in allowing James and Holly to make their own decisions (of course I watch them carefully), because I liked the fact that Mum and Dad never preached to us; they never demanded that we follow a certain path, be it in our education or sport or employment. They trusted us enough for us to make our own choices and when we did— such as my decision to relocate to Sydney to play grade cricket for Sutherland—they only offered support and encouragement. In an age where parents spoil their kids with gadgets and electronics, sometimes support and encouragement is all a child really needs and wants. I can't thank Mum and Dad enough for their guidance and love, because it mattered.

RODNEY MARSH

Rodney Marsh is remembered as one of cricket's great wicket-keepers and he also formed an incredible partnership with his fellow West Australian, Dennis Lillee, in Australia's Test team during the 1970s and '80s to take 95 Test dismissals between them. He finished his 14-year Test career with a record 355 dismissals, and my memories of watching him on the television were of an uncompromising keeper with great glove work and the acrobatic skills of an Olympic gymnast. While his place in Australian cricket is assured, he also had a massive impact on my career when we crossed paths during his days as head coach of the Australian Cricket Academy when it was based in Adelaide during the 1990s. He was a tough disciplinarian, a drill sergeant actually, and we heard stories about the lengths that Rod would take to reinforce that it was not a holiday camp, even though the Academy was based on the beach. One story was about a cadet who had a big night out; when Rod heard he'd decided to miss an early morning training session because he wanted to sleep in, Rod was said to have dragged the bloke to the beach— and I guess he would have to have been a batsman with that attitude—and made him run waist deep in the water in the middle of winter. Legend has it the boy stayed in the water until his lips turned blue. As for me, Rod could see that I thrived on the hard work and the environment at the Academy, and he took me under his wing. What I quickly realised about Rod was that if you were prepared to work hard, give it all you had, he respected you; however, if a player went down there with 'attitude', he shortened them up, hammered them.

I consider myself lucky to have come under Rod's guidance and I liked that everyone at the Academy had to have a job. When I asked why mine was doing repairs and gardening around the place, Rod explained it was due to simple logic. Rod figured that because I was from the country I'd be handy with tools! These days in my role as the head director of the MRF Pace Foundation I channel the basic fundamentals I learnt from Rod all those years ago: account-ability, punctuality, responsibility. But in saying that, we're men with different personalities. While I certainly deliver the message differently, I respect the impact he had on my career and the fact he's given so much back to the sport.

STEVE RIXON

Steve was like Rod in that he was another old-school-style wicketkeeper who had a big influence on my career. He took no nonsense and demanded discipline. While Steve played an important role in my move to Sydney from Narromine, I didn't have much to do with him until I made the NSW team and it was there that he reinforced Rod Marsh's belief that hard work was the foundation for success. Steve worked us and one of his favourite drills was to hit 'high balls'— catches that you have to sprint for. He did it until you couldn't run anymore; it was his way of toughening us up mentally and physically. There were many times when I took a catch in the outfield—like the one I took off Shane Warne's bowling in Adelaide in 2002, after running what seemed like 100 metres, to dismiss Michael Vaughan—and offered 'Stumper' a silent thanks for his torture sessions. Something I really liked about Steve was that in his successful stints as the coach of New South Wales he didn't care about reputations; if you were a member of the national team playing Shield cricket after a series had ended, he demanded that you gave your best and that you showed pride in the baggy blue cap. That expectation did not bother me, I gave everything every time I played. However, there is a mental battle involved in coming down to first-class cricket, because the expectations on a bowler to tear through the opposition's batting line-up or for a batsman to score a bundle of runs are quite incredible. I was very lucky to have both Rod and Steve guide me through the early days of my career, because they both let me know what was expected of me in order for me to succeed, and when I realised I had that in me I gained an incredible amount of confidence. I was also fortunate that I gained the understanding through them that the harder I worked, the more easily success would come. They gave me a great kickstart but the lessons I learned from them— to do the basics and to do them well—remained with me throughout my career. It was simplistic, but that was the beauty of cricket—and life—according to Steve and Rod. You don't overcomplicate it with theory; you work to master the basics and do them well.

ERROL ALCOTT

Errol was someone I had complete trust in during our 11 years together in the Australian team. The physio and the fast bowler are destined to get to know one another because of the time that's needed to tend the numerous injuries and pains 'the art' subjects the human body to. I was fortunate because in Errol I found someone I could confide in about anything, and I knew the matter would stay between us. An athlete needs to be able to have absolute trust in the team's medical staff on so many fronts. For instance, in this age of drugs in sport you need to know if you're taking a vitamin supplement that it does not contain an ingredient that could get you off side with the World Anti-Doping Agency (WADA); once Errol gave a supplement the all clear I didn't even give it a second thought.

For my part I was always upfront and honest with Errol about any problems or pains I had. I never held anything back because that wouldn't have been fair on him—I realised hiding that kind of information wouldn't have allowed him to do his job properly. It was also best to let him know what was wrong because over the years he proved himself to be something of a miracle worker. He made the sports medicine world sit up and take notice during the 2001 Ashes series when his around-the-clock work on Steve Waugh's calf muscle—which had a hole in it the size of a 20-cent piece—defied all expectations. Rather than needing months to recuperate, Steve was not only back at the crease 19 days later but he scored a century. Errol worked a miracle for me when I rolled my ankle on a ball in the outfield during our warm-up for the Second Test of the 2005 Ashes series. I ruptured two ligaments outside of my ankle and tests revealed I suffered some bone damage as well. It was a terrible mess, but Errol put ice on it immediately and he worked on it around the clock with his aim being to break up the scar tissue and to remove the blood. Few gave me any chance of playing again that series, but seven days later I was marking out my run-up and it was all because of a bloke who was as much a trusted friend to me as he was the best physio in the business.

WARREN CRAIG

Warren has been my manager for 20 years and, while he was my best man when Sara and I were married, he sometimes jokes he'd have received less time for murder. Over the years I've put him in a few situations that have tested his patience, but he's unflappable. It says a lot about him that when I know he's on the case, I don't need to worry. He is, as I say, my manager, but when I'm ever asked to describe my relationship with him, the first two words that come to mind are 'great mate'. He's been through thick and thin with me and there have been occasions when he's needed to go beyond the call of duty. Warren played first grade for the old Sydney Cricket Club and for Fairfield as a wicketkeeper and early in our relationship the poor bloke must've wondered what on earth he'd signed on for when he was asked to pad up and face me in the nets at a park in Cronulla. I was returning from an injury and needed someone to bowl to; I can reveal Warren definitely earned his commission that afternoon!

I have no doubt the cornerstone to Warren's success as a manager is that he understands the game and has a good feel for people. While Tom Cruise's celebrated character in the movie *Jerry Maguire* was a highly strung, flashy and over-the-top sports agent, Warren is cool, calm, collected and solid—and he's also the third wicketkeeper who has had a big bearing on my life. When we first met he seemed to be like the Eliot Ness (of The Untouchables fame) of chartered accountants because he was up to his ears in a forensic examination of a 'colourful' Australian, but much to Warren's frustration, the one paper he needed to nail his target proved elusive. He decided to become a sports agent in 1995. The management scene was much different to what it is these days when under-17s players are being courted by managers in the hope they might be cricket's next big thing and the agent's next cash cow. Warren simply went into the old Cricket NSW office and spoke to Neil Maxwell—the former NSW player who worked in the organisation at the time before going on to manage the likes of Brett Lee—and left his name and phone number for any player who was on the lookout for a manager. I'd returned from the West Indies and mentioned to 'Maxy' that I might need a manager, and he put us in touch. It's been a great 20 years and I think the greatest testimony I can offer is that apart from being a trusted friend in all that time, Warren has never let me down.

KEV CHEVELL

When I retired from cricket, the greatest gift I could think to give my fitness instructor Kev Chevell was my baggy green cap, because it was from training with him in his gymnasium at Penrith in Sydney's western suburbs that I became unbreakable in my body and mind. When I returned from the West Indies in 1995, it was painfully obvious to me, and many others, that my body was too light and would not withstand the many rigours of fast bowling. When I met Kev he put me on a path to galvanise my frame and toughen my mental strength, and I have no doubt that had we not crossed paths I would not have had the longevity or success I was able to enjoy. The only question he asked when I sought his help was how far I was prepared to go to be the best I could possibly be. He said the deal was sealed when I replied 'Whatever it takes', because he is only prepared to work with athletes willing to push themselves beyond their comfort zone. It opened a world of hurt to me and there were times when Kev pushed me so hard that I was physically ill. Kevin worked on the philosophy that he wanted to subject me to such a brutal training regime that nothing I encountered during a game, like the stifling subcontinental heat, could compare to it. I note the champion American swimmer Michael Phelps, who has won 18 Olympic gold medals, is coached by a man named Bob Bowman, who has a similar philosophy to Kev about the benefits of training tough.

Kev's training philosophies and principles were learned along the way and as I've said before he's a big believer in the rowing machine; it's his favourite tool of punishment, and he's merciless. While he says it is no coincidence that rowers are considered the fittest of all athletes, he believes another benefit of the machine is it doesn't have the bone-jarring impact of walking, running or jogging. As is the case with my other mentors, Kev doesn't just give orders, he lives what he preaches—he trains every day—and commands great respect from me for that reason. I would never ask anyone to do something that I would not do myself, and Kev is certainly of that ilk. His training was based on common sense, and you should realise by now that what I appreciated was that, like Rod Marsh and Steve Rixon, his key to success was based on one requirement . . .

Hard work.

DENNIS LILLEE

Even if I had never been picked to play cricket at a high level, Dennis would still have played an important role in my life because he was my childhood hero and in my mind's eye I can still see the headband, the moustache, the classic run-up and the aggressive glare. Why wouldn't any kid want to be like him? As a kid, Dennis inspired me to try to be the best I could possibly be. It was from watching him play for Australia that I was motivated to bowl at that battered old 44-gallon drum, because the way he played made me want to follow in his footsteps. As I ran in to bowl at that drum I could sometimes hear that famous 'Lillee' chant in my head—the one the crowds offered him as a tribute whenever he took the ball. I definitely gained a lot from watching him strut his stuff, because while Australia sometimes lost games he played in, I never saw him defeated. He was macho, brave and charismatic, and while he was also a showman, he definitely had substance, and something that's helpful for any fast bowler: the great Dennis Lillee always seemed to have a trick up his sleeve. The more I think of it, the more I believe he could have passed as determination's human form. He was pure class and still holds the title as my No. 1 bowler. I always thought that he left parts of himself on every ground he played at; such was the level of his commitment to the game.

When I made it into the Australian team I learned that others shared my admiration for 'D.K. Lillee'. When we formed the Fast Bowlers Cartel [FBC]—which was in response to the batsmen forming the Platinum Club, where membership involved drinking fancy coffees and cruising shopping arcades to buy clothes that were more about the label than taste and discussing the gossip column's content— we of the FBC ate red meat, watched the footy and worked out ways to humble our foes. We also had a secret greeting, which was to run an index finger along the forehead, just as Dennis did when he wiped the sweat away before he bowled. I think all that salute proves is that a bloke never really grows up. I'm pleased to have formed a friendship with Dennis since the day he came to the Australian Cricket Academy to share the tricks of the trade. He's a great bloke but I definitely can't keep up with him . . . seriously. I don't think he's changed a lot since his playing days. I've learnt a lot from him over the last three years as head coach at the MRF Pace Foundation, and it's through what I have learnt from him that I can now look at a bowler's action and help them to improve upon it.

BOB SIMPSON

Bob is the forgotten hero of Australia's rise to become World Cup winners (just one short year after he was appointed as the coach in 1986). He inherited a team that was regarded by its critics as young and soft, and they certainly did it tough because before beating New Zealand after 'Simmo's' appointment, history notes the Aussies hadn't won a Test series in two years. It wasn't the first time Bob had answered an SOS from Cricket Australia. In 1977, when Kerry Packer's World Series Cricket plundered the likes of Greg Chappell, Rod Marsh, Dennis Lillee, Max Walker, Rick McCosker, David Hookes and just about all of the hardheads from the establishment's stable, Bob returned to the crease aged 41—and ten long years after he'd retired—to offer a young team, which contained no less than six debutants in the opening Test against a strong Indian outfit, with some much needed guidance. He topscored with 89 in the second innings of the First Test and by the time the series ended in a 3–2 triumph to Australia, Bob had hit two centuries and compiled over 500 runs.

As the coach of Australia he certainly demanded a lot from his players, and I have no doubt Steve Rixon was influenced in his outlook as a coach by his time under Bob, because Simmo loved his fielding drills. He'd hit high catches and run the guys as hard as he possibly could, because apart from wanting us to do the basics and to do them well, he believed 'catches win matches' and that philosophy was proven to be correct on numerous occasions during my time in the Australian team's system. He believed every player in the team needed to know their role in the side and that everyone should be proud to have their place in the structure that's called a 'team'. I found Bob was tremendous to talk to and he was happy to offer advice and insights about life on and off the field. It's true to say that Bob had his detractors; all coaches do because they're in a tough gig, and the great coaches will always make calls that some people won't appreciate. Something I have respected about Bob is that he never doubted himself and he stuck to his beliefs. He formed the foundation for those who immediately followed him as coach—Geoff Marsh and John Buchanan—to build on what he'd established, and it resulted in a golden reign for the Australian team.

THE CAPTAINS AND A MAN BORN TO BE KING

Four people who had an important part in my cricket life were my four national skippers: Allan Border, Mark Taylor, Steve Waugh, Ricky Ponting and the bloke called the 'unofficial' skipper, Shane Warne. They understood me and that allowed me to do my 'thing'. Each of them were fine leaders, inspirational and skilful as players, but they were certainly their own men. While they each did things differently, they reinforced to me (and the other players they led) through their actions and words the basic importance of putting the team before everything (and everyone) else. Each of them oversaw a healthy team environment that allowed Australian cricket to prosper and ultimately set the standards that the rest of the world followed.

Allan Border

When I was selected for the Australian Test team I found myself pitchforked into what was a great environment in which players shared their thoughts and advice willingly. However, I was led to believe that in the years before I made my debut, Australia was more or less a team of individuals, and some players did not enjoy the success of others quite as much as they should have. I was blessed to have entered what was a happy and welcoming environment because it set the tone for the rest of my career and I attribute a lot of that team spirit to A.B. He may have been as tough as a boot nail and never gave an inch on the field, but after he took over the captaincy from Kim Hughes he introduced the principles you'd expect from a team of Aussies. While Border's teams might not have had the players that Mark Taylor and Steve Waugh had at their disposal during their reign as skipper, there's no doubt the team improved as a result of what

Border established. Thirty years after he became skipper I think Border ought to be remembered as the architect of the culture that Steve Smith has inherited. The former fast and fiery bowler Rodney Hogg—who took 41 wickets against England in 1978–79—added what I consider an interesting story behind Allan taking over the captaincy. Hoggy is a sought-after speaker and I've heard him say that he fell just one vote short of being named captain. The prospect of Hoggy captaining Australia . . . now, that would have been very interesting.

Mark Taylor

As captain, 'Tubby' brought a different attitude to the game—he was more aggressive in his outlook and he went for the win from the opening delivery of the match. That 'don't take a backwards step' approach was one that I thrived on. Our association went back to the Tooheys Cup match at Parkes when he was one of the stars who played alongside the bush-bashers, and I've reminded him on more than one occasion that the first catch he could have ever taken off my bowling was dropped like a hot spud at first slip. However, I should add that he more than made up for it in the years that followed. Like Border, he was also a very strong character and that was reflected during the 1997 Ashes tour when, despite looking down the barrel after 21 innings where he hadn't scored a 50 (adding to his misery was a stunt by the English tabloid press where they presented him with a metre-wide bat), he was still strong enough to boldly captain the team. Tubby struck back during that tour with a gutsy 129 at Edgbaston that silenced his critics. That innings not only changed his fortunes but I think it summed up Mark—he was a fighter.

Steve Waugh

Even more aggressive than Mark in his desire to win, Steve wanted us to crush the opposition. It didn't matter who we played, Steve didn't ever want the opposition to even get a sniff. I always got along well with Steve, he was one of the guys who I confided in within the team from the outset because I felt as though he could be trusted, and that faith was certainly justified. I value our relationship and I had no hesitation in asking him to be my best man when I married Jane. The fact he also travelled to Sicily when I married Sara shows he's been a big part of my career and my life beyond the boundary. He's yet another person who leads by example but he places an emphasis on the importance of respect. Steve is someone who treasures cricket's values and the history not only of the sport but of Australia. He was instrumental in the team visiting Gallipoli to pay our respects to the Anzacs on our way to England for the 2001 Ashes series. In 2005 we went to Villers-Bretonneux in France to see where the Diggers had fought and died during the push that was said to have helped bring World War I to an end. They were unexpected experiences, and I'm sure I can speak on behalf of the rest of the boys when I say they enriched all of our lives. I also gained a lot by hanging out with Steve when I went on tour, because while most of the boys wanted to play golf on their days off, we traipsed around bazaars, markets and ancient holy sites to get a better sense of the community, culture and beliefs of the places we visited. These days we only live across the water from each other; I can actually see his house from my place, and it's always good to catch up.

Ricky Ponting

We spent two years together in the Academy in Adelaide and even way back then when he was only a teenager, Rick was earmarked by respected judges as a future Test captain. However, something I noticed about Rick was that he didn't really care too much about the hype; he never allowed it to affect him because he worked like someone who didn't take anything for granted. What stood out most about Rick in those early days was he was such an aggressive batsman, he'd take on anything. In my opinion he played the short ball better than anyone else I've seen and it seemed incredible to me that he never tried to duck it. When Rick took over the Australian captaincy, something that really impressed me was the level of maturity in which he handled the role. He spoke with authority and he held himself well, and the reason I guess that made such an impression on me was because I knew him when he was a young bloke, so I had seen him grow up. He developed into a true captain and his knowledge of the game, and the respect he held for it, was outstanding. I think it also says a great deal about Rick's leadership qualities that despite losing seven senior players in a two-year period, he was able to rebuild the national team.

That was extraordinary. Some teams never recover when two or three players retire. I'm pleased to see that Rick is using his knowledge and insights as a coach and it doesn't surprise me that he enjoyed immediate success in his role with the Mumbai Indians in the IPL.

Shane Warne

He wasn't a captain of Australia but I have no doubt he would have done a great job if he had received the chance. Shane is just different—I've never met anyone like him and I doubt I ever will. There were some BIG personalities in the Australian dressing room during our playing days, but I think Warney was bigger than all of them combined. By being bigger than anyone else in the team, I actually think Shane's off-field antics probably saved many of us from too much scrutiny because whatever it was we may have done, it simply paled in comparison to him. Shane and I are very different people, and the truth is I wouldn't want to live his life because it'd be too full-on for my liking. Indeed, I've actually seen people try to do half of what Shane does and it destroys them. However, despite our differences in character I'm extremely proud to be able to call Shane my mate. He was someone who welcomed me into the Australian team with open arms and he was a constant source of support throughout my years in the Baggy Green. I think those of us who played alongside him realised how special a player Warney was— believe it when people say he was a once-in-a-generation player. I think the undisputed rating of his impact on the game as a 'wonder' is that people all over the world were happy to pay to watch him bowl. As a cricketer I was blessed to have Shane bowling at the other end, and I have no doubt many of the wickets I took were the combined result of the pressure he and I applied to batsmen. We enjoyed a good partnership and while we were poles apart in our styles, we both built up pressure by bowling with good control and setting aggressive fields. We gave nothing away and the end result of that was that we took over 1000 Test wickets.

It might be unfair to have restricted my mentors to just a few of the many people who have helped me over the years.

I have benefited from the advice of so many people throughout my life and I've also benefited from the opinions of those people who offered me a view I didn't agree with. I am grateful to them because they made me think a bit deeper about everything from how to dismiss a particular batsman to how to handle a situation in everyday life.

This book was never intended to be a 'how to live your life' or 'self-help' book, but I do hope the message comes through that I feel blessed to have been able to fulfil the dream I had as a young kid who bowled a scuffed ball at a battered 44-gallon drum all those years ago because (despite the opinions of others) I believed I had it in me to one day play for Australia. You will often hear people say 'If I can do it, so can you' but, in my case it really is so very true.

I also hope anyone who might be going through a tough time will take from my story the importance of inner strength and belief. I hope they realise that even though there are those days when they might not want the sun to come up to give them a bit more time to rally their strength, the sun will rise.

Like me, I hope they appreciate through life's many experiences that it is important to make the most of each day and to realise that the love of those around them is a blessing.